A chance invitation to join a walking holiday in Wales led **TRICIA AND BOB HAYNE** to an interest that sees them reaching for their rucksacks as often as possible. From discovering the Buckinghamshire countryside to navigating Hadrian's Wall and encircling the Isle of Wight, they enjoy exploring Britain the best way – on foot.

Tricia was for many years editorial director of Bradt Travel Guides and is now a freelance travel writer. She and Bob research and write Bradt's guide to the *Cayman Islands*, and co-write their *Turks and Caicos Islands*, and have helped to update several others in southern Africa.

Authors

Cotswold Way

First edition: 2009; this second edition 2012

Publisher Trailblazer Publications
The Old Manse, Tower Rd, Hindhead, Surrey, GU26 6SU, UK www.trailblazer-guides.com

British Library Cataloguing in Publication Data
A catalogue record for this book is available from the British Library

ISBN 978-1-905864-48-5

© Trailblazer 2009, 2012: Text and maps

Series Editor: Anna Jacomb-Hood   **Editor**: Jim Manthorpe   **Cartography**: Nick Hill
Proof-reading: Jane Thomas   **Layout**: Nick Hill   **Index**: Jane Thomas
Photographs (flora): C1 – Row 2, left: © Bob Hayne
C1 – Row 1, middle & right; Row 2, middle & right; Rows 3 & 4, right: © Tricia Hayne
C2 – Row 2, right; Row 3, middle & right; Row 4, right: © Tricia Hayne
C3 – Row 1, middle; Row 2 left & right: © Tricia Hayne   C1-3 all others © Bryn Thomas
Other photographs: Stanton (p7), Hailes Abbey, spectacle stocks, sheep and the
Battle of Lansdown site © Bob Hayne; all other photographs © Tricia Hayne

The maps in this guide were prepared from out-of-Crown-copyright Ordnance Survey maps amended and updated by Trailblazer.

Dedication

In memory of Tricia's mum, Mollie

Acknowledgements

Every book of this ilk is something of a joint effort and for this second edition we remain indebted to many people who have helped with advice and information, in particular James Blockley and Don Field at the National Trail Office.

Our thanks go once again to Chris Overton, both for his generous hospitality and for guiding us around the changes in Bath; it was a pleasure to explore the city again. Thanks also to all those readers who wrote with updates and suggestions, in particular, Antoine Bowes, Ann Flavell-Wood, Andrew Guppy, Gerry & Caroline Hoare, David Hofman, Ian Ludford and Michael & Joanna Womack. Thanks, too, to those along the trail who offered us such a warm welcome and helped us – albeit often unknowingly – with information for the guide. Finally, thank you to Bryn Thomas at Trailblazer for the perfect excuse to return to the Cotswolds; to Nick Hill for his input on eateries and watering holes in Bath, and to Anna Jacomb-Hood, Jim Manthorpe and Jane Thomas, also at Trailblazer, for ensuring that the detail was always at the forefront of our minds.

A request

The authors and publisher have tried to ensure that this guide is as accurate as possible. Nevertheless, things change even on these well-worn routes. If you notice any changes or omissions, please write to Trailblazer (address above) or email us at 🖳 info@trailblazer-guides.com. A free copy of the next edition will be sent to persons making a significant contribution.

Warning: long-distance walking can be dangerous

Please read the notes on when to go (pp13-16) and outdoor safety (pp53-6). Every effort has been made by the authors and publisher to ensure that the information contained herein is as accurate and up to date as possible. However, they are unable to accept responsibility for any inconvenience, loss or injury sustained by anyone as a result of the advice and information given in this guide.

Photos: front cover & this page: Folly near Little Sodbury; **overleaf**: Stanley Wood © T Hayne

Printed on chlorine-free paper by D'Print (☎ +65-6581 3832), Singapore

Cotswold Way

44 large-scale maps & guides to 48 towns and villages

PLANNING – PLACES TO STAY – PLACES TO EAT

CHIPPING CAMPDEN TO BATH

TRICIA & BOB HAYNE

TRAILBLAZER PUBLICATIONS

Contents

PART 4: ROUTE GUIDE AND MAPS

Contents

ABOUT THIS BOOK

This guidebook contains all the information you need; the hard work has been done for you so you can plan your trip from home without the usual pile of books, maps, guides and tourist brochures. It includes:

● All standards of accommodation, from campsites to luxurious guesthouses
● Walking companies offering organised tours
● Suggested itineraries for all types of walker
● Answers to all your questions: when to go, degree of difficulty, what to pack and the approximate cost of the whole walking holiday

When you're all packed, boots on and ready to go, there's plenty of information to get you to and from the Cotswold Way, and 44 detailed maps (1:20,000) together with nine town/village plans to help you find your way along it. The route guide section includes:

● Walking times in both directions
● Reviews of accommodation including campsites, hostels, B&Bs and guesthouses
● Cafés, pubs, tea shops, restaurants, and shops for buying supplies
● Rail, bus and taxi information for towns and villages on or near the path
● Town plans of Chipping Campden, Broadway, Winchcombe, Cheltenham, Painswick, Dursley, Wotton-under-Edge and Bath
● Historical, cultural and geographical background information
● GPS waypoints

MINIMUM IMPACT FOR MAXIMUM INSIGHT

We do not inherit the earth from our ancestors: we borrow it from our children.
Native American proverb

By their very nature, walkers tend to be both interested in and concerned about the natural environment. This book seeks to reinforce that interest and concern. There are sections devoted to minimum-impact walking and conservation, with ideas on how to broaden that ethos, as well as a detailed, illustrated chapter on wildlife.

There can be few activities as 'environmentally friendly' as walking. By developing a deeper ecological awareness through a better understanding of nature, and by supporting rural economies, sensitive forms of transport and low-impact methods of farming and land use, we can all do our bit to ensure that the environment remains in safe hands for generations to come.

INTRODUCTION

Asked to conjure up an image of a quintessential Cotswold scene, most people will come up with some combination of a village of honey-coloured houses set against a backdrop of sheep grazing in hillside fields, demarcated by seemingly endless dry-stone walls. For once, the reality and the picture-post-card image still coincide, at least in part. Nevertheless, to walk the Cotswold Way is to discover a far more complex – and arguably more rewarding – environment, characterised in addition by ancient beech woods lining the Cotswold escarpment and wide tracts of arable land.

For once, the reality and the picture-postcard image still coincide...

With the Cotswold villages of tourist brochures along the early part of the route, and the architectural glories of Georgian Bath that await the walker in the south, it's soon clear that Cotswold limestone

Stanton's golden-stone cottages encapsulate the quiet beauty of a Cotswold village.

has been hugely influential in defining the landscape. As you head south, so the stone of the houses gradually fades, from Stanton's golden cottages to the palest ivory of Painswick's villas. Simple parish churches, towering follies and stately homes make their mark, too, all constructed of the same stone. Yet it's not just the stone that hints at the region's history. You won't get far without coming across any number of humps, lumps and bumps, relics of earlier inhabitants who left their mark in burial mounds, hill forts, monasteries and even villas right across the trail. Their chosen spots were often some of those most revered by today's walkers, wide-open expanses on windy hilltops with views west to the wide River Severn and the Malvern Hills.

Almost the entire trail runs through the Cotswolds Area of Outstanding Natural Beauty

Almost the entire trail runs through the Cotswolds Area of Outstanding Natural Beauty, crossing fields still bounded by hedges and walls, and hills where sheep have grazed for centuries. In the early years it was these sheep that led many a merchant to make his fortune in the wool trade, which thus underpinned the foundation of towns from Chipping Campden to Dursley. Where grazing has ended, human intervention has ensured that at least some of the rich grassland can remain a haven for the wild flowers, birds and insects that previous generations took for granted.

Thoughtfully, the Cotswold Way crosses all these places – and perhaps that's the greatest advantage of a man-made trail. While earlier walkers must have taken a direct route on pilgrimage to the abbey at Hailes, today's walkers on the Cotswold Way find themselves twisting and turning along a trail that effectively showcases the very best that the region can offer. That that includes historic castles, more than a passing nod to the Arts and Crafts movement, and some excellent pubs, is to the benefit of all.

History

HISTORY OF THE TRAIL

The Cotswold Way runs for 102 miles (163km) through the Cotswold Hills from Chipping Campden in the north to the Georgian city of Bath. The route was originally devised as a long-distance footpath by members of the Ramblers' Association and was established in conjunction with the Cotswolds AONB in 1970.

Its development as a national trail was approved in 1998, but it was not until May 2007 that the trail was formally launched, one of just 15 in England and Wales. During the transition, several changes were made to the route, and others are still in the offing, although for the most part the original paths remain open.

The path is the responsibility of the National Trail Officer, under the auspices of the Cotswold Way National Trail Office (see box p41).

Opposite: Selsley Common (p130) offers exceptional open walking with far-reaching views.

GEOLOGY

Look at a geological map of England and it is immediately clear that the origins of the present-day Cotswolds lie in the Jurassic period. Geological maps show a continuous swathe of Jurassic-age rocks extending all the way from Dorset to the Yorkshire coast, with the most complete and impressive outcrop making up the Cotswold Hills. These rocks, formed between 145 and 199 million years ago, include silts, clays and sands, as well as the famous Cotswold limestone.

Cotswold stone is an oolitic limestone, a sedimentary rock that was formed primarily in the warm shallow seas of the Jurassic. It is comprised of a large number of almost spherical granules, or oolites, packed closely together, and its origins explain the regular occurrence in the rock of fossils, such as sea urchins. Occasional falls in sea level resulted in dry land where dinosaurs roamed, leaving behind both their footprints and their bones. While most walk-

❑ Dry-stone walls

The dry-stone walls that are so evocative of the Cotswolds are created from irregularly shaped blocks of the local limestone. Deceptive in their simplicity, they require a considerable level of skill to build, with an expert able to complete around six or seven yards (6-7m) a day.

Some beds of Cotswold stone break down naturally into layers of around two or three inches (50-75mm) thick. Typically, the wall is created from two parallel lines of stone, gradually coming together as they near the top. Stones on each side of the wall are fitted together like a jigsaw, laid sloping outwards to draw water away from the centre. Smaller pieces of stone, and offcuts, are used to fill the central cavities, adding strength and durability to the whole wall.

ers will see little difference between the rocks at various places along the trail, to the geologist there are marked distinctions according to the stages at which the sediments were deposited and compressed. In addition, while the surface rock of the Cotswold range is predominantly limestone, the underlying structure is more usually of clays, silts and sands. It is the precise structure of these rocks that both determines the wildlife that populates the hillside and influences the buildings that we see in each part of the region.

The Gloucestershire Geology Trust (☎ 01452-864438, 🖳 www.glosgeo trust.org.uk) is committed to studying and conserving the region's geological heritage, and to recording regionally important geological sites. There are plans in hand to develop a geology trail along the Cotswold Way, but in the meantime, the trust publishes a series of trail guides (£2 each). Entitled *Gloucestershire Uncovered*, each covers locations along the route, including Cleeve Hill Common, Leckhampton Hill and Crickley Hill.

INTRODUCTION

Finally, a layer of slats, or 'combers', is laid along the top at right angles to the wall. The whole is usually around 3ft (1m) high, and some 20in (50cm) at the base, tapering to around 16in (40cm) at the top.

It is estimated that there are some 4000 miles (6000km) of dry-stone walls across the whole of the Cotswolds AONB. Weather, vegetation and accidents take their toll, so regular maintenance is essential. As a result of a revival of interest in traditional crafts, it is possible to go on a course to learn the basics, or to take part as a volunteer to help preserve the region's existing walls. For more information, contact the Cotswolds Conservation Board (see box p58) or the Dry Stone Walling Association of Great Britain (🖳 www.ds wa.org.uk).

INTRODUCTION

How difficult is the path?

Familiarity with the Cotswolds – or at least with the tourist areas in the north – might lead to a sense that the Cotswold Way is little more than a walk in the park. While it would be unreasonable to suggest that it is seriously challenging, it would be equally wrong to underestimate the quite literal ups and downs of a route that takes you from just above sea level to 1066ft (325m) and back over a distance of around 100 miles.

If, as is often suggested, you plan to complete the route in seven days, you're looking at an average of nearly 15 miles, or six to seven hours' actual walking, every day. Some of those hills are steeper than you might expect from a casual glance at the landscape, and poor weather can exacerbate what would otherwise be fairly straightforward. It makes sense, then, to have a reasonable level of fitness before you set off, if only to make sure that what should be an enjoyable week or so's walking doesn't turn into a test of endurance.

The route is well signposted so you shouldn't get lost; look for the acorn logo. This wide view is from the trail south of Wood Stanway.

How long do you need?

This is the great imponderable. Is it reasonable – as is generally suggested – to walk the path from end to end in a week? Well yes, but it's a qualified yes. If you have just seven days' holiday but need two of those to get to and from the trail, you'll be faced with walking 20 miles a day, which isn't for the faint hearted. If, on the other hand, you can spend most of those seven days on the trail, a week is realistic. That said,

> So while the world reckons that this is a week's walk, give it eight days and you'll be adding in time to breathe

averaging almost 15 miles a day won't leave much time for exploring the villages on the route, taking time out for a cream tea in Broadway, or a pint of Donnington's at The Mount Inn in Stanton, or exploring Selsley Common for orchids. You might find yourself casting a wistful backward glance at old churches as you march purposefully past the lych gate, or promising yourself you'll come back to do justice to Hailes Abbey, or Dyrham Park, or even to Bath. So while the world reckons that this is a week's walk, give it eight days and you'll be adding in time to breathe.

If time is really short, you could reasonably leave out the last section, perhaps south of Cold Ashton and down Lansdown Hill into Bath (p163). That isn't to say this isn't worthy of walking – far from it. But Bath is a destination in its own right, so the chances are that you could justify returning on another occasion.

> See p31 for some suggested itineraries covering different walking speeds

Plenty of people can't spare the time to walk from end to end in one go, but still get that sense of achievement by building up the miles over a series of day or weekend walks until they've completed the route. Alternatively, you could simply sample the highlights (though lowlights are few); see p36 for some recommendations.

When to go

SEASONS

Autumn that name of creeper falling and tea-time loving,
Was once for me the thought of High Cotswold noon-air   **Ivor Gurney, *Old Thought***

While English weather is hardly predictable, at least some generalisations can be made. Statistically, the months when the weather is least likely to be inclement are May to September, but statistics – as we all know – can be very misleading. The air temperature at this time is generally at its warmest, with frosts unlikely from the end of May. Rain, though, is another factor. Some

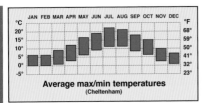

Average max/min temperatures
(Cheltenham)

years can see continuous rain for several weeks and parts of the path will become impassable. While it's tempting to think that this is only likely to happen in winter, the last widespread flooding in Gloucestershire was in the summer of 2007, with 2008 running a close second. April and October often bring days that are bright and breezy when the walking and the surroundings are at their best.

Spring

The weather in spring is as unpredictable as the rest of the year. In **April**, it can be warm and sunny on odd days, but seldom for sustained periods. Although the spring of 2007 upset all the record books, conditions are more likely to be changeable, with blustery showers and cold spells reminding you that winter has only just passed. On the other hand, the days are long, and less rain falls on average in spring than at any other time of the year. This, coupled with the milder weather of **May** and **June**, and the proliferation of wild flowers early in the year, makes it one of the best times to tackle the trail.

Summer

July and **August** are the traditional holiday months and the conditions can be especially good for walking with generally mild temperatures and still many hours of daylight. This, however, is also the time when the Cotswolds experience a surge in visitors, especially around the tourist honeypots of Broadway and Bath. For the most part, though, the trippers won't be out in the fields and on the hills, so here at least you can leave the hordes behind.

Autumn

Many connoisseurs consider autumn, especially early autumn, the best time of year for walking. **September** and **October** can be lovely months to get out on the trail, especially when the leaves begin to turn. Although the air temperature usually remains relatively mild, October can see the first frosts and rain is an ever-present threat.

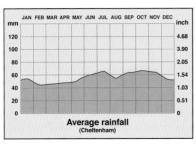

Average rainfall
(Cheltenham)

Winter

Only the very hardiest of souls will attempt the Cotswold Way in winter. The days are shorter, and once the clocks have gone back at the end of October, until mid March, you will need to be at your destination by 4.30-5pm to avoid walking in the dark. Cold weather, wind and driving rain are not the best recipe for a day's walking, although a crisp winter morning takes a lot of beating.

DAYLIGHT HOURS

If you're planning to walk in autumn, winter or early spring, you'll need to take into account how far you can walk in the available daylight. It will not be possible to cover as many miles or to be out for as long as you would in the summer.

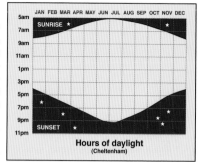

Hours of daylight
(Cheltenham)

The table (right) gives the sunrise and sunset times for the middle of each month at latitude 52° North, which runs through the Cotswold Hills, giving a reasonably accurate picture for daylight along the Cotswold Way. Depending on the weather, you should get a further 30-45 minutes of usable light before sunrise and after sunset.

❏ FESTIVALS AND ANNUAL EVENTS

The following events may need to be considered when planning your walk since all will affect the availability and sometimes price of accommodation in their area. Those with a particularly strong impact locally are the National Hunt Festival in Cheltenham in March, and Badminton Horse Trials in May.

In addition to the following annual fixtures, it's as well to be aware that events held at the Prescott Speed Hill Climb (🖥 www.bugatti.co.uk) outside Winchcombe can put a lot of pressure on the town's resources.

February
● **Cheltenham Folk Festival** (☎ 0844-576 2210, 🖥 www.cheltenhamtownhall .org.uk/folk-festival) Folk music comes to town for three days in mid February.

March
● **Bath Literature Festival** (☎ 01225-463362, 🖥 www.bathlitfest.org.uk) Ten days at the beginning of March see Bath's literary scene come alive. Authors as diverse as Colin Thubron and Kazuo Ishiguro were among those at the 2011 event.
● **National Hunt Festival, Cheltenham** (☎ 0844-579 3003, 🖥 www.chelten ham.co.uk) Now dubbed simply The Festival, this four-day event in mid March is one of the racing calendar's highlights – both in racing terms and socially – culminating in every jump jockey's dream, the Cheltenham Gold Cup. Tickets are hard sought after, and accommodation throughout the area is often booked a year ahead. If you have no choice but to walk in this week, make sure you plan well ahead.

April/May
● **Wotton-under-Edge Arts Festival** (🖥 www.wottonartsfestival.org.uk) This ten-day festival takes place around the end of April and early May.

May
● **Annual Cheese Rolling** Cooper's Hill (🖥 www.cheese-rolling.co.uk) The last official competition took place in 2009, but there's still strong support for this village event, traditionally held on the last May Bank Holiday Monday; see box p119.

INTRODUCTION

❏ FESTIVALS AND ANNUAL EVENTS   *(continued from p15)*

● **Badminton Horse Trials** (☎ 01454-218375, 🖳 www.badminton-horse
.co.uk) Hugely important among the riding fraternity, this four-day event takes place
east of the trail near Old Sodbury in early May. Accommodation is limited in this
area, and guesthouses, pubs and hotels for miles around get prebooked months in
advance: you've been warned!
● **Cheltenham Jazz Festival** (☎ 01242-505444, 🖳 www.cheltenhamfestivals
.com) A week of jazz is celebrated in early May.
● **Chipping Campden Music Festival** (☎ 01386-849018, 🖳 www.campden
musicfestival.co.uk) A local two-week festival dedicated to classical music, based in
the town's revered St James's Church.
● **Cotswold Olimpicks** Dover's Hill, Chipping Campden (🖳 www.olimpick
games.co.uk) Friday after the last May Bank Holiday, followed the next day by the
Scuttlebrook Wake; see box p78.
● **Winchcombe Walking Festival** (☎ 01242-602925, 🖳 www.winchcombe
welcomeswalkers.com) was inaugurated in 2010 to promote walking in this area of
the Cotswolds. It takes place from Friday to Sunday over the penultimate weekend in
May with a series of graded walks and evening events.

June
● **Bath International Music Festival** (☎ 01225-463362, 🖳 www.bathmusic
fest.org.uk) Held for two weeks at the end of May and early June, the festival showcases music ranging from classical to jazz and folk.
● **Cheltenham Science Festival** (☎ 01242-505444, 🖳 www.cheltenham
festivals.com) Held over six days in mid June.
● **Cheltenham Food and Drink Festival** (☎ 01242-521997, 🖳 www.garden-
events.com) Three days of foodie heaven in Montpellier Gardens; mid to late June.
● **Cotswold Way Relay** (🖳 www.cotswoldwayrelay.co.uk) It might be best to avoid
walking on the last Saturday in June. On the other hand, you'll have the one-upman-
ship of taking the time to savour the trail's attractions while others steam past with
eyes only on the clock. For details, see box p34.

July
● **Cheltenham Music Festival** (☎ 01242-505444, 🖳 www.cheltenham
festivals.com) Popular two-week festival at the beginning of July with international
artists playing an eclectic mix of primarily classical music.
● **Cotswold Beer Festival** (🖳 www.gloucestershirecamra.org.uk/cbf) One of
CAMRA's national beer festivals, usually held at Postlip Hall outside Winchcombe
over the last weekend in July (although the 2012 date could be brought forward to
avoid a clash with the Olympics).
● **Cheltenham Cricket Festival** (☎ 0117-910 8000, 🖳 www.gloscricket.co.uk)
Founded in 1872, the festival is held in the grounds of Cheltenham College around
the end of July/early August.

August
● **Frocester Beer Festival** (🖳 www.dursleylions.org/frocesterbeerfestival.htm) Two
days of tasting and camaraderie, held near Stonehouse; August Bank Holiday weekend.

October
● **Cheltenham Literature Festival** (☎ 01242-505444, 🖳 www.cheltenham
festivals.com) This ten-day festival in mid October goes from strength to strength,
attracting literary giants such as Roger McGough, as well as Man Booker prize win-
ners, and offering a range of workshops.

PLANNING YOUR WALK

1

Practical information for the walker

ROUTE FINDING

Having been opened as a national trail only in 2007, it's no surprise that the Cotswold Way is clearly signposted along almost its entire length. On the few occasions – usually in a field, but also around the Ebley Canal – where there might be some ambiguity, the maps in this guide should quickly put you straight.

The waymark throughout is the National Trails' acorn symbol, to be found on stiles, kissing gates, fingerposts and guideposts. Sometimes as an alternative you will find the standard yellow or blue footpath or bridlepath roundel overprinted with the words 'Cotswold Way', and the authorities in Bath have devised a more discreet sign, a metallic acorn on a black background.

Using GPS with this book

I never carried a compass, preferring to rely on a good sense of direction. I never bothered to understand how a compass works or what it is supposed to do. To me a compass is a gadget, and I don't get on well with gadgets of any sort.
Alfred Wainwright

While modern Wainwrights will scoff, more open-minded walkers will accept GPS technology as an inexpensive and well-established, if non-essential, navigational aid. To cut a long story short, within a minute of being turned on and with a clear view of the sky, GPS receivers will establish your position and altitude anywhere on earth in a variety of formats, including the British Ordnance Survey grid system, to an accuracy of within a few metres.

One thing must be understood, however: treating a GPS as a replacement for maps, a compass and common sense is a big mistake. Although current units are robust, it only takes the batteries to go flat or some electronic malfunction to leave you in the dark. A GPS is merely a navigational aid or backup to conventional route finding and, in almost all cases, is best used in conjunction with a paper map. All a GPS does is stop you exacerbating navigational errors or save you time in correcting them.

The maps in the route guide include numbered waypoints; these correlate to the list on pp184-5, which gives the latitude/longitude position in a decimal minute format as well as a description. Typically a waypoint has been given for most of the high spots and significant places of interest along the route, as well as several of the towns and villages. You can download the complete list of these waypoints for free as a GPS-readable file (that doesn't include the text descriptions) from the Trailblazer website: 💻 www.trailblazer-guides.com (click on GPS waypoints).

It's anticipated that you won't tramp along day after day, ticking off the book's waypoints as you pass them, because the route description and maps are more than adequate most of the time. Only when you're **unsure of your position** or which way to go might you feel the need to turn on the unit for a quick affirmation.

It's also possible to buy state-of-the-art digital mapping to import into your GPS unit, assuming that you have sufficient memory capacity, but it's not the most reliable way of navigating and the small screen on your pocket-sized unit will invariably fail to put places into context or give you the 'big picture'.

Despite these possibilities, almost everyone who has ever walked the Cotswold Way has done so without GPS so there's no need to rush out and buy one. The route is exceptionally well waymarked, and with the maps in this guide, there is little chance that you will get lost. That said, it offers a good opportunity to try out new technology before tackling something more navigationally challenging.

ACCOMMODATION

The Cotswold Way is generally well served with bed-and-breakfast and pub accommodation, but there are one or two areas, particularly between the Cheltenham area and Dursley, where the options are quite limited and you may be faced with up to a mile further at the end of the day's walk. That said, most places listed in this guide are either on or within easy reach of the trail. Campers, though, will find themselves with quite a challenge, and may have to combine camping with the odd night at a B&B. A comprehensive selection of places to stay is given in each section of the route guide, Part 4, though do bear in mind that even the most long-standing establishments can change hands, or close without warning.

Although smoking in enclosed public spaces is banned in England, places to stay are able to designate rooms for smokers. In practice, however, very few B&Bs do this, so check if it is important to you (see p27).

Booking

It's best to reserve your accommodation in advance, especially at peak periods and weekends, when there can be stiff competition for beds, and in winter, when several B&Bs close for the season. Very few B&B owners appreciate someone turning up on the doorstep without warning, and you don't want to find yourself with nowhere to stop. The suggested itineraries on p31 should help with planning ahead.

PLANNING YOUR WALK

Most hotels and some B&Bs offer online or email booking but for the majority you will need to phone. In many cases you will be asked for a deposit of around 50%, rising to 100% for one-night bookings, which is generally non-refundable if you cancel at short notice. While larger places may take credit or debit cards, many B&Bs accept only cheques or payments by bank transfer for the deposit, with the balance settled by cash or cheque.

If you do have to cancel, be sure to give as much notice as you can so they can offer your room to someone else.

Prices

Prices given in this guide are, unless otherwise stated, for a room with breakfast for one night. The trend towards flexible pricing according to the time of year, the time of the week, and the occurrence of festivals, is spreading beyond hotels to pubs and even B&Bs, especially in tourist hotspots, so do ensure you check the rate before confirming a reservation.

For a guide to rates, see under Hostels (below), B&Bs (pp20-1), Pubs (p21), and Hotels (p21).

Camping

Man is born free under the stars, yet we lock our doors and creep to bed.
Robert Louis Stevenson

There are few official campsites along the Cotswold Way, especially along the northern part of the trail between Winchcombe and the Ebley Canal area. **Wild camping** is not permitted anywhere, which is no help to those who prefer the great outdoors to a B&B. It may be worth asking at a farm along the route if you can pitch a tent in a field, but please don't just turn up and risk it. Farmers used to be more amenable to the odd inconspicuous tent but attitudes have changed and if you were discovered you would certainly not be made welcome.

Rates for camping range from £3.50 per tent to £7.50 per person, so it still remains the most economical way to walk the trail.

Hostels

Cheap hostel-style accommodation along the Cotswold Way itself is available only in Bath, although there at least you'll have a choice, with beds from £12 a night. The city's youth hostel, where accommodation discounts are available to members of Hostelling International (🖳 www.hihostels.com), and the **Youth Hostels Association** (☎ 01629-592700, 🖳 www.yha.org.uk), is a good mile east of the centre, so a fair trek for walkers. The cost of annual YHA membership is currently £15.95 per person, or £9.95 for those under 26, with family membership at £22.95 for two adults at the same address.

B&Bs and guesthouses

Although historically there is a distinct difference between a guesthouse and the more personal B&B, the edges are becoming increasingly blurred. Traditionally, those staying in a B&B, where overnight visitors are limited to no more than six at any one time, will find themselves very much as guests in a private house. Establishments accommodating greater numbers have to be registered as a guesthouse.

Staying in **B&Bs** brings you into contact with local people in a way that hotels and guesthouses can't. For anyone unfamiliar with the concept, you get a bedroom in someone's home along with a cooked breakfast the following morning. The accommodation is invariably clean and comfortable, traditionally with the emphasis on floral patterns and chintz – although things are changing fast, and rooms in many B&Bs along the Cotswold Way compete with the best for style and elegance. If one night you find yourself in a modern bungalow, the next could be in a picture-perfect cottage, or on a working farm.

Guesthouses, which effectively bridge the gap between B&Bs and hotels, may be more structured in approach. In reality, especially in some of the towns along the trail, many walkers have no idea whether they're in a B&B or a guesthouse. What matters is a warm welcome, a comfortable room, and – ideally – someone who understands that walkers tend to have muddy boots and wet clothes.

Where visitor numbers are high, such as in Bath or Broadway, you may well find that a minimum two-night stay is imposed, which can cause problems for walkers. Others simply charge a higher rate for one-nighters. Such restrictions are most likely to be the case at weekends or in the height of the tourist season.

What to expect For most long-distance walkers, tourist-board star-rating systems have little meaning. At the end of a long day you'll simply be glad of a place with hot water and a smiling welcome. It is these criteria that have been used for places included in this guide, rather than whether a room has tea- and coffee-making facilities, a shaver point or TV – though many of them have.

In the trend towards making rooms **'en suite'**, many places have carved out a tiny area for a shower and a loo. Yet a larger room with a bathroom across the corridor, often for your own private use, could well be preferable – and the option of a hot bath has significant appeal if you're cold and wet; establishments with baths are indicated in this guide with a ☛ symbol. Finding anywhere with a **single** room is increasingly difficult, and those there are tend to be pretty small. A **double** room is supposed to have one double bed, and a **twin** room two singles, but sometimes the two are interchangeable, allowing greater flexibility. The concept of a **family room** – defined in this guide as any room that will sleep three or more – is becoming increasingly popular, and can work well for walkers travelling as a group.

Some B&Bs and guesthouses have a **sitting room** exclusively for guests' use, a real bonus at the end of a day when retiring to your room instead of relaxing in a comfy chair can seem something of an anti-climax. Others will welcome guests to sit out in the **garden** on a summer's evening.

An **evening meal** is sometimes on offer at the more isolated establishments, though you should always pre-book this or you could go hungry. If you're expecting a meal, but are delayed, do ring ahead. Nobody wants to serve (or eat) dried-up lasagne and limp salad. If meals are not available, many owners will offer you a lift to the nearest pub if it's too far to walk.

Rates The image of B&B as a cheap option is no longer valid; costs have soared in recent years. For the most part, you can expect to pay around £50-60 per night for a double room sharing a bathroom (which is increasingly unusual), rising to at least £60-75 en suite, and often significantly more. A lot depends on location and facilities, of course. The touristy towns tend to command a premium, and some of the classier establishments quote rates on a par with those at a boutique hotel, with £120 a room not untypical.

Most rates in this guide are quoted for two people sharing a double room, reflecting the increasing trend even in family-run B&Bs to operate on this basis. That said, some places still charge per person, and a few charge more for a twin room than for a double – which may not seem logical to ordinary mortals. Few places along the Cotswold Way offer single rooms, but most will discount the rate of a twin or double room for lone walkers by about £5-15 a night.

Transport Where places offering accommodation are not right on the Cotswold Way, B&B owners may offer to collect walkers at an agreed rendezvous and deliver them back to the trail next day. It's a service that is usually provided free of charge, but do check first. It is important to agree lift arrangements at the time of making the booking. If you are walking with a mobile phone, it might be helpful to ring ahead to warn of your impending arrival at the pick-up point.

Pubs

Many pubs offer B&B accommodation, and some supply every modern convenience – including luxuries such as four-poster beds. Obviously they tend to be less personal than B&Bs, but for some walkers that's a bonus – and you don't have far to go to the bar, either. Of greater concern for most people is that pubs can be quite noisy, especially at weekends, so bear this in mind if you fancy an early night.

In general, pub prices along the Cotswold Way are similar to those at B&Bs, averaging £70 B&B for an en suite double room. In tourist areas, many pubs – like B&Bs – charge extra at weekends (including Friday night), whereas at more business-orientated establishments, prices drop at weekends.

Hotels

At first glance, a hotel may not seem the obvious venue for a walker. Muddy boots and a rucksack might seem at odds with the surroundings, and having something suitable to change into could pose a problem, but if you can get over that hurdle, you're down to issues of cost and style.

Most hotels charge per room rather than per person, and while some will negotiate a rate for single occupancy, this is by no means the norm. The increasing use of 'dynamic pricing' – where rates vary almost daily in line with demand – means that prices can vary significantly, especially if booked online, and makes it difficult to generalise. While you might expect to pay at least £80 for a double or twin room with breakfast, booking early can make a big difference, especially out of season. Conversely, during festivals or at similar times, rates can be extortionate. Do check whether or not breakfast is included, and watch out for hidden extras such as service charge and VAT.

Holiday cottages

The inclusion of holiday cottages is outside the scope of a guide dedicated to walkers on the move. However, for those who would prefer to stay at a fixed base, covering different parts of the route each day, self-catering may be the perfect option. Typically cottages are let on a weekly or fortnightly basis, with prices starting at around £300 a week for four people in the low season. For details, contact the relevant tourist information centre (see box p41). And if you're after something more individual, you could try one of the properties owned by the Landmark Trust (see box p60).

❏ **Real ale along the trail**

Much of the beer found in pubs along the path is pasteurised and manufactured in millions of gallons and distributed throughout Britain. Known as keg beer, it has been reviled by real ale drinkers in its time but is invariably smooth and tastes the same wherever you are.

However, traditional real ale, the product of small-scale local breweries, is always in demand. Real ale continues to ferment in the cask so can be drawn off by hand pump or a simple tap on the cask itself. Keg beer, on the other hand, has the fermentation process stopped by pasteurisation and needs the addition of gas to give it fizz and sparkle.

Keep an eye out for pubs displaying the CAMRA sticker, which shows they have been selected by the Campaign for Real Ale (🖳 www.camra.org.uk). This invaluable organisation, which publishes the annual *Good Beer Guide*, has been largely responsible for the revival of independent breweries in the UK. Their 'LocAle' initiative goes further, encouraging pubs to stock at least one locally brewed ale. Many also have a selection of guest ales from surrounding counties to add variety. Look out, too, for the Cask Marque emblem, indicating ales served to a specified standard.

Local brews you'll find along the Cotswold Way are those by Donnington, Goffs, Cotswold Spring, Wickwar, Severn Vale, Stanway, Uley, Stroud (their Budding was voted best bitter by the Gloucester branch of CAMRA in 2011), Bath Ales, and Abbey Ales. You'll find offerings from the Hereford-based Wye Valley Brewery, too, while the Cornish contingent is represented by Sharp's. All create good pints, but try the brews above 4% ABV for better taste and flavour.

Whether you're after a quick half at lunch or putting your feet up in the evening, there are many pubs offering good-quality ales. The *Crown and Trumpet* (see p86) in Broadway has ales from the small brewery based at Stanway House, which might include Stanney Bitter or Cotswold Gold. An evening meal at *The Mount Inn* (see p90) at Stanton washed down with a pint of Donnington's is hard to beat, or if you time it right a lunch break at *The Edgemoor Inn* (see p127) will offer Wickwar's BOB amongst others. While wandering around Painswick drop into *The Royal Oak* (see p126) for a selection from the Stroud Brewery. Well worth a short detour is *The Old Crown* (see p136) at Uley which, as well as supporting its own local brewery (Pig's Ear was an award winner in 2011), offers an ever-changing choice of other beers; if it all gets too much you can stay overnight, too.

Further south you arrive at ale-seekers' heaven, *The Old Spot* (see p141) in Dursley, voted best cask ale pub at the Great British Pub Awards in 2011, it offers a wonderful array of bitters, including Old Ric (named after owner Ric Sainty who died in 2008). *The Beaufort Arms* at Hawkesbury Upton has an ever-changing range and is a 'LocAle' pub, while continuing along the trail, *The Dog Inn* (see p156) at Old Sodbury has Sharp's Doom Bar.

And when you finish in Bath (see p179), you could celebrate at *The Star* or the *Old Green Tree* with a pint of Bellringer (Abbey Ales). The *Volunteer Rifleman's Arms* and *The Raven* are other good choices offering a wide range, while for a pint of Gem (Bath Ales), look no further than *The Salamander*.

FOOD AND DRINK

The Cotswolds area isn't known for its haute cuisine. Historically at least, this is a region of simple, farmhouse fare, based on good ingredients, rather than fine cooking. In Bath you'll come across a few regional specialities (see box p178), but elsewhere savvy travellers seek out the delights of Old Spot pork, Cotswold honey or Double Gloucester cheese. Tea rooms do a fine trade in cream teas, too, though it would be stretching a point to suggest that this is typical of the region.

Breakfast and lunch

For breakfast, a fry-up of bacon, eggs and sausages is considered *de rigueur* by many walkers – and supplied by all good B&B hosts. Most offer a buffet of cereals and fruit juice and toast as well, so if a 'full English' isn't for you, you'll always be able to fall back on something lighter.

Unless you're planning to stop at a pub en route, you will probably need a packed lunch. Many B&B owners will provide one for around £5, and will also fill your flask with coffee or tea. If you don't fancy breakfast, it's worth asking if you could have a packed lunch instead. Alternatively you could pick up the makings of a picnic lunch at village shops along the trail: rolls, cheese, apples and cereal bars survive well in a rucksack for a couple of days. Be careful to plan ahead, though, as there are sections of the walk when you won't come across any shops at all. In any event, you should always carry some form of high-energy food in case of emergency (see p39).

Evening meals

Perhaps more than any other national trail, the Cotswold Way is abundantly supplied with **pubs** and **inns**, not to mention some pretty exclusive **restaurants**. Where B&Bs are off the beaten track, most owners will provide an evening meal by prior arrangement, or will drive you to the nearest pub. Occasionally, however, you'll have to fend for yourself, which could involve considerable extra mileage at the end of a long day.

Aside from the ubiquitous pub grub, the choice on menus continues to widen, and almost everywhere will have at least one vegetarian option. If you're keeping a strict eye on costs, stick to pubs rather than restaurants, or look for fixed-price menus – often available early in the evening before the place gets busy.

Alternatively, there are numerous **takeaways** in towns along the route, from fish and chips, pizza parlours and kebab joints to Indian and Chinese cuisine.

Self-catering

There are enough shops along the path to allow you to buy supplies frequently, so in general you should not need to carry food for longer than a couple of days. Most village shops are open seven days a week, often from 8am to 8pm or even later, taking full advantage of casual trade and the sale of alcohol. Fuel for camp stoves may not always be available, though, and, while Camping Gaz and meths can usually be found in the towns, it makes sense not to let supplies run low.

Drink

During licensing hours you can get a pint of beer or any other drink in licensed premises. The key lies in the words 'during licensing hours'. Gone are the days when pubs were permitted to sell alcohol only during limited hours between 11am and 11pm Monday to Saturday and from 12 noon on Sundays. Instead, each landlord has to apply for a licence relating to the maximum number of hours in which drinking is permitted on the individual premises. As a result, hours are far more flexible, and while many pubs in rural areas still close during the afternoon on weekdays, if not at weekends, you've at least a chance of finding a thirst-quenching pint when you want it.

Note that the opening times given for pubs in Part 4 are those for which food is served, not necessarily the full licensing hours.

Drinking water Carry at least a litre of water, and top it up at public toilets during the day: these are marked on the trail maps in Part 4. Alternatively, ask locally; most people are happy to fill a bottle of water, though it's only fair to buy something first in a pub or café. Drinking from streams is not advisable.

MONEY

Plan your money needs carefully. It makes sense to carry cash for day-to-day spending and to pay for campsites. Most pubs and all but the smallest village shops accept credit cards, but in B&Bs, payment by cheque is the norm. Even those that have facilities for card payments will often levy an extra charge.

If you're planning to stick to cash, start with about £200 and expect to replenish along the way. All the towns you pass through have ATMs, either in banks or in supermarkets. Cash can also be drawn at post offices against many UK bank accounts: for full details, see 🖳 www.postoffice.co.uk. Note that you need to have your cheque book or debit card with you, and your PIN number. Travellers' cheques can be exchanged in banks, foreign exchange bureaux and the larger hotels, but these are of least use to the walker.

For more on money, see p40; for budgeting, see pp28-9.

OTHER SERVICES

Many of the villages and all the towns along the trail have at least one public **telephone**, a small **shop** and a **post office**. Apart from getting cash, post offices may be used for sending home unnecessary equipment that may be weighing you down. In Part 4, mention is given to other services that may be of use to the walker such as **outdoor equipment shops**, **launderettes**, **internet access**, **pharmacies** and **tourist information centres**. The latter can be used, among other things, for finding and (sometimes) booking accommodation.

TAKING DOGS ALONG THE COTSWOLD WAY

For many walkers a dog is an inseparable companion and there is no reason why yours shouldn't accompany you, provided you act responsibly and keep it under control at all times. The deal with dog mess is the same on a national trail as it is in the local park: clear it up. It is a legal requirement to keep dogs under control on public rights of way. On most 'access land' (ie open country and common land, as against public paths) you must keep a dog on a short lead between 1 March and 31 July, and at all times when you're near farm animals. Farmers are legally entitled to shoot a dog found worrying sheep – and they do. That said, if you or your dog is chased by a farm animal, it may be safer to let the dog off the lead rather than risk injury. Dogs running free in standing crops can also cause damage, so do take care to prevent this. Be aware, too, that ground-nesting birds are active between March and June. A dog on the loose at this time could inadvertently frighten them off and possibly cause them to desert their nests.

Some B&Bs positively welcome dogs, others are less keen. In Part 4 of this guide, a symbol 🐾 indicates that dogs are usually welcome, though you should still always check ahead; some may accept only small dogs, for example. Few B&Bs charge for dogs but hotels often do, with rates varying from £5 a night to £20 per stay. Hostels generally don't accept dogs at all, with the exception of assistance dogs.

DISABLED ACCESS

Many areas of the trail are inaccessible to the majority of wheelchair and scooter users, and those of limited mobility, either because the terrain is unsuitable or because of the not inconsiderable number of kissing gates to be negotiated. Some sections, however, are more forgiving – particularly near country parks which also have nearby parking.

The Cotswolds Conservation Board (see p58) offers a series of walks within the Cotswolds AONB. Entitled *Walks on Wheels*, they can be downloaded from the website. Another initiative involves the hire of off-road mobility scooters at Crickley Hill Country Park. Known as Trampers, the scooters can be hired between April and September for £2.50 an hour, on completion of a short training session, and can be used on any of four waymarked trails. For more on countryside access for the disabled, contact Disabled Ramblers (💻 www.disabledramblers.co.uk).

WALKING COMPANIES

For walkers wanting to make their holiday as easy and trouble-free as possible there are several specialist companies offering a range of services, from baggage carrying to fully guided group tours.

Baggage carriers/accommodation booking

The thought of carrying a heavy pack puts a lot of people off walking long-distance trails, but it need not be an issue. Using a **baggage-carrying service** to deliver your bags to your accommodation each night will leave you free to walk unencumbered (well, with just a day pack) during the day. Charges during 2011 were around £7-8 per bag for each leg of the journey.

Alternatively, some of the **taxi** firms listed in Part 4 will provide a similar service on request, or you could make an arrangement with your B&B host, some of whom handle baggage transport themselves. Prices vary widely, depending on the mileage involved and the individual concerned, but generally you can expect to pay at least £20 a day which makes using a specialised baggage carrier much better value.

Note that Sherpa Van also provides an **accommodation booking** service.

● **Carryabag** (☎ 01242-250642, 🖳 www.carryabag.co.uk; Cheltenham)
● **Cotswold Luggage Transfers** (☎ 01386-840688, 🖳 www.luggage-transfers. co.uk; Chipping Campden)
● **Sherpa Van** (☎ 01748 826917 for baggage transfer only; ☎ 01609 883731, 🖳 www.sherpavan.com; Richmond, N Yorks). Minimum two bags.

Self-guided walking holidays The following companies provide customised packages for walkers, which usually include detailed advice and notes on itineraries, maps, accommodation booking, daily baggage transfer and trans-

---

PLANNING YOUR WALK

❑ **Information for foreign visitors**
● **Business hours** Most **shops** and main **post offices** are open at least from Monday to Friday 9am-5pm and Saturday 9am-12.30pm, but many, shops in particular, choose longer hours and some open on Sunday as well. Occasionally, especially in rural areas, you'll come across a local shop that closes at midday during the week, usually a Wednesday or Thursday, a throwback to the days when all towns and villages had an early-closing day. Many **supermarkets** remain open 12 hours a day; the Spar chain usually displays '8 till late' on the door. **Banks** typically open Monday to Friday at 9.30am until 3.30pm or 4pm, but of course ATM machines are open all the time. **Pub** hours are less predictable, but common opening hours are 11am-2.30pm and 6-11pm Mon-Sat, opening an hour later on Sunday evenings.
● **Holidays** Most business premises close on 1 January, Good Friday and Easter Monday (March/April), the first and last Monday in May, the last Monday in August, Christmas Day and Boxing Day (25-26 December), all of which are designated as 'bank holidays'. **School holidays** in England are generally as follows (though these can vary slightly, especially if Easter is very early or late): a one-week break late October, two weeks over Christmas and the New Year, a week mid-February, two weeks around Easter, one week at the end of May/early June (to coincide with the end-May bank holiday) and five to six weeks from late July to early September. Private school holidays fall at the same time, but tend to be slightly longer.
● **Money** The British pound (£) comes in notes of £100, £50, £20, £10 and £5, and coins of £2 and £1. The pound is divided into 100 pence (usually referred to as 'p', pronounced 'pee') which comes in silver coins of 50p, 20p, 10p and 5p, and copper coins of 2p and 1p. Up-to-date **rates of exchange** can be found on 🖳 www.xe.com/ucc, at some post offices, or at any bank or travel agent.
● **Time** During the winter, the whole of Britain is on Greenwich Meantime (GMT). The clocks move forward one hour on the last Sunday in March, remaining on British Summer Time (BST) until the last Sunday in October.
● **Travel insurance and EHICs** Although Britain's National Health Service is free at the point of use, that is only the case for residents. All visitors to Britain should be properly insured, including comprehensive health coverage. EC residents can obtain essential health treatment during a temporary visit to Britain on production of a valid EHIC card. For details, contact your national social security institution.

port at the start and end of your walk. If you don't want the whole package, some companies will arrange just accommodation-booking or baggage-carrying services on their own.

- **British and Irish Walks** (☎ 01242-254353, 🖥 www.britishandirishwalks.com; Cheltenham) Covers only some sections of the Cotswold Way not the entire route.
- **Celtic Trails** (☎ 01291-689774, 🖥 www.celtrail.com; Chepstow)
- **Compass Holidays** (☎ 01242-250642, 🖥 www.compass-holidays.com; Cheltenham)
- **Contours Walking Holidays** (☎ 01629-821900, 🖥 www.contours.co.uk; Derbyshire)
- **Cotswold Journeys** (☎ 01242-237775, 🖥 www.cotswoldjourneys.com; Cheltenham)
- The **Cotswold Walking Company** (☎ 01242-604190, 🖥 www.thecotswold walkingcompany.com; Cheltenham).

- **Smoking** A ban on smoking in public places came into force in England in July 2007. The ban relates not only to pubs and restaurants, but also to B&Bs, hostels and hotels. These latter have the right to designate one or more bedrooms where the occupants can smoke, but the ban affects all enclosed areas open to the public – even if they are in a private home such as a B&B. Should you be foolhardy enough to light up in a no-smoking area, which includes pretty well any indoor public place, you could be fined £50, but it's the owners of the premises who carry the can if they fail to stop you, with a potential fine of £2500.

- **Telephone** From outside Britain the international country access code for Britain is ☎ 44 followed by the area code minus the first 0, and then the number you require. Within Britain, to call a number with the same code as the phone you are calling from, the code can be omitted: dial the number only. It is cheaper to ring at weekends, and after 6pm and before 8am on weekdays. If you're using a mobile phone that is registered overseas, consider buying a local SIM card to keep costs down. See also p40 for details about using a public phone. For the **emergency services** (police, ambulance, fire or coastguard), dial ☎ 999.

- **Churches** Although some churches are open to visitors during daylight, many nowadays are kept locked for security reasons. If you'd like to take a look around, it is worth seeing if there is a note about a keyholder, or – if you are staying in a town or village – asking locally who you could contact.

- **Weights and measures** Following a European Commission directive, milk in Britain can still be sold in pints (568ml), as can beer in pubs, though most other liquid including petrol (gasoline) and diesel is now sold in litres. Road distances will also continue to be given in miles (1.6km) rather than kilometres. Most food is sold in metric weights (g and kg) but the imperial weights of pounds (lb) and ounces (oz) are frequently displayed too.

The population remains split between those who still use inches and feet and those who are happy with centimetres and millimetres; you'll often be told that 'it's only a hundred yards or so' to somewhere, rather than a hundred metres or so. The weather – a frequent topic of conversation – is also an issue: while most forecasts predict temperatures in °C, many people continue to think in terms of °F.

● **Cotswold Walking Holidays** (☎ 01242-518888, 🖳 www.cotswoldwalks
.com; Cheltenham)
● **Discovery Travel** (☎ 01904-632226, 🖳 www.discoverytravel.co.uk; York)
● **Explore Britain** (☎ 01740-650900, 🖳 www.explorebritain.com; Co Durham)
● **Footpath Holidays** (☎ 01985-840049, 🖳 www.footpath-holidays.com; Nr
Warminster, Wilts)
● **HF Holidays** (☎ 0845-470 8558, 🖳 www.hfholidays.co.uk; Elstree, Herts)
● **Let's Go Walking** (☎ 01837-880075, 🖳 www.letsgowalking.com; Devon)
● **Macs Adventure** (☎ 0141-530 8886, 🖳 www.macsadventure.com; Glasgow).
● **Sherpa Expeditions**(☎ 020-577 2717, 🖳 www.sherpa-walking-holidays
.co.uk; Middlesex). Northern section only.
● **UTracks** (☎ 0845-241 7599, 🖳 www.utracks.com; Wimbledon). Part of the
northern section only.
● **The Walking Holiday Company** (☎ 01600-713008, 🖳 www.thewalkinghol
idaycompany.co.uk; Monmouth).

Group/guided walking tours Fully guided tours are ideal for individuals
wanting to travel in the company of others and for groups of friends wanting the
reassurance of a guide. The packages usually include meals, accommodation,
transport arrangements, minibus back-up and baggage transfer, as well as a
qualified guide. Companies' specialities differ widely, with varied sizes of
group, standards of accommodation, age range of clients and professionalism of
guides, so it's worth checking carefully before making a booking.
    There is also an annual series of guided walks along the trail run out of
Winchcombe by the Cotswold Voluntary Wardens (see p97).
● **Footpath Holidays** (see above) Tours take in only parts of the Cotswold Way.
● **HF Holidays** (see above) Covers Chipping Campden to Wotton-under-Edge.
● **Let's Go Walking** (see above)
● **Ramblers Countrywide Holidays** (☎ 01707-331133, 🖳 www.ramblersholi
days.co.uk; Welwyn Garden City). Four-day 'highlights' of the Cotswold Way.

Budgeting

How you budget for your trip will depend largely on the type of accommodation you use and where you have your meals. If you camp and cook for yourself, you will be able to keep costs to a minimum. These escalate as you go up
the accommodation and dining scales and will also be affected by the extent to
which you use the services offered to guests, such as transportation of luggage,
packed lunches and other refinements.

CAMPING

The cost of camping along the Cotswold Way varies from £3.50 to £7.50 per person, sometimes plus an extra £1 or so for the use of a shower. Living frugally,

you could get by on as little as £10-15 per person per night, pitching your tent at official sites and cooking your own food. Most walkers, however, will indulge in the occasional cooked breakfast (around £5), the odd pint of beer (around £2.50), or a pub meal after a long hard day (£9-11), so it's probably more realistic to reckon on at least £15-20 per day. That said, places where you can camp along the Cotswold Way are limited, so you'll almost certainly have to budget for the occasional night in a B&B if you plan to complete the whole trail in one go.

HOSTELS

In reality, the only hostels you're going to find along the route are in Bath and (some way off) in Cheltenham, where you'll pay somewhere between £14.40 and £35 for the night, in some cases including a continental breakfast. Typically prices are higher at weekends and in the summer months than at quieter periods. Most hostels have some form of self-catering facility, although where an evening meal is available, you can expect to pay upwards of around £9 for it.

B&Bs AND PUBS

If you're sharing a room, allow around £30-40 per head for an overnight stay with breakfast, perhaps more in the tourist towns over a summer weekend. Add on the cost of an evening meal, at around £9-16, without drinks, and you won't be far wrong on £40-50 per person per day. Buying a packed lunch will cost an extra £5 or so. Those travelling alone will almost certainly find that a single room, or single occupancy of a double room, will cost more – so anticipate an additional £5-15 a day.

EXTRAS

Don't forget to set aside some money for the inevitable extras, such as batteries, postcards, buses and taxis, drinks, cream teas, snacks and entrance fees – or, rather more crucially, any changes of plan. Around £50-100 should be about right.

Itineraries

All walkers are individuals. Some like to cover large distances as quickly as possible. Others are happy to amble along, stopping whenever the whim takes them. You may want to walk the Cotswold Way in one go, tackle it in a series of days or weekends, or use it as the basis for individual linear walks; the choice is yours. To accommodate these different options, this guide has not been divided up into strict daily sections, which could impose too rigid a structure on how you should walk. Instead it has been designed to make it easy for you to plan the itinerary that suits you. If you need an added spur, consider signing up for the Cotswold Way Hall of Fame which recognises those who have completed the entire walk. For details, see 'planning a trip' on the National Trails' website (p41).

The **planning map** opposite the inside back cover and the **table of facilities** on pp32-3 summarise the essential information for you to make a plan of your own, in conjunction with the **distance chart** on pp186-7. Alternatively, to make it even easier, see the **suggested itineraries** (opposite) and simply choose your preferred speed of walking. There are also suggestions on p36 for those who want to experience the best of the trail over a day or a weekend. The **public transport map** (p46) may help at this stage.

Having made a rough plan, turn to **Part 4** where you will find summaries of the route, full descriptions of accommodation, places to eat and other services in each town and village, with detailed trail maps.

WHICH DIRECTION?

Most guidebooks to the Cotswold Way assume you will walk from north to south, which is the direction that has been followed in the layout of this book. There are some compelling reasons for this. To start with, although the prevailing wind is from the west, the Cotswolds frequently experience some vicious north-easterlies, and walking into the teeth of these can be decidedly unpleasant. Then there's the fact that the north Cotswolds have more than their fair share of attractive villages and towns with plenty of places to stay and eat – so that distances can be kept shorter in the initial stages, and there's a good choice of restaurants and B&Bs at the end of a walking day. And for those in need of an incentive, what better way to celebrate the end of the walk than by relaxing in Bath's spa?

Of course, starting from Bath has its advantages, too. Some walkers prefer not to have the sun in their eyes, which can be a deciding factor (although less so than you might think, since the route takes a considerable number of twists and turns). Others may wish to explore one of the quintessential Cotswold villages at leisure once the walk is over. The maps in Part 4 give timings for both directions and, as route-finding instructions are on the maps rather than in the text, it is perfectly straightforward to walk from south to north using this guide.

SUGGESTED ITINERARIES

The itineraries opposite are suggestions only, based on the location of places to stay. How you plan your walk will depend on several factors, from the availability of accommodation to personal interests, as well as the distance you choose to walk each day. Don't forget to add travelling time before and after the walk, and to allow additional time for photography and breaks – or simply to stop and stare.

SIDE TRIPS

Most people embarking on the Cotswold Way do so with the express aim of completing the walk from A to B, and there's certainly enough of interest to justify spending at least a week along the trail. Yet it's always tempting to take off the blinkers occasionally and consider what happens to left and right.

(cont'd on p35)

❏ SUGGESTED ITINERARIES

All itineraries assume that walkers take the route via Selsley Common and around Stinchcombe Hill. Not all places have a campsite; those that have (with or without B&Bs) have been asterisked.

● Itinerary for slower walkers and those who want to linger

Walking an average of 10-12 miles (16-19km) a day, with two longer days of around 13 miles (21km) and three shorter days of 7-8½ miles (11-13.5km).

Day	Daily schedule	Miles/km	B&B-style accommodation/ Campsite*
1	Chipping Campden to Stanton	10½/17	Stanton
2	Stanton to Winchcombe	7½/12	Hailes*, Winchcombe*
3	Winchcombe to Dowdeswell Res	11/17.5	Dowdeswell Reservoir
4	Dowdeswell to Birdlip	10½/17	Birdlip
5	Birdlip to Randwick	13½/21.5	Randwick, Westrip*
6	Randwick to Dursley	10½/17	Dursley, North Nibley*
7	Dursley to Wotton-under-Edge	7/11	Wotton-under-Edge
8	Wotton-under-Edge to Little Sodbury	13/21	Little Sodbury*
9	Little Sodbury to Cold Ashton	8½/13.5	Cold Ashton*
10	Cold Ashton to Bath	10/16	Bath*

● Itinerary for steady walkers

Walking an average of 12-15miles (21-22½km) a day with two shorter days of 10½ miles (25.5km)

Day	Daily schedule	Miles/km	B&B-style accommodation/ Campsite*
1	Chipping Campden to Wood Stanway	12½/20	Wood Stanway, Hailes*
2	Wood Stanway to Cleeve Hill	11½-13½/18.5-21.5	Cleeve Hill
3	Cleeve Hill to Birdlip	13½-15½/21.5-25	Birdlip
4	Birdlip to Randwick	14/22.5	Randwick, Westrip*
5	Randwick to Dursley	10½/17	Dursley, North Nibley*
6	Dursley to Hawkesbury Upton	14½/23	Hawkesbury Upton
7	Hawkesbury Upton to Pennsylvania	14/22.5	Pennsylvania, Cold Ashton*
8	Pennsylvania to Bath	10½/17	Bath*

● Itinerary for faster walkers

Walking 14-16 miles (22½-25.5km) a day with one short day of 9 miles (14½km)

Day	Daily schedule	Miles/km	B&B-style accommodation/ Campsite*
1	Chipping Campden to Hailes	16/25.5	Hailes*, North Farmcote
2	Hailes to Seven Springs	16/25.5	Coberley, Upper Coberley, Leckhampton
3	Seven Springs to Painswick	14/22.5	Painswick
4	Painswick to Uley	15½/25	Uley, North Nibley*
5	Uley to Wotton-under-Edge	9/14.5	Wotton-under-Edge
6	Wotton-under-Edge to Tormarton	15/24	Tormarton*
7	Tormarton to Bath	14½/23	Bath*

VILLAGE AND

Place name (Places in brackets are not directly on the Cotswold Way)	Distance from previous place directly on Way approx miles/km (via Selsley & Stinchcombe)	Cash machine (ATM)	Post office	Tourist information centre (TIC) or point (TIP)
Chipping Campden	Start of Cotswold Way	✔	✔	✔
Broadway	6/9.5	✔	✔	✔
(Buckland)				
(Snowshill)				
Stanton	4.5/7			
Stanway				
Wood Stanway	2/3			
(North Farmcote)				
Hailes	3.5/5.5			
Winchcombe	2/3	✔	✔	✔
Postlip	4/6.5			
Cleeve Hill	2/3			
(Cheltenham)		✔	✔	✔
(Ham Hill)				
(Charlton Kings)				
Dowdeswell Reservoir	5/8			
(Upper Coberley)				
Seven Springs	3/5			
(Coberley)				
(Leckhampton)				
(Little Shurdington)				
Crickley Hill	5/8			
Birdlip	2.5/4			
(Little Witcombe)				
Cranham Corner	2/3.25			
Painswick	2.5/4	✔	✔	✔
(Edge)				
(Randwick/Westrip)				
Stonehouse/Ebley	8.5/13.5			
(King's Stanley)	(quick route)	✔	✔	
Middleyard	1/1.5 (quick route)			
Selsley	1.5/2.5 (scenic route)			
(Nympsfield)				
(Uley)			✔	
Dursley	7.5/12 (alternative route)	✔	✔	
	6/9.5 (direct route)			
North Nibley	5/8	✔	✔	
Wotton-under-Edge	2/3	✔	✔	✔
(Hillesley)				

(cont'd on p34)

PLANNING YOUR WALK

TOWN FACILITIES

Eating place ✔=one; ✔✔=two; ✔✔✔=three +	Food store	Campsite	Hostel	B&B-style accommodation ✔=one ✔✔=two; ✔✔✔=three +	Place name (places in brackets are a short walk off the Cotswold Way: see opposite for distances)
✔✔✔	✔			✔✔✔	Chipping Campden
✔✔✔	✔			✔✔✔	Broadway
				✔	(Buckland)
✔				✔	(Snowshill)
✔				✔✔✔	Stanton
✔					Stanway
				✔✔	Wood Stanway
				✔	(North Farmcote)
✔		✔		✔	Hailes
✔✔✔	✔	✔		✔✔✔	Winchcombe
				✔	Postlip
✔✔✔				✔✔✔	Cleeve Hill
✔✔✔	✔		✔	✔✔✔	(Cheltenham)
				✔✔	(Ham Hill)
✔				✔✔	(Charlton Kings)
✔				✔	Dowdeswell Reservoir
				✔	(Upper Coberley)
✔					Seven Springs
				✔	(Coberley)
				✔	(Leckhampton)
				✔	(Little Shurdington)
✔					Crickley Hill
✔				✔	Birdlip
✔				✔✔	(Little Witcombe)
✔✔				✔	Cranham Corner
✔✔✔	✔			✔✔✔	Painswick
✔				✔✔	(Edge)
✔✔✔		✔		✔	(Randwick/Westrip)
				✔	Stonehouse/Ebley
✔	✔	✔		✔✔	(King's Stanley)
				✔✔	Middleyard
✔					Selsley
✔				✔	(Nympsfield)
✔	✔			✔	(Uley)
✔✔✔	✔			✔✔✔	Dursley (alternative route)
					Dursley (direct route)
✔	✔	✔		✔✔	North Nibley
✔✔✔	✔			✔✔✔	Wotton-under-Edge
✔				✔	(Hillesley)
					(cont'd on p35)

(cont'd on p35)

PLANNING YOUR WALK

VILLAGE AND

Place name (Places in brackets are not directly on the Cotswold Way)	Distance from previous place directly on Way approx miles/km (via Selsley & Stinchcombe)	Cash machine (ATM)	Post office	Tourist information centre (TIC) or point (TIP)
(cont'd from p32)				
Lower Kilcott	6/10			
Hawkesbury Upton	1.5/2.5		✔	
Little Sodbury	3.5/5.5			
Old Sodbury	2/3			
Coomb's End	0.5/1			
Tormarton	1.5/2.5			
(South of M4)				
Pennsylvania	6/10			
Cold Ashton	0.5/1			
Bath	10/16	✔	✔	✔

TOTAL DISTANCE   102 miles/163km or 100.5 miles/161km

❑ **Cotswold Way Relay**

It's been 18 years since the first Cotswold Way Relay, and the event continues to attract a considerable number of teams each year. Today, though, improved way-marking along the trail means fewer runners take the 'scenic' route – something that gains considerably in significance when you realise there are no marshals to guide the way.

The record for the fastest ladies' team is held by the organisers, Team Bath Athletic Club, who in 2008 knocked five minutes off the previous time to clock up an impressive 14 hours, 6 minutes and 13 seconds. The senior men's record, though, has stood since 1995 at precisely 11 hours and 55 minutes, set by Stroud & District Athletic Club.

The race starts in Chipping Campden at 7am on the last Saturday in June, finishing at Bath Abbey as evening draws in. It follows the official route of the Cotswold Way, which is divided into ten stages of varying lengths and difficulty. The shortest, between Dursley and Wotton-under-Edge, covers just 7¼ miles (11½km), but some runners contend with distances of 12 miles (19km) or more, and one group faces an ascent of 513m into the bargain.

Each stage sees a mass start, triggered by the expected arrival time of the first runner from the previous leg. With the tally in 2011 totalling 740 participants – so 74 runners per leg – you might just want to step off the path and let them pass!

TOWN FACILITIES

Eating place ✔=one; ✔✔=two; ✔✔✔=three +	Food store	Campsite	Hostel	B&B-style accommodation ✔=one ✔✔=two; ✔✔✔=three +	Place name (places in brackets are a short walk off the Cotswold Way: see opposite for distances)
(cont'd from p33)					
				✔	Lower Kilcott
✔✔	✔			✔✔	Hawkesbury Upton
		✔		✔	Little Sodbury
✔✔				✔✔✔	Old Sodbury
				✔	Coomb's End
✔✔		✔		✔✔✔	Tormarton
✔	✔				(South of M4)
				✔	Pennsylvania
✔		✔		✔✔✔	Cold Ashton
✔✔✔	✔	✔	✔	✔✔✔	Bath

PLANNING YOUR WALK

(*cont'd from p30*) With over 3000 miles (4800km) of footpaths in the Cotswolds AONB alone, and several long-distance trails crossing the region, there's a tantalising number of **side routes** you could follow.

Winchcombe is a great place to get sidetracked, for as well as the Cotswold Way, the town is a junction for several trails. Newest of these is the **Winchcombe Way**, a 42-mile (67km) figure-of-eight route with the focus firmly on the town. Others include the **Gloucestershire Way** (which meanders for 100 miles (160km) between Chepstow and Tewkesbury, taking in the Forest of Dean and the River Severn). Altogether more manageable – and offering the option of an interesting two-day loop – are the **Warden's Way** and the **Windrush Way**, which run over different routes between Winchcombe and Bourton-on-the-Water, covering 13 and 14 miles (21km and 22.5km) respectively.

If the idea of joining up the dots appeals, you could hardly do better than look at the 55-mile (88km) **Wysis Way**, which crosses the Cotswold Way north of Painswick, en route between two other national trails, Offa's Dyke Path and the Thames Path.

Further south, around Lower Kilcott, the **Monarch's Way** runs alongside the Cotswold Way for a short distance before continuing along its 615-mile (984km) journey between Worcester and Shoreham in Sussex. The route mirrors that taken by Charles II during his escape to France after the Battle of Worcester in 1651. The journey took the king six weeks to complete – with Parliamentary forces in hot pursuit. It's certainly food for thought.

❏ HIGHLIGHTS: THE BEST DAY AND WEEKEND WALKS
Day walks

The suggestions below take in various stretches of the Cotswold Way. The trail authorities have also implemented a series of circular walks, ranging from 1¹/₂ to 6¹/₂ miles and varying in difficulty. Although the walks are in part waymarked with a green roundel stating 'Cotswold Way Circular Walk', these waymarks are designed merely to complement the detailed and regularly updated route directions that can be downloaded from 💻 www.nationaltrail.co.uk/cotswold/text.asp?PageId=54.

● **Chipping Campden to Broadway** (see pp80-4) A good 6-mile (9.5km) introduction to the Cotswold Way, taking in two of the trail's most attractive towns, and some superb views from Dover's Hill and Broadway Tower. If you don't want to retrace your steps, there are buses between the two towns.

● **Broadway to Winchcombe** (see pp88-97) From one of the Cotswolds' most popular villages, this 12-mile (22km) stretch leads to one of the prettiest at Stanton – where there's an excellent pub to break up the day. The route drops down alongside the ruins of Hailes Abbey before continuing to the attractive wool town of Winchcombe. A regular bus service links the two towns.

● **Winchcombe to Cleeve Hill** (see pp100-4) A bracing 6¹/₂-miles (10.5km) will see you steadily climbing from Winchcombe up to Belas Knap long barrow (see box p101), and on through woodland to emerge on the edge of Cleeve Hill Common and the highest point of the trail, Cleeve Hill. To return, retrace your steps to the golf club and thence to the road, where a regular bus runs to Winchcombe.

● **Dowdeswell Reservoir to Crickley Hill** (see pp112-18) This 8-mile (12.5km) walk is ideal for nature lovers, taking in both ancient beechwoods and areas of unimproved limestone grassland, as well as the Devil's Chimney at Leckhampton, and some prehistoric sites. Finish at the Air Balloon pub. Public transport at both ends of the walk is via Cheltenham.

● **Crickley Hill to Painswick** (see pp116-24) More woods characterise this lovely 9-mile (14.5km) walk along the Cotswold escarpment, broken up by Cooper's Hill and Painswick Beacon, and finishing in the attractive town of Painswick. Buses serve both ends of the route.

● **Circular walk around Selsley Common** (see pp132-4) Start in King's Stanley and follow the road and cycle path parallel to the Stroudwater Canal, and thence to Selsley Common, for a 5-mile (8km) round trip that takes in some spectacular views, a fascinating Arts and Crafts church, and the two alternative routes along this stretch of the Cotswold Way.

● **Bath to Dyrham Park** (see pp167-160) ie reverse of the route description) Climb out of Bath towards the racecourse and the battlefields near Freezing Hill, then continue on to Dyrham Park. It's about 12¹/₂ miles (20km), so you might have enough time to explore the house or grounds before getting a taxi back to Bath.

Weekend walks

● **Chipping Campden to Cleeve Hill** (see pp81-104) If there's one walk along the trail that showcases the quintessential Cotswolds, this is it. Villages of Cotswold stone, rolling hills, woodland and some excellent views: they're all in this 24-mile (38.5km) route. Buses serve both ends of the walk.

● **Dursley to Tormarton** (see pp141-57) Most of this 22-mile (35km) walk follows the edge of the Cotswold escarpment, sometimes wooded, at others more open, with numerous small villages and the final stretch through Dodington Park. There are buses at both ends of the route.

What to take

How much you take with you is a very personal decision which takes experience to get right. For those new to long-distance walking the suggestions below will help you strike a sensible balance between comfort, safety and minimal weight.

KEEP IT LIGHT

If there's one maxim that is crucial to long-distance walking, it's 'keep it light'. It is all too easy to take things along 'just in case' but such items can soon mount up. If you are in any doubt about anything on your packing list, be ruthless and leave it at home. You're rarely far from a shop on the Cotswold Way, so if you find you've left out something that turns out to be essential, the chances are you'll be able to pick up an equivalent easily enough.

HOW TO CARRY IT

The size of your rucksack depends on how you plan to walk. If you are staying in B&Bs or pubs, you should be able to get all you need into a 40- to 50-litre pack: large enough for a change of clothes, waterproofs, essential toiletries, a water bottle and a packed lunch. Pack similar things in different-coloured stuff sacks or plastic bags so they are easier to pull out of the dark recesses of your pack, then put these inside a waterproof rucksack liner, or tough plastic sack, to protect everything if it rains. Those camping will also need space for a tent, sleeping bag, cooking equipment, towel and food: 65 to 75 litres' capacity should be about right.

Whatever its size, make sure before you set off that your rucksack is comfortable. Ideally it should have a stiffened back system and either be fully adjustable or exactly the right size for your back. Carrying the main part of the load high and close to your body with a large proportion of the weight on your hips (rather than on your shoulders) by means of the padded waist belt should allow you to walk in comfort for days on end. Play around with different ways of packing your gear and adjust all those straps until you get it just right. A useful extra is a bum/waist bag or a very light daypack to carry a camera, wallet and other essentials if you go off sightseeing.

Of course, if you decide to use a baggage-carrying service (see pp25-6) you can pack most of your things separately and simply carry a daypack with the essentials for a day's walking.

FOOTWEAR

A comfortable, well-fitting pair of leather or Gore-Tex-lined **boots** is the best footwear you can take, and essential if you're carrying a heavy rucksack. In addition to offering proper ankle support, which is particularly important on rough ground, they are most likely to keep your feet dry. Make sure they are properly waxed or waterproofed, both before you set out and during your walk.

Traditionally walkers wear two pairs of **socks**, one thin pair, with a thicker pair on top. Aside from adding warmth, this is a good blister-avoidance strategy, though modern walking socks with two inbuilt layers can do the job just as well. Taking three pairs of socks should be ample.

In summer you could get by with a light pair of trail **shoes** if you're carrying only a small pack, though it's not generally advisable. A second pair of shoes to wear in the evening is well worth taking, and they can be useful in case of injury, too. Lightweight trainers are best for the cooler months; in summer sports sandals are equally suitable.

CLOTHES

Wet and cold weather can catch you out even in summer, while spring and summer can be glorious at times, so go prepared for the unexpected. Most walkers pick their clothes according to the versatile layering system, which consists of a base layer to transport sweat away from your skin; a mid-layer or two to keep you warm; and an outer layer or 'shell' to protect you from the wind and rain.

Thermal material is ideal for **base layers** as it draws moisture away from the skin, keeping you drier (and thus warmer when you stop for a break) than a conventional cotton T-shirt. A **mid layer** of micro-fleece is ideal, being both warm and light, with an additional sweater or fleece useful for colder days or when you stop, when you can get cold very quickly. Both thermal tops and fleeces have the added advantage that they dry relatively quickly.

All this pales into insignificance when it comes to **waterproofs**. A waterproof jacket is essential year-round and will be much more comfortable (but also more expensive) if it's also 'breathable' to prevent the build-up of condensation on the inside. This layer can also be worn to keep the wind off. Waterproof trousers are important most of the year but in summer could be left behind if your main pair of trousers is reasonably windproof and quick-drying. Gaiters are rarely necessary except perhaps in winter if it's very wet.

Trousers and **shorts** should be light and quick-drying: trousers with zipped legs that convert into shorts can be ideal, especially in summer when the weather can change rapidly. Never wear denim jeans for walking: if they get wet they become heavy, cold and very uncomfortable. In winter, or if you're camping, consider a pair of thermal **longjohns** or thick tights.

What you take in the way of **underwear** is very much a personal preference, but if you want to change every day, you'll need three sets to ensure you always have one dry. Women may find a **sports bra** more comfortable because pack straps can cause bra straps to dig into your shoulders.

A **warm hat** is important at any time of the year, and **gloves**, too, except perhaps in the height of summer. It's surprising how quickly you can get cold if it's raining. In summer a **sunhat** will help to keep you cool and prevent sunburn, and **swimming gear** would be useful if you plan to take advantage of one of the pools en route. Finally, don't forget a **change of clothes** for the evenings. While wearing the same kit all week suits some, putting on clean clothes after a shower is a great morale boost – and will probably make you feel more comfortable if you're eating out.

TOILETRIES

Take only the minimum. In addition to **toothpaste** and a **toothbrush**, **sunscreen** is invaluable, and you'll need a small bar of **soap** if you're camping. Also take a suitable supply of any **medication** and, for women **tampons/sanitary towels**. A roll of **loo paper** in a plastic bag is handy, as is a lightweight **trowel** if you get caught out far from a toilet (see p51 for the code of the outdoor loo). What you pack in the line of deodorants, razors, hairbrushes etc is a matter of personal preference.

FIRST-AID KIT

Medical facilities in Britain are good so you only need the essentials to cover basic problems and emergencies. Ideally take a waterproof bag containing the following: **plasters/Band Aids** for minor cuts; **Compeed**, **Moleskin** or **Second Skin** for blisters; a selection of different-sized **sterile dressings** for wounds; **porous adhesive tape**; a **stretch bandage** for holding dressings or splints in place and for supporting a sprained ankle; a **triangular bandage** to make a sling for a broken or sprained arm; **elastic knee support** for a weak knee; **antiseptic wipes**; **antiseptic cream**; **safety pins**, **tweezers** and **scissors**; and **aspirin** or **paracetamol** for mild to moderate pain and fever.

Most importantly, do make sure you have a modicum of first-aid knowledge, or much of your kit will be rendered useless.

GENERAL ITEMS

Essential

Essential items you should carry are a **whistle** to attract attention if you get lost or find yourself in trouble; a **torch** (flashlight) with spare bulb and batteries in case you end up walking after dark; a one- or two-litre **water bottle/pouch**; **emergency food** such as chocolate, cereal bars or dried fruit; a **penknife** and a **watch**.

If you're not carrying a sleeping bag or tent you could also consider carrying an emergency plastic **bivvy-bag** – although at no stage on the route are you far from civilisation. A **compass** can be invaluable, especially in poor visibility, but do make sure you know how to use it.

Useful

Many would list a **camera** (and **spare memory cards** or **film** and **batteries**) as essential but a **notebook** or **sketchbook** are other good ways of recording your impressions, and **binoculars** mean you can observe wildlife more easily. A pair of **sunglasses** is useful, as is a **vacuum flask** for hot drinks. A **walking stick** or **pole** helps to take the shock off your knees (some walkers use two poles but this leaves no free hand).

A **mobile phone** is useful, although there are areas without any signal. For this reason, make sure that you always have the wherewithal to call from a public phone box in case you have no signal at the crucial moment. Calls to the emergency services (☎ 999, or ☎ 112 from a mobile) are free of charge, but those urgent calls to book a night's accommodation can catch you out. Calls cost a minimum of 40p, but increasingly you will need a credit, debit, BT or prepaid card instead. (Insert the card then follow the instructions.)

A **GPS** (see p17) device could also be useful in an emergency, but not as an alternative to a compass: batteries have been known to fail at the crucial moment.

CAMPING GEAR

If you're camping you will need a decent **tent** able to withstand wet and windy weather; a two- or three-season **sleeping bag**; a **sleeping mat**; a **stove** and **fuel**; **cooking equipment** (a pan with frying pan that can double as a lid/plate is fine for two people); a **bowl**, **mug** and **cutlery** (don't forget a can/bottle opener); and a **scourer** for washing up.

MONEY

The best way to carry your money is as **cash**. There are banks in most of the towns along the path, and ATMs in some others, so withdrawing money along the route with a **debit (or credit) card** is fairly straightforward. Cards are also the easiest way to pay in restaurants, hotels and supermarkets, many of which offer a cash-back facility. For most B&Bs you'll need to pay in cash or – for those with a British bank account – by **cheque**. For more details, see p24.

TRAVEL INSURANCE

Do consider insurance cover for loss or theft of personal belongings, especially if you are camping or staying in hostels, as there will be times when you'll have to leave your belongings unattended. Most British walkers will be covered under their home insurance policy, but it's worth checking this. For health insurance for visitors from overseas, see p26.

MAPS

The hand-drawn maps in this book cover the trail at a scale of 1:20,000, with plenty of detail and information to keep you on the right track. The **Ordnance Survey** (☎ 0845-456 0420, 🖥 www.ordnancesurvey.co.uk) covers the whole route at a scale of 1:25,000 on the following five maps: Outdoor Leisure series (double-sided maps with an orange cover) OL45, and Explorer series (also with orange covers) Nos 179, 168, 167 and 155. None of these is strictly necessary if you pay careful attention to the maps in this guide, which should lighten the load somewhat, as all five weigh about 1¹/₂lbs (0.7kg). They're expensive, too, at £7.99 for the single Explorer maps or for Explorer OLs, or £13.99 for the waterproof Explorer All Weather maps. That said, it's a good idea for safety's sake to carry the map covering the highest point of the walk, Cleeve Hill

Common (Explorer 179). Although the area is not particularly isolated, visibility up there can be seriously compromised when the mist comes down, making it easy to become disorientated and wander dangerously close to the edge of the escarpment. In such conditions a map from which you can take compass bearings is essential. Another useful option is the Harvey map (🖳 www.harveymaps.co.uk) which covers the whole route at 1:40,000 on a single, waterproof sheet, and costs £12.95.

While it may be extravagant to buy all these maps, Ramblers (see box below) allows members to borrow them at just 50p per map, or £1 for waterproof maps. Alternatively, members of Backpackers are entitled to discounts.

❏ SOURCES OF FURTHER INFORMATION

Trail information
Cotswold Way National Trail Office (tel 01451-862000, 🖳 www.nationaltrail.co.uk/cotswold) The website includes information on any diversions in place as well as details of events happening.

Tourist information offices
Tourist information offices provide all manner of locally specific information for visitors, although generally they are not there to proffer advice. A few – specifically in Bath and Cheltenham – have paid staff and offer an accommodation-booking service (for which there may be a charge). Others along the Cotswold Way are staffed by volunteers who usually have information on accommodation but may not be able to book it for you.

There are tourist offices on or near the Cotswold Way in **Chipping Campden** (see p76), **Broadway** (see p85), **Winchcombe** (see p98), **Cheltenham** (see p106), **Painswick** (see p123), **Wotton-under-Edge** (see p146) and **Bath** (see p168).

Tourist boards
Cotswolds Tourism (☎ 01452-328321, 🖳 www.cotswolds.com) has responsibility for all matters touristic throughout the region. Bath, though, is covered by its own authority, **Visit Bath** (see p168).

Another excellent source of information is the **Cotswolds Conservation Board** (see p58).

Organisations for walkers
● **Backpackers' Club** (🖳 www.backpackersclub.co.uk) A club aimed at people who are involved or interested in lightweight camping through walking, cycling, skiing, canoeing, etc. They produce a quarterly magazine, provide members with a comprehensive advisory and information service on all aspects of backpacking, organise weekend trips and also publish a farm-pitch directory. Membership is £12 per year.
● **Long Distance Walkers' Association** (🖳 www.ldwa.org.uk) Annual membership, at £13, includes three copies of *Strider* magazine a year giving details of challenge events and local group walks as well as articles on the subject. Information on 730 long-distance paths is presented in their *UK Trailwalkers' Handbook*.
● **Ramblers** (formerly Ramblers' Association; 🖳 www.ramblers.org.uk) Looks after the interests of walkers throughout Britain. They publish a large amount of useful information including their quarterly *Walk* magazine (£3.60 to non-members). The website also has a discussion forum. Membership costs £31/41/19.50 individual/joint/concessionary; £10 discount for individual/joint membership if paid by direct debit.

PLANNING YOUR WALK

RECOMMENDED READING

Field guides
There are plenty of good field guides on the market, though deciding which, if any, will justify space in a rucksack is a tough decision. The series published by Collins is unfailingly practical, if a little dated, though for identification purposes the RSPB's bird guides come out ahead.

● *Insects of Britain and Western Europe* by Michael Chinery (Collins, 1993)
● *The Mammals of Britain and Europe* by David Macdonald and Priscilla Barrett (Collins, 2005)
● *RSPB Pocket Birds* by Jonathan Elphick and John Woodward (Dorling Kindersley, 2009)
● *Trees of Britain and Northern Europe* by Mitchell and Wilkinson (Collins, 2001)
● *Wild Flowers of Britain and Northern Europe* by Richard Fitter, Alastair Fitter and Marjorie Blamey (Collins, 1996)

General reading
● *The Hidden Landscape: A Journey into the Geological Past* by Richard Fortey (Bodley Head, 2010) brings vividly and clearly to life the evolution of a landscape which most of us take for granted.
● *The Arts and Crafts Movement* by Elizabeth Cumming and Wendy Kaplan (Thames & Hudson, 1991) is a clear introduction to the complexities of the movement (see box p75), from its roots in Britain to continental Europe and the United States.

Biography
No journey through the Cotswolds is complete without Laurie Lee's classic childhood autobiography, *Cider with Rosie* (Vintage Classics, 2002).

Fiction
The novelist Jane Austen lived in Bath for five years, and set two of her novels, *Northanger Abbey* and *Persuasion*, in the city. Both can be found in several editions, including Penguin Classics, and afford a rather different perspective on the city and society to that seen by today's visitors. More recently, JK Rowling of *Harry Potter* fame hails from the Cotswolds; indeed, the town of Dursley is evoked in the surname of Harry's unpleasant uncle and aunt – though there the connection ends. If you're in to crime fiction, those written by Rebecca Tope with titles such as *A Grave in the Cotswolds* (Allison and Busby, 2011) should give you something to ponder as you walk along the trail.

Poetry
Most prolific among the poets whose work has been influenced by the Cotswolds is the war poet Ivor Gurney (1890-1937), who was born in Gloucester and served in World War I, before suffering severe mental problems and being confined to an institution. Others include James Elroy Flecker (1884-1915), who was buried in Cheltenham; and WH Davies (1871-1940), known the world over for his poem, *Leisure* (see p56), who made his home in Gloucestershire. Their work can be found in numerous poetry anthologies.

PLANNING YOUR WALK

Getting to and from the Cotswold Way

While Bath at the southern end of the trail is easily reached by train, bus, National Express coach or car, getting to and from Chipping Campden is more of a challenge. The nearest railway station is at Moreton-in-Marsh, from where there's a local bus, but taking a train to Stratford-upon-Avon, followed by a bus or taxi, is a viable alternative. For details, see p75 in Part 4 under Chipping Campden and the public transport tables on pp44-8.

Although there are no other railway stations on the trail itself, trains do service Stonehouse, some about half a mile (1km) to the west of Ryeford on the

PLANNING YOUR WALK

❑ **GETTING TO BRITAIN**
● **By air** Most international airlines serve London Heathrow (🖳 www.heathrowairport.com) and London Gatwick (🖳 www.gatwickairport.com). A number of budget airlines fly from many of Europe's major cities to the other London terminals at Stansted (🖳 www.stanstedairport.com) and Luton (🖳 www.london-luton.com). From London it takes about two hours to get to Bath by train; getting to Chipping Campden, which is not on the railway network, will take closer to three hours. There are a few flights from Europe to Bristol (🖳 www.bristolairport.co.uk) and Birmingham (🖳 www.birminghamairport.co.uk), which are closer to the Cotswold Way than London.
● **From Europe by train** Eurostar (🖳 www.eurostar.com) operates a high-speed passenger service via the Channel Tunnel between Paris/Brussels and London. Trains arrive and depart London from the international terminal at St Pancras station, which itself has connections to the London Underground and to all other main railway stations in London.

For more information on rail travel from Europe contact Rail Europe (🖳 www.raileurope.co.uk). A second site, 🖳 www.raileurope.com, is designed specifically for the needs of visitors from North America.
● **From Europe by coach** Eurolines (🖳 www.eurolines.com) works with 32 long-distance coach operators across Europe to provide an integrated network connecting some 500 destinations, as far flung as Moscow, Helsinki, Casablanca and London, in the UK, where it links in with the National Express network (see p45).
● **From Europe by car** Three companies operate **ferries** on the shorter cross-Channel route to Dover, usually taking around 75 minutes. Of these, P&O Ferries (🖳 www.poferries.com) and SeaFrance (🖳 www.SeaFrance.com) operate out of Calais. An alternative point of embarkation is Dunkerque, a two-hour crossing operated by DFDS (🖳 www.dfdsseaways.co.uk). There are also numerous other ferries linking the major North Sea and Channel ports of mainland Europe with ports along Britain's eastern and southern coasts.

Both 🖳 www.ferrysavers.com and 🖳 www.directferries.com have a full list of companies and services.

Eurotunnel (🖳 www.eurotunnel.com) operates the shuttle train service for vehicles via the Channel Tunnel between Calais and Folkestone, taking about an hour between the motorway in France and the motorway in Britain.

❏ RAIL SERVICES

Chiltern Railways (☎ 0845-600 5165, 🖳 www.chilternrailways.co.uk)
● London Marylebone–Leamington Spa–Warwick–**Stratford-upon-Avon**, Mon-Sat 6/day, Sun 5/day.

Cross Country (☎ 0844-811 0124, 🖳 www.crosscountrytrains.co.uk)
● Newcastle-upon-Tyne–York–Leeds–Birmingham New Street–**Cheltenham Spa** –Bristol, Mon-Sat 14/day, Sun 16/day. Some services continue to Exeter and Plymouth; others link in to destinations that include Aberdeen, Glasgow, Reading, Southampton and Bournemouth.

First Great Western (☎ 0845-700 0125, 🖳 www.firstgreatwestern.co.uk)
● London Paddington–Reading–Swindon–Chippenham–**Bath Spa**–Bristol Temple Meads, Mon-Fri 19/day, Sat 32/day, Sun 19/day (some services continue to Cardiff and Swansea).
● London Paddington–Swindon–Stroud–**Stonehouse**–Gloucester–**Cheltenham Spa** (some services require a change at Swindon), Mon-Fri 18/day, Sat 14/day, Sun 12/day
● London Paddington–**Moreton-in-Marsh**–**Evesham**–Worcester, Mon-Fri 19/day, Sat 14/day, Sun 12/day
● **Cheltenham Spa**–Gloucester–**Cam & Dursley**, Mon-Sat 9/day, Sun 6/day (additional trains require a change in Gloucester).

South West Trains (☎ 0845-600 0650, 🖳 www.southwesttrains.co.uk)
● London Waterloo–Woking–Basingstoke–Andover–Salisbury–**Bath Spa**–Bristol Temple Meads, Mon-Sat 3/day, Sun 2/day.

Ebley Canal, and there is a station north of Dursley with a linked bus service into the town centre. Connections to Cheltenham, about $2^{1}/_{2}$ miles (4km) west of the trail, are excellent. It is also possible to take the train to Stroud or Gloucester, then transfer by bus from there.

A network of local buses links most other villages along the Cotswold Way, making access for walkers relatively straightforward. As a result it is perfectly possible to create a series of linear walks without having to retrace your steps.

NATIONAL TRANSPORT

By rail

The rail services of most relevance to walkers along the Cotswold Way are from London Paddington to Moreton-in-Marsh (for Chipping Campden) and Bath, although there are also trains to Cheltenham Spa from the same London station, with connections from there to Cam & Dursley. A viable alternative to Chipping Campden is the Chiltern Railways service from London Marylebone to Stratford-upon-Avon.

Fares vary very widely, but significant savings can be made by booking well in advance, and by travelling at the quietest times of day. For the latest on train times, fares and rail information, contact **National Rail Enquiries** (☎

❑ COACH SERVICES

National Express

(☎ 0871-781 8178, ⌨ www.nationalexpress.com)

403 London Victoria–**Bath**, via Heathrow Airport, 10/day; some services call at stops that include Reading, Newbury, Swindon and Chippenham

302 Bristol–Northampton via **Bath**, Corsham, Chippenham, Swindon & Oxford, 1/day

444 London Victoria–Gloucester via **Cheltenham**, 9/day; some call at stops that include Reading, Cirencester and Stroud

London Victoria to Hereford via **Cheltenham**, 4/day; three services via Newent and Ross on Wye

London Victoria to Worcester via **Cheltenham**, 2/day (one service via Evesham, the other via Tewkesbury and Malvern)

222 London Heathrow–Gloucester via Swindon, Cirencester, **Charlton Kings** and **Cheltenham**, 10/day

335 Poole–Halifax via Bournemouth, Salisbury, Marlborough, Swindon, Cirencester, Gloucester, **Cheltenham**, Leicester and Huddersfield, 1/day

460 London–Stratford-upon-Avon via Coventry, Leamington Spa and Warwick, 3/day

---

0845-748 4950, or – from overseas – +44 (0)20-7278 5240, ⌨ www.national rail.co.uk).

To get to Moreton-in-Marsh from Bath, or vice versa, at the end of your walk, the most direct route (ie the one with the least number of changes) is via Reading, with both trains operated by First Great Western.

If you think you may need to book a taxi when you arrive, check the relevant place in the route guide or visit ⌨ www.traintaxi.co.uk for details of taxi companies operating at rail stations throughout England. It is also possible to book train tickets that include bus travel to your ultimate destination: enquire when you book your train ticket.

By coach

National Express (☎ 0871-781 8178, ⌨ www.nationalexpress.com) is the principal long-distance bus operator in Britain. The service of greatest use to Cotswold Way walkers is that to Bath, but coaches also run regularly from London to Cheltenham Spa, from where local buses connect to several points along the trail. See coach services box, above.

Travel by coach is usually cheaper than by train but takes rather longer. Advance bookings can carry significant discounts so it makes sense to book at least a week ahead.

By car

Chipping Campden lies west of Oxford, so the best access is via the M40 from London or Birmingham, leaving at junction 8 (northbound) or 9 (southbound) to link up with the A44 towards Evesham. The turning to Chipping Campden is the B4081 beyond Moreton-in-Marsh.

PLANNING YOUR WALK

PLANNING YOUR WALK

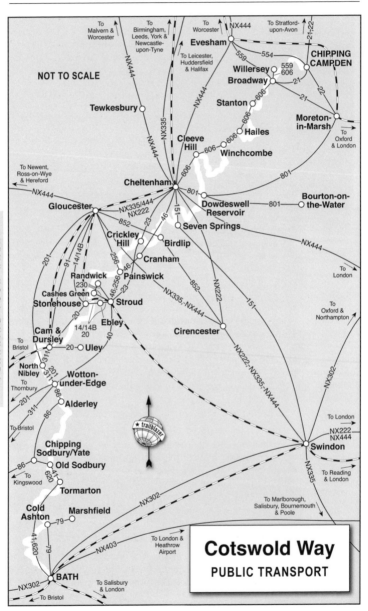

Cotswold Way
PUBLIC TRANSPORT

Getting to **Bath** is infinitely more straightforward: leave the M4 at junction 18, then take the A46. The greater problem is what to do with your car while you are tramping along the trail – and how to get back to it when you reach the end.

Parking in Bath is possible in one of the multi-storey car parks, but a long stay would be extremely expensive, and safety is also a consideration; parking on the road is not an option. In Chipping Campden, on-street parking is unrealistic, though the occasional B&B may have sufficient space to let you park for a week or so, provided you stay with them for a night or two. Given the logistics of returning to their starting point, many walkers choose to leave the car at home.

LOCAL TRANSPORT

The public transport map opposite gives an overview of the most useful bus and train routes for walkers. For contact details and the approximate frequency of services in both directions, see the boxes on rail services (p44), coach services (p45) and local buses below.

❑ **LOCAL BUS SERVICES**
Note that most local bus companies have no service on bank holidays, and very few operate on a Sunday either.

● **Andybus** (☎ 01666-825655)
41   Malmesbury–Yate via Tormarton and Old Sodbury, Mon-Sat 5/day

● **Castleways** (☎ 01242-602949, ☎ 01242-603715, 🖳 www.castleways.co.uk)
559   Willersey–Broadway–Evesham, Mon-Fri 5/day, Sat 4/day
606   Willersey–Broadway–Cheltenham via Stanton turn (approx ¹/2 mile from
        village), Winchcombe & Cleeve Hill, Mon-Fri 5/day, Sat 4/day; or
        Winchcombe-Cheltenham only, Mon-Fri 10/day, Sat 8/day.

● **Cotswold Green** (☎ 01453-835153)
211   Cam–Dursley 2/day
230   Stroud circular route via Cashes Green & Randwick, Mon-Fri 4/day, Sat
        3/day
256   Stroud–Gloucester via Painswick & Cranham Corner, Wed 2/day

● **Faresaver** (☎ 01249-444444, 🖳 www.faresaver.co.uk)
79   Marshfield–Bath via Cold Ashton, Mon-Thu & Sat 1/day, Fri 2/day

● **First** (☎ 0845-606 4446, 🖳 www.firstgroup.com)
311   Thornbury–Dursley via Wotton-under-Edge & North Nibley, Mon-Fri
        8/day, Sat 7/day

● **Johnsons** (☎ 01564-797000, 🖳 www.johnsonscoaches.co.uk)
21   Stratford-upon-Avon–Moreton-in-Marsh via Chipping Campden and
        Broadway, Mon-Sat 3/day
22   Stratford-upon-Avon–Moreton-in-Marsh via Chipping Campden, Mon-Fri
        6/day, Sat 5/day

(cont'd overleaf)

PLANNING YOUR WALK

❏ **LOCAL BUS SERVICES** (*cont'd from p47*)

● **Mike's Travel** (☎ 01454-281417)

201	Gloucester–Thornbury via North Nibley & Wotton-under-Edge, Mon-Sat 1/day

● **Pulhams Coaches** (☎ 01451-820369)

801	Cheltenham–Bourton-on-the-Water or Moreton-in-Marsh via Dowdeswell Reservoir (*request only*), Mon-Sat 12/day, Sun 3/day (May-Sep),
852	Gloucester–Cirencester via Birdlip, Mon-Fri 4/day, Sat 6/day

● **Stagecoach** 🖥 www.stagecoachbus.com
Stagecoach in the Cotswolds ☎ *01453-755563*

14, 14B	Stroud–Gloucester via Selsley, King's Stanley & Stonehouse, Mon-Sat 17/day, Sun 4/day
20	Stroud–Uley via Ebley & Dursley, Mon-Fri, 13/day, Sat Stroud–Dursley only 12/day
40	Stroud–Wotton-under-Edge, Mon-Sat 5/day
46	Cheltenham–Forest Green via Cranham, Painswick & Stroud, Mon-Fri 12/day, Sat 11/day, Sun 6/day

● **Stagecoach** 🖥 www.stagecoachbus.com
Stagecoach in Swindon ☎ *01793-521415*

151	Cirencester–Cheltenham via Seven Springs, Mon-Sat 12/day

● **Swanbrook Transport** (☎ 01452-712386, 🖥 www.swanbrook.co.uk)

210	Cam–Dursley rail-link service, linked to trains into Cam & Dursley station, Mon-Sat 12/day, Sat 11/day

● **Wessex Connect** (☎ 0117 986 9953, 🖥 www.wessexconnect.com)

86	Kingswood–Wotton-under-Edge via Yate, Chipping Sodbury, Horton, Hawkesbury Upton, Hillesley & Alderley, Mon-Fri 5/day, Sat 4/day
620	Old Sodbury–Bath, Mon-Fri 6/day, Sat 4/day

While individual timetables are available from operators, more useful is a series of leaflets published by the Cotswolds Conservation Board, entitled *Explore the Cotswolds by Public Transport*. These are updated twice a year, in January and July, and are available online at www.nationaltrail.co.uk/Cotswold, or from most tourist information centres along the route.

All bus timetables for services operating in Gloucestershire (which excludes Broadway in the north, and Bath in the south) can be found on 🖥 www.gloucestershire.gov.uk/bustimetables.

In addition to the companies listed in the boxes on p44, p45 and pp47-8, information can be obtained from the national public transport information line, **traveline** (☎ 0871-200 2233, 🖥 www.traveline.org.uk).

Although much of the trail is well served by local bus services, there is little in the way of an integrated service, particularly between the northern and southern parts of the route. Most operators issue timetables twice a year, and while these vary less than in some areas, it is important to check ahead to make sure the service you want is running.

2

MINIMUM IMPACT & OUTDOOR SAFETY

Minimum-impact walking

Walk as if you are kissing the Earth with your feet
Thich Nhat Hanh, *Peace is every step*

Simply by visiting the Cotswolds you are making a positive impact on the local community – as well as on your well-being. Your presence brings money into the local economy, and creates jobs for local people. It ensures that the area maintains a high profile and helps to strengthen the value of local crafts such as dry-stone walling (see box p10) that could otherwise be left to die out. So much for the positives.

On the other side, there is the risk that large numbers of tourists can unwittingly destroy the very place they have come to enjoy. If such tourists adopt a blinkered approach, damage – both environmental and social – is inevitable. But if visitors make the effort to work with local communities to protect the environment, everyone will benefit.

The following guidelines are designed to help you reduce your impact on the environment where you are a visitor, to encourage conservation and to promote sustainable tourism in the area.

ECONOMIC IMPACT

Communities along the Cotswold Way are no strangers to crises that range from foot-and-mouth disease to widespread flooding. More generally, political and economic expediency threatens the closure of rural post offices and local hospitals. Yet walkers can play their part in helping to keep such communities economically viable. The watchword is 'local': buy local, support local businesses, encourage local skills, all of which bring significant social, environmental and psychological benefits.

Buy local

Look and ask for local produce to buy and eat. Not only does this cut down on the amount of pollution and congestion that the transportation of food creates, so-called 'food miles', but it also ensures that you are supporting local farmers and producers: the very people who have moulded the countryside you have come to see and who are in the best position to protect it. If you can find local food that is also organic, so much the better.

Support local businesses

It's a fact of life that money spent at local level – perhaps in a market, or at the greengrocer, or in an independent pub – has a far greater impact for good on that community than the equivalent spent in a branch of a national chain store or restaurant. While no-one would advocate that walkers should boycott the larger supermarkets, which after all do provide local employment, it's worth remembering that businesses in rural communities rely heavily on visitors for their very existence. If we want to keep these shops and post offices, we need to use them. The more money that circulates locally and is spent on local labour and materials, the greater the impact on the local economy and the more power the community has to effect the change it wants to see.

ENVIRONMENTAL IMPACT

By choosing to walk you have already made a positive step towards minimising your impact on the wider environment. By following these suggestions you can also tread lightly through the Cotswolds.

Use public transport whenever possible

Using public transport rather than private cars benefits both visitors and locals, as well as the environment. Local buses (see pp47-8) service many of the villages through which you'll pass and it's often possible to use them at the end of a day or several days on the trail to get back to a convenient point. Also of use are local taxi firms, which are only too happy to ferry walkers or their luggage around.

Never leave litter

Leaving litter shows a total disrespect for the natural world and others coming after you. As well as being unsightly and unhygienic, litter kills wildlife, pollutes the environment and can be dangerous to farm animals. **Please** remove your rubbish and dispose of it in a bin in the next village. It would be very helpful if you could pick up litter left by other people too.

● **The lasting impact of litter** A piece of silver foil left on the ground takes 18 months to decompose; a plastic bag 10 years; clothes 15 years; and an aluminium can 85 years. Would you want your great-grandchildren to find your discarded lemonade can next to their picnic?

● **Is it OK if it's biodegradable?** Not really. Apple cores, banana skins and the like are unsightly, encourage flies, ants and wasps, and can ruin a picnic spot for others. Orange peel left on the ground takes six months to decompose.

Erosion

● **Stay on the waymarked trail** Please. The effect of your footsteps may seem minuscule but when they are multiplied by several thousand walkers each year they become rather more significant. Avoid taking shortcuts, widening the trail or creating more than one path; your boots will be followed by many others.

● **Consider walking out of season** As the weather warms up, so plants start to grow and walkers appear on the hillsides. Thus areas of the trail subject to the greatest pressure are often prevented from recovering. Walking at less busy times eases this pressure on the environment. It can also be more rewarding, with fewer people on the trail, and a more relaxed atmosphere prevalent among local communities.

Respect all wildlife

Care for all wildlife you come across on the path; it has just as much of a right to be there as you. Tempting as it may be to pick wild flowers, leave them so the next person who passes can enjoy them too. Don't break branches off or damage trees in any way.

If you come across wildlife, keep your distance and don't watch for too long. Your presence can cause considerable stress, particularly if the adults are with young or in winter when the weather is harsh and food scarce. Young animals are rarely abandoned. Never interfere if you find young deer or fledgling birds that are apparently alone; their mother will almost certainly return as soon as you have moved on.

The code of the outdoor loo

As more and more people discover the joys of the outdoors, sorting the toilet issue is of increasing importance. Even the least sensitive of people are offended by loo paper strewn across a path, or by the ill-disguised sight of human excrement. Not only is it offensive to our senses but, more importantly, it can infect water sources.

● **Where to go** Wherever possible wait until you come to **a public toilet**. These are marked on the trail maps in this guide. If you do have to go outdoors, choose a site at least **30m away from running water**. Use a strong stick to **dig a small hole** about 15cm (6") deep in which to bury your excrement. It decomposes quicker when in contact with the top layer of soil or leaf mould, and using a stick to stir loose soil into your deposit will speed up decomposition even more. Do not squash it under rocks as this slows down the composting process. If you have to use rocks to hide it make sure they are not in contact with your faeces.

● **Toilet paper and tampons/sanitary towels** Toilet paper takes a long time to decompose, whether buried or not. Like **tampons** and **sanitary towels**, it is easily dug up by animals and could end up in water sources or on the trail. The best method for dealing with such items is to **pack them out**. Put them inside a paper bag, then inside a plastic bag (or two). Then simply empty the contents of the paper bag at the next toilet you come across and throw the bag away.

ACCESS

Respect, Protect, Enjoy **The Countryside Code**

Rights of way

As a designated national trail, the Cotswold Way is a public right of way, a path that anyone has the right to use on foot provided they stay on the path and do not cause damage or obstruct it in any way. The trail takes in several public rights of way which fall largely into one of three categories:

● A **footpath** (marked with a yellow arrow) is open to walkers only, not to cyclists, horse-riders or vehicles

MINIMUM-IMPACT & OUTDOOR SAFETY

● A **bridleway** (blue arrow) is open to walkers, horse-riders and cyclists
● A **restricted byway** (purple arrow) is open to walkers, riders and cyclists, but not to motorised vehicles.

That said, not all footpaths are necessarily rights of way. Sometimes a landowner will allow a path across his land to be used for the convenience of walkers, although it may not be recognised as a right of way. This is known as a **permissive path**.

The maintenance of rights of way is down to the landowner in conjunction with the county council through whose area it passes, and sometimes the local authority. Farmers and land managers must ensure that paths are not blocked by crops or other vegetation, or otherwise obstructed, that the route is identifiable, and that the surface is restored soon after cultivation. If crops are growing over the path, you have every right to walk through them, following the line of the right of way as closely as possible. Should you find a path blocked or impassable, report it to the appropriate highway authority.

Right to roam

Following a concerted effort by groups such as the Ramblers (see p41) and the British Mountaineering Council, the principle of access to the countryside was finally allowed under the Countryside and Rights of Way Act 2000, affectionately known as CroW. In England, the act came into effect in full in 2005, creating a new right of access to the English countryside for recreation on foot. There are restrictions, of course: some land (such as gardens, parks and cultivated land) is excluded, and high-impact activities such as driving a vehicle, cycling, and horse-riding may not be permitted. The act also gives greater protection to SSSIs (see p59) and AONBs (see p58); it lists habitats and species important to biological diversity in England; and it covers the conduct of those walking with dogs (see pp24-5). While much of this is only of background interest for those walking the Cotswold Way, it will have a significant impact on the future of walking in the countryside generally.

❏ **Walking through fields of cattle**
It is very rare that cows will attack walkers but it does happen. Cows get particularly nervous when dogs are about and cows with calves can be even more twitchy. Most of the time they will just watch you pass but very rarely they will wander over out of curiosity. The Ramblers offer the following guidelines:
● Try not to get between cows and their calves
● Be prepared for cattle to react to your presence, especially if you have a dog with you
● Move quickly and quietly, and if possible walk around them
● Keep your dog close and under proper control
● Don't hang onto your dog. If you are threatened by animals – let it go as the cow will chase after that
● Don't put yourself at risk. Find another way round the cows and rejoin the footpath
● Don't panic! Most cows will stop before they reach you. If they follow just walk on quietly.
● Report any problems to the highway authority.

Land over which access has been granted may be marked with a circular brown-and-white waymark, depicting a Morph-like creature walking across a hill. For full details and to search a particular area, take a look at 'Countryside access' on the Natural England website, 🖳 www.naturalengland.org.uk.

The Countryside Code

Much of the route followed by the Cotswold Way is across farmland, frequently passing through ploughed fields, farm buildings, and areas with grazing livestock, to the point that it is impossible to be unaware of the business of farming. Farmers are faced with a harsh environment, a short grazing season and severe weather conditions; let's not add the nuisance of irresponsible walkers to their problems.

In the context of the CroW Act, the Countryside Code has been revised and simplified under a new banner: 'Respect, Protect, Enjoy':

● **Be safe, plan ahead and follow any signs** Check on any restrictions and follow local signs, such as diversions, which may be for safety reasons or to protect livestock.

● **Leave gates and property as you find them** While a farmer will normally close a gate to keep livestock in, he may sometimes leave it open so they can reach food and water. If you're walking in a group, make sure that the last person through knows how to leave the gates. And talking of gates (or stiles or other means of access), they're there to be used. Climbing over walls, hedges and fences causes damage and can increase the risk of farm animals escaping. Finally, don't interfere with any animal, even if it appears to be in distress; you could do more harm than good. Try to contact the farmer instead.

● **Protect plants and animals, and take your litter home**

● **Keep dogs under close control**

● **Consider other people** If you're walking along country roads do consider both yourself and drivers. Ideally walk facing the oncoming traffic, and carry a torch or wear highly visible clothing when it's getting dark and in bad weather. If you're driving yourself, reduce your speed, watch out for pedestrians, and make sure that you park your car considerately.

Health and outdoor safety

HEALTH

Prevention

Water and dehydration You need to drink lots of water while walking – probably more than you think. Many health specialists recommend 2-4 litres a day, depending on the weather and your physique. If you're feeling drained, lethargic or just out of sorts it may well be that you haven't drunk enough. Thirst is not always a reliable indicator of how much you should drink. The frequency and colour of your urine is a more useful guide: the clearer the better.

Sunburn Even on overcast days, the sun still has the power to burn. Sunburn can be avoided by regularly applying sunscreen, remembering your lips and ears, and by wearing a hat to protect your face and the back of your neck. Those with fair skin should consider wearing a light, long-sleeved top and long trousers rather than T-shirt and shorts.

Blisters Worn-in, comfortable boots are a must, as are good, well-fitting socks. How many people set out on a long walk in new boots and live to regret it!

Look after your feet, too: air them at lunchtime, keep them clean and change your socks daily. If you feel any 'hot spots' on your feet while you are walking, stop immediately and apply a few strips of zinc oxide tape and leave on until it is pain free or the tape starts to come off.

If you have left it too late and a blister has developed, surround it with 'moleskin' or any other 'blister kit' to protect it from abrasion. Popping it can lead to infection. If the skin is broken, keep the area clean with antiseptic and cover with a non-adhesive dressing material held in place with tape.

Joints and muscles If you're susceptible to joint problems – in particular knees and ankles – do invest in a pair of walking poles and use one or both of them, especially during steep ascents or descents. Properly used, they can lessen the impact of long-distance walking on the joints, and thus can help to prevent injury.

Even the fittest athlete warms up before exercise and stretches afterwards – and it's good practice for walkers. It's surprising how much easier it is to set off in the morning without aching muscles, and this, too, lessens the risk of injury.

More serious problems

Hypothermia Hypothermia, or exposure, occurs when the body can't generate enough heat to maintain its core temperature. Since it is usually as a result of being wet, cold, unprotected from the wind, tired and hungry, it is easily avoided by wearing suitable clothing (see pp38-9), carrying and consuming enough food and drink, being aware of the weather conditions, and checking on the morale of your companions. Early signs to watch for include feeling cold and tired with involuntary shivering. If in doubt, find shelter as soon as possible and warm the person up with a hot drink and chocolate or other high-energy food. If possible, give them another warm layer of clothing and allow them to rest.

If the condition is allowed to worsen, strange behaviour, slurring of speech and poor co-ordination will become apparent and the victim can quickly progress into unconsciousness, followed by coma and death. Quickly get the victim out of the wind and rain, improvising a shelter if necessary. Rapid restoration of body warmth is essential, and best achieved by bare-skin contact: someone should get into the same sleeping bag as the patient, both having stripped to their underwear, with any spare clothing laid under and over them to build up heat. This is an emergency: send for help.

Hyperthermia At the other end of the scale, hyperthermia occurs when the body is allowed to overheat. **Heat exhaustion** is often caused by water depletion and is a serious condition that could eventually lead to death. Symptoms include thirst, fatigue, giddiness, a rapid pulse, raised body temperature, low urine output and, later on, delirium and coma. The only remedy is to re-establish the balance of water. If the victim is suffering severe muscle cramps it may be due to salt depletion.

Heat stroke is caused by the failure of the body's temperature-regulating system and is extremely serious. It is associated with a very high body temperature and an absence of sweating. Early symptoms can be similar to those of hypothermia, such as aggressive behaviour, lack of co-ordination and so on. Later the victim goes into a coma or convulsions, and death will follow if effective treatment is not given. Sponge the victim down or cover with wet towels, then vigorously fan them. Get help immediately.

Dealing with an accident

● Ensure both you and the casualty are out of further risk of danger, but otherwise do not move someone who may be seriously injured.

● Use basic first aid to treat the injury to the best of your ability.

● Try to attract the attention of anybody else who may be in the area: the **emergency signal** is six blasts on a whistle, or six flashes with a torch.

● If you have to go for help, ideally leave someone with the casualty. If there is nobody else, make sure the casualty is warm, sheltered and as comfortable as possible: leave spare clothing, water and food within easy reach, as well as a whistle and/or torch for attracting attention.

● Telephone ☎ 999 (or ☎ 112 from a mobile phone) and ask for the police or other rescue service. Be sure you know exactly where you are before you call.

● Report the exact position of the casualty and his or her condition.

OUTDOOR SAFETY

The Cotswold Way is not a hazardous undertaking and presents no greater risk than you would encounter on an average day's walk in the countryside. Nevertheless, there are some sensible precautions that can help to prevent problems.

❏ Lyme disease

Ticks are small blood-sucking insects that live on cattle, sheep and deer and cannot fly. When you are walking with bare arms or legs through long grass or bracken small ticks can brush off and attach themselves to you, painlessly burying their heads under your skin to feed on your blood. After a couple of days of feasting they will have grown to about 10mm and will drop off.

There is a very small risk that they can infect you with Lyme disease, although affected ticks have to be attached to you for 24-36 hours before they are likely to infect you. Check your body after a walk and remove any by pinching the head, not the body, and twisting. Keep the area clean with disinfectant. If you suffer flu-like symptoms, or lasting irritation at the site of the bite for a week or more, see a doctor. Wear boots, socks and trousers when walking through, or sitting on, long grass, heather and bracken.

Check the weather forecast (see below) before you set out and go properly equipped (see pp37-41). Be sure to carry plenty of food to last you through the day and at least a litre of water. Drinking from streams is not recommended since they are likely to contain traces of pesticides and other chemicals used on the land. Should the weather close in, take particular care to stay on the route, especially if you are on one of the stretches of the Cotswold Way that runs along the escarpment. If in doubt, stop and check – using a compass and map, and perhaps a GPS.

Weather information

Anyone familiar with the British weather will know that it can change quickly. What started out as a warm sunny day can be chilly and wet by lunchtime, so don't be fooled. Newspapers, television and radio stations all give the forecast for the day ahead and local people will have plenty of advice on the subject. Weather forecasts can be found online at 🖳 www.metoffice.gov.uk and 🖳 www.bbc.co.uk/weather. The Met Office's telephone weather forecasting service was withdrawn in November 2011.

Walking alone

If you enjoy walking alone you must appreciate and be prepared for the increased risk. Try to tell someone where you are going. One way of doing this is to telephone your booked accommodation and let them know you are walking alone and what time you expect to arrive. If you leave word with someone else, don't forget to let them know you have arrived safely. Carrying a mobile phone is useful, though there's no guarantee of good reception.

What is this life if, full of care,
We have no time to stand and stare.
No time to stand beneath the boughs
And stare as long as sheep or cows.
No time to see, when woods we pass,
Where squirrels hide their nuts in grass.
No time to see, in broad daylight,
Streams full of stars, like skies at night.
No time to turn at Beauty's glance,
And watch her feet, how they can dance.
No time to wait till her mouth can
Enrich that smile her eyes began.
A poor life this if, full of care,
We have no time to stand and stare.
William Henry Davies, *Leisure*

THE ENVIRONMENT AND NATURE

3

Given its route within the relatively narrow range of the Cotswold Hills, the Cotswold Way runs through an unexpectedly broad range of habitats. Among these, grasslands and beechwoods stand out from the dominant farmland, where grazing land and arable farming have created their own habitats. Open moorland contrasts with long-established towns and villages, and there's even a river and a canal across the trail. To do justice to the flora and fauna of such an area would take a book several times the size of this one. What follows, then, is a brief description of the animals, birds and plants you may come across – and a few that are there, but which you're unlikely to spot. To find out more, take a look at one of the field guides listed on p42.

While it's interesting in itself to be able to identify individual plants and creatures, far more valuable is to understand their place within their environment, and how we as walkers can help to protect that fragile relationship. Conservation is part of that relationship, which is why these issues are explored here.

Conserving the Cotswolds

It's the business of government to see that the countryside is preserved for the pleasure and sanity of all of us. The fatal mistake has been to imagine that the interests of the countryside are in some way different from the interests of farmers. The countryside can only be maintained by a healthy agriculture. If farming dies, a most precious part of Britain dies with it. **John Mortimer**

Perhaps John Mortimer had the Cotswolds in mind when he penned these words. He certainly could have done, for farming has been an intrinsic part of these hills for many centuries, shaping the countryside – and the towns and villages – that we see today.

Yet for all that the Cotswolds draws tourists in their droves, the pressure for development, the economic reality of maintaining small communities, and the red tape imposed on Britain's farmers all conspire against maintaining an equable balance with nature. If it's taken just over 70 years for over 96% of the region's unimproved limestone grassland (that's permanent grassland which has not been regularly cultivated) to disappear, how much longer will it be before there's nothing left?

There are plenty of organisations that are determined not to let the unthinkable happen, some of them are listed on p60. Environmental issues are of growing interest on the political field and thanks to the efforts of these groups, many of them voluntary, the fight-back is gaining ground. Their work relies on the active participation of everyone who cares.

GOVERNMENT AGENCIES AND SCHEMES

Primary responsibility for countryside affairs in England rests with **Natural England** (see box below), which bring under one umbrella the work of the former Countryside Agency, English Nature and the Rural Development Council.

The organisation is responsible for enhancing biodiversity, landscape and wildlife in rural, urban, coastal and marine areas; promoting access, recreation and public well-being; and contributing to the way natural resources are managed. One of its roles is to designate national trails, national parks, areas of outstanding natural beauty (AONBs), which afford the second level of protection after a national park, sites of special scientific interest (SSSIs), and national nature reserves (NNRs), and to enforce regulations relating to these sites.

Cotswolds AONB

Now for some statistics. Some 95% of the Cotswold Way national trail falls within the Cotswolds Area of Outstanding Natural Beauty, the largest of the 38 AONBs in England and Wales. Established in 1966, and extended in 1990, it runs from north to south for 78 miles (126km), and covers a total of 790 square miles (2038sq km).

The area has been inhabited for around 6000 years, and today some 157,000 people live within its boundaries. Despite that, more than 80% of the land is still farmland, its fields demarcated by an estimated 4000 miles of dry-stone walls. A further 9% or so is woodland, especially beech, though the walker on the Cotswold Way could be forgiven for thinking that the woods accounted for a significantly higher proportion than this!

Significantly, in terms of the area's natural history, over half of the UK's total Jurassic limestone grassland is to be found here, much of it protected within sites of special scientific interest (SSSIs). That figure, though, tells only a part of the story. While the region's flower-rich limestone grasslands as a whole covered 40% of the AONB in 1935, that area has shrunk to just 1.5% today. Given that such habitats can harbour almost 400 species of plants, and 25

❏ **Statutory bodies and other countryside authorities**
● **Cotswolds Conservation Board** (🖥 www.cotswoldsaonb.org.uk) Body responsible for the administration of the Cotswolds AONB.
● **English Heritage** (☎ 0870-333 1181, 🖥 www.english-heritage.org.uk) Government body responsible for the care and preservation of ancient monuments in England, including several of the long barrows along the Cotswold Way.
● **Natural England** (☎ 0845-600 3078, 🖥 www.naturalengland.org.uk).

species of butterfly, it's hardly any wonder that conservation of what little remains is such a vital issue.

A team of Cotswold Voluntary Wardens is responsible for much of the work involved in running the AONB, including the Cotswold Way, from footpath maintenance and hedge laying to publicity and fundraising. Others lead walks, including an annual series along the Cotswold Way (see p97). A half-yearly newspaper, the *Cotswold Lion*, ensures that both local people and visitors are kept informed of what's going on across the region.

Sites of special scientific interest (SSSIs) and National nature reserves (NNRs)

The designation SSSI affords protection to specific areas against anything that threatens their unique habitat or environment. There are over 80 SSSIs across the Cotswolds, including parts of Cleeve Hill Common (🖳 www.cleevecom mon.org), Leckhampton Hill, Crickley Hill and Painswick Beacon along the Cotswold Way.

'Triple SIs' are managed in partnership with the owners and occupiers of the land who must give written notice of any operations likely to damage the site and who cannot proceed until consent is given. Many SSSIs are also designated as national nature reserves (NNRs), including several that combine to make up the Cotswolds Commons and Beechwoods NNR.

Geoparks

The European Geoparks initiative was originally set up to help the development and management of deprived areas which nevertheless benefit from a rich geological heritage. The concept has since moved on, with today's geoparks designed to raise awareness of an area and to educate the general public.

The Cotswold Way runs through the Cotswold Hills Geopark (🖳 www.cotswoldhillsgeopark.net), which was established by the Gloucestershire Geology Trust (see p11), in partnership with the Cotswolds AONB and Natural England. Currently reaching as far south as Stroud, it may in future be extended to include Bath.

CAMPAIGNING AND CONSERVATION ORGANISATIONS

Voluntary organisations started the conservation movement back in the mid-1800s and are still at the forefront of developments. Independent of government but reliant on public support, they can concentrate their resources either on acquiring land which can then be managed purely for conservation purposes, or on influencing political decision-makers by lobbying and campaigning.

The **National Trust** (NT) with its four million members now protects over 255,000 hectares in the United Kingdom. NT properties on or close to the trail include Snowshill Manor (p90), Hailes Abbey (p94), Horton Court (p152) and Dyrham Park (p158), while in addition there are significant tracts of land protected by the trust. Of these, some of the most interesting are Dover's Hill just

❏ **Campaigning and conservation organisations**
● **British Trust for Conservation Volunteers** (BTCV; ☎ 01302-388883, 🖳 www2
.btcv.org.uk) Encourages people to value their environment and take practical action
to improve it.
● **Butterfly Conservation** (☎ 01929-400209, 🖳 www.butterfly-conservation.org)
● **Campaign to Protect Rural England** (CPRE; ☎ 020-7981 2800, 🖳 www.cpre
.org.uk)
● **Landmark Trust** (general enquiries ☎ 01628-825920, booking enquiries ☎ 01628-
825925, 🖳 www.landmarktrust.org.uk)
● **National Trust** (NT; ☎ 0844-800 1895, 🖳 www.nationaltrust.org.uk)
● **Royal Society for the Protection of Birds** (RSPB; ☎ 01767-680551, 🖳 www.rspb
.org.uk)
● **Woodland Trust** (☎ 01476-581111, 🖳 www.woodland-trust.org.uk).

outside Chipping Campden, and Haresfield Beacon, as well as several areas of
woodland.

The **Royal Society for the Protection of Birds** (RSPB) has over a million
members and around 200 nature reserves, but the nearest to the trail is at
Highnam Woods, some 3¾ miles (6 km) west of Gloucester.

Rather smaller in scale is the work of **Butterfly Conservation**, which
owns and manages the 31-hectare Prestbury Hill Reserve, to the south of
Cleeve Hill. The two-part reserve, incorporating both Masts Field and the Bill
Smyllie Reserve, features a diversity of habitat and is home to some 30 species
of butterfly.

The **Woodland Trust** aims to conserve, restore and re-establish trees, particularly broadleaved species. Their properties along the Cotswold Way include
Lineover Wood, Stanley Wood, and Coaley Wood.

In a different mould altogether is the **Landmark Trust**, which works to
preserve historic or architecturally interesting buildings and to make them suitable for short-term holiday lets. The trust has accommodation options along the
trail that include Campden House at Chipping Campden (see p74), Beckford's
Tower (see box p163), and two very close to Bath Abbey.

BEYOND CONSERVATION

There is a sufficiency in the world for man's need but not for man's greed.
                                                          Mohandas K Gandhi

For most of us, thoughts of conservation tend to fall into several compartments.
First there are the conservation organisations, which many of us join, secure in
the knowledge that we're doing our bit. Then there's the issue of recycling –
conscientiously ensuring that the content of our bins is properly sifted so that as
little as possible goes to landfill. And then of course there are all those areas
protected by law as national parks, AONBs and others, so that no-one can
develop them further. Often it's not until something that's right on our doorstep
is threatened that we'll get involved in anything more.

Yet to be realistic, why are we in such a position? Why do we need to have so much protection in place? If everyone were to work with, rather than against, the environment, there should be no need to have statutes to control pollution, waste and over-development. Fragmented government departments and international bodies are at loggerheads over issues that to most of us – at least in environmental terms – are reasonably straightforward. Surely it's time that we worked together to preserve what is left of the world's natural resources or – in business parlance – engaged in some serious joined-up thinking before it's too late.

Flora and fauna

TREES AND SHRUBS

While the Cotswold Hills are widely revered for their hills and steep cliffs, among their less-sung attractions are the magnificent woods of **beech** (*Fagus sylvatica*) that define the edge of the escarpment. Some veteran species are at least 250 years old, and one – in Lineover Wood south-east of Cheltenham – dates back over 400 years. They are seen at their best in spring, when the soft green of the new leaves adds texture rather than darkness to the woodland panorama. Time is inevitably taking its toll on these old timers, which are threatened by factors such as disease, wind damage and erosion, as well as the vigorous seedlings of

Ash (with seeds)

other species such as **ash** (*Fraxinus excelsior*).

Also interspersed with the beech are **sycamore** or **sycamore maple** (*Acer pseudoplatanus*), and **oak** (*Quercus robur*), as well as **horse chestnut** (*Aesculus hippocastanum*), **lime** or **linden** (*Tilia vulgaris*) and **birch** (*Betula pubescens*). Another species, the **large-leaved lime** (*Tilia platyphyllos*), is one of the rarest trees in Britain, but there's a bank of them in Lineover Wood, whose name derives from the Anglo-Saxon word for 'lime bank'.

Amongst mixed woodland you will come across trees such as **rowan** or **mountain ash**

Birch (with flowers)

(*Sorbus aucuparia*), popular with birds who seek out its bright orange berries around August, **silver birch** (*Betula pendula*), **aspen** (*Populus tremula*), alder (*Alnus glutinosa*), and **hazel** (*Corylus avellana*).

While there are **conifers** to be found, most are incidental to the deciduous trees; there are none of the dark conifer plantations so prevalent in many woodland areas.

In the hedgerows, the white, star-like blossom of the **blackthorn** (*Prunus spinosa*) heralds the beginning of spring, giving way as the year progresses to dark-blue, almost dusty-looking sloes which make great sloe gin. Later, a mass

Alder (with flowers)

of creamy flowers proclaims the **hawthorn** (*Crataegus monogyna*), whose fruit adds a splash of red in autumn. Then, in early summer, the glory goes to the **elder** (*Sambucus nigra*), with its sweet-smelling clusters of cream flowers which by September have formed into a purplish-black fruit, ripe for making jelly or wine.

WILD FLOWERS

[see colour plates opposite p64]

On Cotswold edge there is a field and that
Grows thick with corn and speedwell and the mat
Of thistles, of the tall kind
Ivor Gurney, *Up There*

Of speedwell and thistles there are indeed plenty, but Gurney – writing after World War I – does little more than hint at the richness of the flora to be found in his native Cotswolds. While much has changed since then, and habitats have declined significantly, there are still wild flowers aplenty along the trail.

Limestone grassland

Until the 1950s, sheep grazed the limestone grasslands that are so characteristic of the Cotswolds (some say the name derived from the Saxon words *wold*, referring to high, open country, and *cod* meaning 'found', but others claim it came from the Cotswold sheep), encouraging a broad range of wild flowers and an attendant population of butterflies and other insects. With changes in agriculture, what was left of this 'unimproved' grassland became overgrown, but several areas are now managed to ensure that this unique habitat can continue to prosper. Over 200 species of wild flower have been identified at Crickley Hill alone, with other similar areas including Leckhampton Hill, Painswick Beacon, Coaley Peak, Selsley Common and Prestbury Hill Reserve, as well as a small patch of ground at Great Witcombe Roman Villa.

Many of the wild flowers that grow in this habitat, such as **cowslips** (*Primula veris*), are also to be found along hedgerows and in fields, but some are specific to this environment. In spring there's the **early purple orchid** (*Orchis mascula*), but it's in summer that the wild orchids really come into their own. Relatively easy to find among colourful patches of **birdsfoot trefoil**

(*Lotus corniculatus*), purple **self-heal** (*Prunella vulgaris*) and red or white **clover** (*Trifolium* spp) are the bright pink **pyramidal orchid** (*Anacamptis pyramidalis*), and **common spotted orchids** (*Dactylorhiza fuchsii*), which can be pink, pale lilac or white. The **bee orchid** (*Ophrys apifera*), named for its close resemblance to a bee, is a rarity, and is carefully protected where it does grow. Also present are the **fly orchid** (*Ophrys insectifera*) – which does look like a fly – and the rather inconspicuous **musk orchid** (*Herminium monorchis*).

Striking in their summer glory are the tall spikes of startlingly blue **viper's bugloss** (*Echium vulgare*), and the **thistles** (*Cirsium* spp) and **knapweeds** (*Centaurea scabiosa*), their colourful purple flowers a magnet for bees. The delicate **harebell** (*Campanula rotundifolia*) is also at home here, as is the **scabious** (*Knautia arvensis*), their pale-blue flowers contrasting with bold **ox-eye daisies** (*Leucanthemum vulgare*) and the rather less flamboyant **yellow rattle** (*Rhinanthus minor*), named for the sound made by its seeds when they're ripe. Lower down is the **common rock rose** (*Helianthemum nummularium*), its bright-yellow, five-petalled flowers familiar to many gardeners. Look out, too, for the pinkish-purple flowers of wild herbs such as **basil** (*Clinopodium vulgare*), **marjoram** (*Origanum vulgare*) and the ground-hugging **thyme** (*Thymus serphyllum*).

Moorland
Up on the hills and on open spaces such as Cleeve Hill Common you'll come across plenty of **bracken** (*Pteridium aquilinum*), its fronds turning to a crisp brown as the year progresses. Here, too, the bright-yellow flowers of **gorse** (*Ulex europaeus*) brighten up the hillside.

Hedgerows and field boundaries
As the days grow longer and the air begins to warm up, wild flowers start to appear along the hedgerows. Needing little introduction are the more common species which even the uninitiated will soon recognise, such as **primrose** (*Primula vulgaris*), **common dog violet** (*Viola riviniana*), **common speedwell** (*Veronica officinalis*), which can cure indigestion, gout and liver complaints, **bugle** (*Ajuga repans*), **tufted vetch** (*Vicia cracca*), **lesser celandine** (*Ranunculus ficaria*), not unlike the related buttercup, and **red campion** (*Silene dioica*). Here, too, you might find the occasional **green alkanet** (*Pentaglottis sempervirens*) which, with its bright-blue flowers and soft, hairy leaves, is often mistaken for borage, and the tall, deep-purple **honesty** (*Lunaria redivia*), whose flat, translucent seedpods are sought after by flower arrangers.

Later, from May to September, these will be joined by **buttercup** (*Ranunculus acris*), the flowers of which children will use to tell you if you like butter, and the small pink-flowered **herb robert** (*Geranium robertianum*). The **dandelion** (*Taraxacum officinale*) grows almost everywhere, including on waste ground, as does the tall **rosebay willowherb** (*Epilobium angustifolium*). Equally tall is the purple **foxglove** (*Digitalis purpurea*). Its flowers are attractive to bees but the plant is poisonous to humans – although it's from the foxglove that the drug Digitalin is extracted to treat heart disease. Unmistakable is the vivid red splash of the **field poppy** (*Papaver rhoeas*). Then there are the tall

white-flowering heads of members of the carrot family such as **cow parsley**
(*Anthrisus sylvestris*), **yarrow** (*Achillea millefolium*) and **hedge parsley**
(*Torilis japonica*).

Summer is when the climbers and ramblers come into their own. Almost
everyone is familiar with the common **bramble** (*Rubus fruticosus*), sought out
in autumn by blackberry pickers. **Honeysuckle** (*Lonicera periclymenum*), also
known as woodbine, makes its appearance growing through hedges and in
woodland from June to September, the fruits ripening to red in the autumn.
Hedge bindweed (*Calystegia sepium*), with its white trumpet-shaped flowers,
and the related pink **field bindweed** (*Convolvulus arvensis*) are a common sight
during the summer months, as is the pale-pink **dog rose** (*Rosa canina*), which
later produces rosehips, an excellent source of vitamin C and used to make a
subtle-flavoured jelly. Then there's another autumn beauty, the almost translucent scarlet berries of the **white briony** (*Bryonia cretica*) that tumble in profu-
sion down many a hedgerow. Beware, though: they're extremely poisonous.

Woodland
Spring has to be the best time to walk through the Cotswolds' beech woods.
This is when the air is pungent with the smell of densely packed white **ramsons**
(*Allium ursinum*), widely known as **wild garlic**. In some places, carpets of **bluebells** (*Hyacinthoides non-scripta*) appear, while others are favoured by **dog's
mercury** (*Mercurialis perennis*) – no floral beauty, this, but its bright green
leaves make a splendid floor covering. Beneath the still-open tree canopy, the
woodland floor is liberally sprinkled with white **wood anemones** (*Anemone
nemorosa*), whose petals close up at night and in bad weather. With a similar
night-time habit but with more rounded leaves is the smaller **wood sorrel**
(*Oxalis acetosella*). The plant with the red stem, dark green leaves and soft
green bracts is the **wood spurge** (*Euphorbia amygdaloides*). A little later you
might see the occasional patch of **lily-of-the-valley** (*Convallaria majalis*), or
the much taller **Solomon's seal** (*Polygonatum multiflorum*).

In darker areas, especially along rocks and walls (look out for them in Pen
Wood and Coaley Wood), are **hart's tongue ferns** (*Phyllitis* or *Asplenium
scolopendrium*), their long narrow leaves slightly furled; this is the only British
fern whose leaves are undivided.

In summer and autumn, there's often the opportunity to supplement a packed
lunch with wild **alpine strawberries** (*Fragaria vesca*) and to a lesser extent **wild
raspberries** (*Rubus idaeus*). Steer well clear, though, of the poisonous purple
fruits of **bittersweet** or **woody nightshade** (*Solanum dulcamara*).

Riverbanks and wet areas
You won't have much opportunity to spot plants along riverbanks as you're
walking the trail, but there is the occasional stream, and the alternative route
along the Ebley Canal offers a few water-loving specimens. In summer, the soft
cream heads of **meadowsweet** (*Filipendula ulmaria*), which has similar medic-
inal properties to aspirin, contrast with tall **purple loosestrife** (*Lythrum sali-
caria*). On the edge of water courses bright-yellow **marsh marigolds** (*Caltha*

Early Purple Orchid
Orchis mascula

Spotted Orchid
Dactylorhiza fuchsii

Pyramidal Orchid
Anacamptis pyramidalis

Honesty
Lunaria redivia

Field Scabious
Knautia arvensis

Woolly Thistle
Cirsium eriophorum

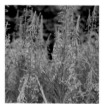

Rosebay Willowherb
Epilobium angustifolium

Herb-Robert
Geranium robertianum

Black Knapweed
Centaurea nigra

Red Campion
Silene dioica

Rowan (tree)
Sorbus aucuparia

Field Poppy
Papaver rhoeas

Common Dog Violet
Viola riviniana

Dog Rose
Rosa canina

Honeysuckle
Lonicera periclymemum

Ramsons (Wild Garlic)
Allium ursinum

Germander Speedwell
Veronica chamaedrys

Wood Spurge
Euphorbia amygdaloides

Self-heal
Prunella vulgaris

Green Alkanet
Pentaglottis sempervirens

Wood Anemone
Anemone nemorosa

Foxglove
Digitalis purpurea

Bluebell
Hyacinthoides non-scripta

Viper's Bugloss
Echium vulgare

Meadow Buttercup
Ranunculis acris

Rock Rose
Helianthemum nummularium

Gorse
Ulex europaeus

Lesser Celandine
Ranunculus ficaria

Birdsfoot-trefoil
Lotus corniculatus

Marsh Marigold
Caltha palustris

Yarrow
Achillea millefolium

Primrose
Primula vulgaris

Cowslip
Primula veris

Colour photos (following pages)

● **C4 Top left**: Approaching Broadway Tower (see p83) from the north. **Right**: Broadway's St Michael and All Saints' church nestles at the foot of the Cotswold Hills. **Bottom left**: The Market Hall, Chipping Campden (p74). **Right**: Fresh produce catches the eye in Broadway.

● **C5 Top left**: A thatched fox in Stanton (p90). **Centre left**: Carved detail on a kissing gate at Stanway. **Right**: Cleeve Hill Common. **Bottom left**: The ruins of Hailes Abbey (p94) lie right beside the trail. **Bottom right**: The ancient long barrow of Belas Knap (p101).

● **C6 Top left**: The Devil's Chimney (p115) on Leckhampton Hill. **Bottom left**: The traditional Cotswold Lion is distinctive for its unkempt fringe. **Centre**: The Tyndale Monument (p143) offers sweeping views across the Cotswolds landscape. **Top right**: Stone stile by the site of the 1643 Battle of Lansdown (p162). **Bottom right**: Bluebells in springtime.

● **C7 Top left & centre**: All Saints' Church at Selsley (p133) features a window with panels by William Morris, Dante Gabriel Rossetti and Edward Burne-Jones. **Top right**: Dyrham Park (p158). **Bottom, Painswick**: Flights of fancy abound at Painswick Rococo Garden (**left**, p123). Millennium Clock on St Mary's Church (**centre**). Spectacle stocks (**right**, p125).

C4

Peacock
Inachis io

Small Tortoiseshell
Aglais urticae

Large Blue
Maculinea arion

Large Garden/Cabbage White
Pieris brassicae

Small Heath
*Coenonympha
pamphilus*

Red
Admiral
Vanessa atalanta

Small Garden/Cabbage White
Artogeia rapae

Painted Lady
Cynthia cadui

Small Copper
Lycaena phlaeus

Silver-washed Fritillary *Argynnis paphia*

palustris) may be seen, while on the water itself (take a look on the canal) are large **yellow waterlilies** (*Nuphar lutea*). You might also see the pink **cuckoo flower** (*Cardamine pratensis*), **ragged robin** (*Lychnis flos-cuculi*), as well as **watermint** (*Mentha aquatica*), easily identified by its smell, and **hemp agrimony** (*Eupatorium cannabinum*), with its large pink flowers.

BUTTERFLIES

The existence of unimproved limestone grasslands is one of the major features that make butterflies so important to the Cotswolds region. Some 34 species are found in this environment, with the area significant for both the **small blue** (*Cupido minimus*), and the **Duke of Burgundy fritillary** (*Hamearis lucina*). Part of the Cotswolds AONB near Stroud has seen the reintroduction of the **large blue** (*Maculinea arion*), which, along with the **Adonis blue** (*Lysandra bellargus*), had been declared extinct in this area.

Those with a serious interest would be well advised to spend some time at the Prestbury Hill Reserve south of Cleeve Hill, where many species are protected within a reserve managed by Butterfly Conservation. Some, such as the **large whites** (*Pieris brassicae*) and **small whites** (*Artogeia rapae*), and the nettle feeders like **red admiral** (*Vanessa atalanta*) and **painted lady** (*Cynthia cadui*), are familiar to many of us from our gardens and parks and are easily spotted in many other places. Other, rarer species, such as the **large skipper** (*Ochlodes venata*), **brown argus** (*Aricia agestis*), **chalk-hill blue** (*Lysandra coridon*), **green hairstreak** (*Callophrys rubi*), **dark green fritillary** (*Argynnis aglaja*), **marbled white** (*Melanargia galathea*), **grayling** (*Hipparchia semele*), **small copper** (*Lycaena phlaeus*), **small heath** (*Coenonympha pamphilus*) **speckled wood** (*Pararge aegeria*), **comma** (*Polygonia c-album*), **peacock** (*Inachis io*), **tortoiseshell** (*Aglais urticae*), and **meadow brown** (*Maniola jurtina*), benefit significantly from this protection. Some of these are also found in other reserves, including Leckhampton Hill or at Painswick Beacon. Elsewhere, perhaps in Buckholt Wood, you may be lucky enough to spot the **silver-washed fritillary** (*Argynnis paphia*), the largest of the British fritillaries with a wingspan of almost three inches (70mm).

There may be considerable difference between the male and female of a species, which can be particularly frustrating for the novice attempting to identify a creature that scarcely holds still for a moment. Many of the blue butterflies, for example, take their name from the male; the female is often a rather insignificant brown.

BIRDS

High overhead ran frenzied larks, screaming, as though the sky were tearing apart
Laurie Lee, *Cider with Rosie*

To most of us, the song of a skylark overhead is decidedly more appealing than to Laurie Lee's childhood ears. And fortunately, there are still several places along the Cotswold Way where skylarks can be seen. Of the 86 species of bird

THE ENVIRONMENT & NATURE

that have been identified in the region as a whole, the skylark is considered to be one of 20 that are designated as 'nationally important' – along with the linnet, starling, house sparrow and yellowhammer.

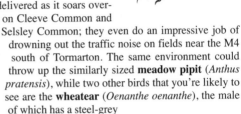

SKYLARK
L: 185mm/7.25"

Open farmland and upland areas

Out on the hills is where you'll find the **skylark** (*Alauda arvensis*), which is often heard long before it is seen, its clear song delivered as it soars overhead. Look out for them on Cleeve Common and Selsley Common; they even do an impressive job of drowning out the traffic noise on fields near the M4 south of Tormarton. The same environment could throw up the similarly sized **meadow pipit** (*Anthus pratensis*), while two other birds that you're likely to see are the **wheatear** (*Oenanthe oenanthe*), the male of which has a steel-grey back and crown and often bows and flicks its tail and perches on walls or rocks, and the **stonechat** (*Saxicola torquata*), much smaller and darker in plumage and identifiable by its call, a single sharp 'teck'. In autumn, flocks of **redwings** (*Turdus iliatus*) and **fieldfares** (*Turdus pilaris*) arrive from their breeding grounds in northern Europe to feed on wild fruit and berries.

STONECHAT
L: 135mm/5.25"

YELLOWHAMMER
L: 160mm/6.25"

Most easily spotted on hedgerows alongside farmland is the **yellowhammer** (*Emberiza citronella*), its familiar song widely translated as 'little-bit-of-bread-and-no-cheese'. This bright yellow bird with a reddish-brown back is regularly seen at Dover's Hill and Leckhampton Hill, too.

Out on the fields and across the hills is big crow country. You can't miss these gregarious birds, collectively known as corvids, whether the grey-headed **jackdaws** (*Corvus monedula*), the **rooks** (*Corvus frugilegus*), or the **carrion crows** (*Corvus corone corone*). If you doubted their community instincts, look out for jackdaws in particular at Wontley Farm near Belas Knap, where they have taken over the

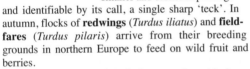
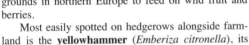

LAPWING/PEEWIT
L: 320mm/12.5"

derelict buildings en masse. In a similar environment you'll find **lapwings** (*Vanellus vanellus*), with their smart crests; during the breeding season the male performs a spectacular display, tumbling through the air to attract its mate.

WOODCOCK
L: 330MM/13"

Increasingly seen near urban dumps, or anywhere that they can pick up scraps, are **lesser black-backed gulls** (*Larus fuscus*), usually in the company of the noisy and closely related **herring gulls** (*Larus argentatus*). Despite their prevalence, these two still seem entirely incongruous in a rural setting.

In an area where such a large proportion of land is given over to agriculture, the presence of gamebirds comes as no surprise. **Pheasants** (*Phasianus colchicus*) and **partridges** (*Perdix perdix*) are found practically everywhere, so don't be surprised if one suddenly flies up just in front of you, startled at your approach. You may also put up a **snipe** (*Gallinago gallinago*), which has a zig-zag flight when flushed, or in wooded areas the **woodcock** (*Scolopax rusticola*), easily distinguished from the snipe by its larger size and more rounded wings. Its camouflage makes it difficult to observe during the day.

Lording it over them all are the birds of prey. Both the **kestrel** (*Falco tinnunculus*) and the **sparrowhawk** (*Accipiter nisus*) can be seen, but it's the much larger **buzzard** (*Buteo buteo*), with its brown colouring and cruel yellow talons, that attracts most attention. Its mewing cry can send a shiver down the spine as it soars over fields, woods or moorland in search of its prey, anything from a beetle to a rabbit. The buzzard's fierce reputation won't stop other birds from defending their nests: rooks in particular will sometimes gang up to chase it away, although if sufficiently provoked the buzzard could well retaliate. The occasional **red kite** (*Milvus milvus*) is starting to put in an appearance, presumably encroaching west following its successful re-introduction in the Chiltern Hills. It is easily distinguished in flight from other birds of prey by its forked tail.

RED KITE
L: 650MM/25"

Woodland

Many of the woodland residents such as the **chaffinch** (*Fringilla coelebs*), **greenfinch** (*Carduelis chloris*), **robin** (*Erithacus rubec-*

ula), **song thrush** (*Turdus philomelos*), **blackbird** (*Turdus merula*), **blue tit** (*Parus caeruleus*) and **great tit** (*Parus major*), are familiar to us from our gardens, although less well known is the **long-tailed tit** (*Aegithalos caudatus*), which is distinguished from other tits by its very long tail: it tends to frequent woodland fringes and clearings.

Of the finches, the **goldfinch** (*Carduelis carduelis*) and **linnet** (*Acanthis cannabina*) are relatively common, too, but you might also spot the **siskin** (*Carduelis spinus*), which is smaller and more streaked than the greenfinch, and more yellow in colour. The **brambling** (*Fringilla montifringilla*), which often mixes with chaffinches in winter, is easily distinguished from them by its distinct white upper rump. The **bullfinch** (*Pyrrhula pyrrhula*) is notable for the male's brilliant red chest; the female is like a monochrome copy of her mate. They feed on berries, buds and seeds in the trees and bushes, their movements slow and deliberate. A much smaller bird is the **goldcrest** (*Regulus regulus*), which is the smallest European bird, recognised by its yellow crown with black edges.

The **willow warbler** (*Phylloscopus trochilus*) and **chiffchaff** (*Phylloscopus collybita*) will keep you guessing since distinguishing between them is quite difficult. The chiffchaff is generally rather browner than the willow warbler and its legs are blackish. More obviously, the willow warbler has the more melodic song.

Even if you're unfamiliar with the **treecreeper** (*Certhia familiaris*), it's not difficult to put a name to this small, brown bird with a curved bill that does exactly that: creeps up trees searching for insects. A similar location might also throw up the **nuthatch** (*Sitta europaea*), with its bluish-grey upper side and pinkish-cream chest, though this species tends to make its way down the trunk head first. Similar in size, although not in habit, is the **blackcap** (*Sylvia atricapilla*), quite easy to identify not just for the said black head (as well as brown back and lighter chest), but also for its pretty song. Usually a summer visitor, it nests in woods or dense shrubs. Another summer visitor is the inconspicuous **tree pipit** (*Anthus trivialis*); this one happiest on woodland fringes or any rough country, from where it delivers itself into the air, singing as it goes.

Larger and far more conspicuous are members of the woodpecker family. The **green woodpecker** (*Picus viridis*), a striking bird with a bright green body and red head, is also notable for its curious call, a kind of laughing cry that carries a long way. More often heard than seen are the **lesser spotted woodpecker** (*Dendrocopos minor*) and the much larger **great spotted woodpecker** (*Dendrocopos major*), distinctive for its striking black-and-white plumage, with a bright red patch under the tail and – in the male – similarly coloured crown. Both habitually drum on trees, usually to mark

GREEN WOODPECKER
L: 330MM/13"

their territory and extract insects rather than to bore holes for a nest site.

It is highly likely that you'll see the **magpie** (*Pica pica*) in its handsome black, white and blue plumage, and the colourful **jay** (*Garrulus glandarius*) is becoming more common everywhere; both are highly efficient at cleaning eggs out of birds' nests and even taking young birds. Rarely seen, although its distinctive call is known even to children as the first harbinger of summer, the **cuckoo** (*Cuculus canorus*) is grey or occasionally brown in colour, not unlike a heavy male sparrowhawk. Among the dove family, **wood pigeons** (*Columba palumbus*) and **collared doves** (*Streptopelia decaocto*) can be seen – and heard – everywhere.

Finally, there are the birds of the night, of which the one you're most likely to see – even occasionally in the daytime – is the **tawny owl** (*Strix aluco*). It can be quite unnerving to look up from a lunchtime picnic to find you're being observed from on high.

Streams, canals, rivers and reservoirs

Large tracts of open water are not something you'd associate with the Cotswolds, with the notable exceptions of the canal near Ebley, and the parallel River Frome, but reservoirs and the occasional stream or ornamental pond are enough to attract **swallows** (*Hirundo rustica*), **house martins** (*Delichon urbica*) and **swifts** (*Apus apus*). Watch their acrobatics in summer as they swoop low, picking up insects on the wing. You'll also spot these birds further afield, too. House martins often build their nests under the eaves of houses or churches, while swifts can often be seen rising on the currents; look out for them above Selsley Common. Distinctive in flight for its scimitar-shaped wings, the swift cannot perch like the swallow and martin, and spends almost its entire life aloft. The less-common **sand martin** (*Riparia riparia*) nests in colonies in holes in steep riverbanks and cliffs such as those in Witcombe Wood, near the reservoir.

In evidence along the canal are the familiar **mute swans** (*Cygnus olor*), **mallards** (*Anas platyrhynchos*), **coots** (*Fulica atra*) and **moorhens** (*Gallinula chloropus*), but there are other birds around too. The **grey wagtail** (*Motacilla cinerea*) in particular, with a blue-grey head and a bright-yellow underside, can be seen year-round bobbing up and down by the bridge on the river where the stream flows fast.

SWIFT
L: 200MM/8"

MAMMALS

You might occasionally spot a **roe deer** (*Capreolus capreolus*) in the woods along the Cotswold escarpment. Small in stature, with an average height of 60-75cm at the shoulder, they are reddish brown in summer, but grey in winter, and have a distinctive white rear end which is conspicuous when the deer is alarmed.

THE ENVIRONMENT & NATURE

Males have short antlers with no more than three points. They are active at dawn and dusk and can sometimes be heard barking. If you come across a young kid apparently abandoned, leave it alone and go away; it's normal behaviour for the mother to leave her kid concealed while she goes off to feed.

An enclosure of **red deer** (*Cervus elaphus*) can be seen at Broadway Tower, but these animals are not found in the wild in the Cotswolds.

❏ Farm animals

Dotted across the hills, **sheep** seem to take on the colour of Cotswold stone, rather dirty in the rain, but a soft warm cream in the sun, their lambs improbably white. In the Middle Ages, Cotswold sheep, or 'Cotswold Lions' as they were known, were bred for their long, thick fleeces, which brought immense fortunes to local merchants, enabling them to build the splendid manor houses and imposing 'wool' churches that still grace the region's towns. The animal is distinctive to the layman both for its long coat and a rather unkempt fringe.

Today, because of the widespread crossing of breeds, most of the sheep seen in the fields are cross-breeds, reared primarily for their meat. Yet some of the old breeds are still used, particularly for grazing on Cleeve Hill, so don't be surprised to see the occasional flock of Cotswold sheep. Just to the west of the trail, on land between Cheltenham and Cleeve Hill, there's a flock of Soay sheep, small animals with an unusual light brown fleece.

While the majority of grazing animals in the Cotswolds are sheep, there are still **cattle** to be found, particularly further south along the trail. Many are the familiar black-and-white Friesians, but more conspicuous are the occasional belted Galloways, almost entirely black but with a broad white belt around the girth. The 'local' breed, Gloucester cattle, are distinctive, too, though you'll be lucky to see them. Once bred for Double Gloucester cheese, they have smart, near-black coats (occasionally spotted) enlivened by a bold white streak running from mid spine and through the tail. Other distinguishing features are a black head and legs, and black-tipped horns. And near Lower Kilcott you may spot a herd of Highland cattle, their shaggy coats looking decidedly out of place on the neatly cropped hillside.

No summary of farm animals in Gloucestershire would be complete without a nod to the **Gloucestershire Old Spot**. Named for the large black spots that dot their otherwise pink skins, these pigs once thrived in the outdoors, foraging on scraps and windfall apples. In fact, the spots are said to be bruises from falling apples in the orchards. You're unlikely to see one along the Cotswold Way itself, but at least you'll know something about it if you visit the Dursley pub of the same name!

Finally, there are the **horses**. Lots of them – though nowadays they scarcely fall into the bracket of farm animals. From children's ponies to thoroughbred racehorses, you'll find plenty that points to man's passion for equines. Riding stables are much in evidence, especially in the north of the region, and many's the day when you'll come across a rider or party of riders as you walk along the trail. With this obvious local involvement, it's no accident that two of the country's biggest events in the horsey calendar, the Cheltenham Gold Cup and the Badminton Horse Trials, take place in the Cotswolds.

If you want a closer look at many of these animals and more rare breeds, pay a visit to the **Cotswold Farm Park** (☎ 01451-850307, 🖳 www.cotswoldfarmpark .co.uk; mid/late March to early Nov daily, 10.30am-5pm), east of Winchcombe, about four miles (6.4km) from the trail at Stumps Cross, off the B4077.

Far more visible is the **rabbit** (*Oryctolagus cuniculus*). While many town-ies consider them to be cute relatives of Peter Rabbit, to the farmer they're a pest, responsible each year for damage to crops that can be counted in the millions. Despite being prey to buzzards, foxes, feral cats, stoats and man, they breed rapidly, bucks mating at four months old and does at three-and-a-half months, so their numbers are on the increase.

The **brown hare** (*Lepus europaeus*) is larger than the rabbit with large powerful hind legs and very long, black-tipped ears. They are found on upland such as Leckhampton Hill, and rely for escape on their great acceleration, capable of attaining speeds of up to 45mph (70km/h).

Badgers (*Meles meles*) are nocturnal animals and rarely seen during the day, lying up in their underground burrows, or setts. Litters of cubs are born in February. Like rabbits, they are responsible for considerable damage on farmland, but unlike rabbits they are a protected species and cannot be destroyed. There is also some suggestion that cattle can catch the TB virus through contact with badgers. Although calls from the National Farmers' Union for them to be culled were rejected in July 2008, in 2011 the coalition government gave the go-ahead for culling in two trial areas with a view to extending it across the country.

Red foxes (*Vulpes vulpes*) are becoming common in spite of occasional persecution by man, and the British roads. Readily identifiable by their colour and bushy tail, foxes are shy animals that come out mainly at night to hunt for food. Their supposed habit of killing all the hens in a coop and taking only one is apparently not the result of vicious rage but done to take advantage of abundance while it is available to compensate for times when food is scarce. Although the issue remains controversial, a ban on fox hunting was implemented in 2005.

The ubiquitous **grey squirrel** (*Sciurus carolinensis*) needs no introduction, having driven the native red squirrel into just one or two strongholds since the former's arrival here from North America in the 19th century.

The **weasel** (*Mustela nivalis*), one of Britain's smaller carnivores, is found in a wide range of habitats and is not a protected species. In fact, it may be trapped and killed by gamekeepers out to protect their birds from its claws. Mainly nocturnal and preferring dry areas, the weasel is smaller than the **stoat** (*Mustela erminea*), the tip of whose tail is always black. Other small creatures that hide away in hedgerows include the nocturnal **hedgehog** (*Erinaceus europaeus*), which curls into a tight prickly ball when startled, as well as **shrews** (*Sorex sp.*), **voles** (*Microtus arvalis*) and **harvest mice** (*Micromys minutus*).

Of the 18 species of **bat** to be found in the UK, several are found in the Cotswolds. The most obvious place to spot them is at Woodchester Mansion (see p136) where six different species roost in the house and grounds. These include the endangered **greater horseshoe bat** (*Rhinolophus ferrumequinum*), with a wingspan of around 14in (35cm), and its cousin, the **lesser horseshoe bat** (*Rhinolophus hipposideros*), as well as the tiny **pipistrelle** (*Pipistrellus pipistrellus*), which is Britain's most common species of bat – and the smallest, with a wingspan of just 8in (20cm).

❏ The smaller things in life

While you're looking out for things at ground level, perhaps you'll spot two other

grassland natives that are both now rare, but can still be found in this habitat. The **glow worm** (*Lampyris notciluca*) was once so common that people could read by the light of several found together. And **Roman snails** (*Helix pomatia*, left) were considered a delicacy by the Romans, which is presumably how they acquired their name. Look out for them around Leckhampton and Crickley Hill, their cream-coloured shells up to two inches wide.

REPTILES

The **adder** (*Vipera berus*) is the only venomous snake in Britain but poses very little risk to walkers and will not bite unless provoked or unwittingly disturbed; if you're lucky enough to see one, leave it in peace. Their venom is designed to kill small mammals such as mice and shrews; human deaths are rare.

You are most likely to encounter an adder in spring when they come out of hibernation, and during the summer, when pregnant females warm themselves on open ground in the sun. They are easily identified by the striking zigzag pattern on their back and a 'V' on the top of their head behind the eyes.

Grass snakes (*Natrix natrix*) are Britain's largest reptile, growing up to a metre in length. They prefer rough ground with plentiful long grass in which to conceal themselves, laying their eggs in warm, rotting vegetation such as garden compost heaps, the young hatching in August. The body has vertical black bars and spots running along the sides and usually has a prominent yellow collar round the neck. They are sometimes killed by people mistaking them for adders but are neither venomous nor aggressive.

The equally harmless **slow worm** (*Anguis fragilis*) looks like a snake but is actually a legless lizard. It has no identifying marks on the body, which varies in colour from coppery brown to lead grey and is usually quite shiny in appearance. Like lizards, they are able to blink; snakes have no eyelids. They love to sun themselves and are also found in old buildings under stones or discarded roofing sheets. Also present is the **common lizard** (*Lacerta vivipara*), which like other reptiles is partial to sunning itself during the day to warm up its body temperature.

ROUTE GUIDE & MAPS

Using this guide

The route guide and maps have not been divided into rigid daily stages since people walk at different speeds and have different interests. The **route summaries** below describe the trail between significant places and are written as if walking the path from north to south. To enable you to plan your own itinerary, **practical information** is presented clearly on each of the trail maps. This includes walking times in each direction, and places to stay and eat, as well as shops where you can buy supplies. Further service details are given in the text under the entry for each place; note that the hours stated for pubs relate, for the most part, to when food is served; most venues serve drinks outside these hours.

For an overview of this information, see Itineraries, p31.

TRAIL MAPS

Scale and walking times
The trail maps are to a scale of 1:20,000 (1cm = 200m; $3^1/_8$ inches = one mile). Walking times (see box below) are given along the side of each map and the arrow shows the direction to which the time refers. Black triangles indicate the points between which the times have been taken. The time-bars are a tool and are not there to judge your walking ability. There are so many variables that affect walking speed, from the weather conditions to how many beers you drank the previous evening. After the first hour or two of walking you will be able to see how your speed relates to the timings on the maps.

Up or down?
The trail is shown as a dotted line – – –. An arrow across the trail indicates the slope; two arrows show that it is steep. Note that the arrow points towards the higher part of the trail. If, for example, you are walking from A (at 80m) to B (at 200m) and the trail between the

---

❏ **Important note – walking times**
Unless otherwise specified, **all times in this book refer only to the time spent walking**. You will need to add 20-30% to allow for rests, photography, checking the map, drinking water etc, not to mention time simply to stop and stare. When planning the day's hike count on 5-7 hours' actual walking.

two is short and steep it would be shown thus: A– – – >> – – – B. Reversed arrow heads indicate a downward gradient.

Accommodation

Accommodation marked on the map is usually either on or within easy reach of the trail. Where accommodation is scarce, however, some of the places listed are a little further away. If that is the case, many B&B proprietors will collect walkers from the nearest point on the trail and deliver them back again next morning, if requested. Details of each place are given in the accompanying text.

Unless otherwise specified, the rates quoted are for the summer high season and are for two people sharing a room. Most places deduct between £5 and £15 for single occupancy, although there are considerable variations. In tourist towns, particularly, you can expect to pay extra at weekends (whereas in the odd business establishment the rate is likely to be higher during the week). The number of rooms of each type is given after each entry: S = single room, T = twin room, D = double room, F = family room (sleeping at least three people). Note that some places accept only a two-night stay, particularly at weekends.

The text also mentions whether the premises have **wi-fi** (WI-FI); if a **bath** is available (●) in at least one room; and whether **dogs** (🐾) are welcome.

Other features

The numbered **GPS waypoints** refer to the list on pp184-5. Generally, other features are marked on the maps when they are pertinent to navigation. In order to avoid cluttering the maps and making them unusable, not all features have been marked each time they occur.

The route guide

CHIPPING CAMPDEN   MAP 1a, p77

The 'Best-Kept Village' sign that takes centre stage says much for this beguiling town that lies almost at the most northern point of the Cotswolds Area of Outstanding Natural Beauty. It feels fitting to start the trail here, where the classic Cotswold images of warm honey-coloured stone and rolling green hills are so perfectly balanced. The start – or finish – of the trail is marked by a low stone next to the 18th-century **Town Hall** [25], stating simply 'Cotswold Way: the beginning and the end'.

The Chipping Campden we see today was founded on the wool industry in the 14th and 15th centuries, largely due to one of the country's most successful wool merchants, William Grevel. His home, **Grevel House** [12], still stands on the High St, and

to him and other wealthy benefactors the town owes the outstanding **St James's Church**. Over two hundred years later, another local worthy, Sir Baptist Hicks, trumped Grevel House with his **Campden House** [8]; parts of the house are now used by the Landmark Trust (see p60). Hicks was also responsible for the **Market Hall** [26], today owned by the National Trust and still in regular use, and for the **almshouses** [10] in Church St.

Fast forwarding through the centuries brings us to the **Arts and Crafts movement** (see box opposite), which played an influential role in reversing the town's decline following years of agricultural doldrums. Now tourism is the key to the economy, with plenty of restaurants and a range of accommodation suited to walkers and sightseers alike.

Every year in May the town hosts a two-week music festival (🖳 www.camp-denmusicfestival.co.uk) and – on Dover's Hill – the Olimpick Games (see box p78).

Transport

Access to Chipping Campden is relatively straightforward by road, but by public transport is more challenging. The nearest railway station is at Moreton-in-Marsh, on the line from London Paddington, with up to 19 **trains** a day operated by First Great Western, and continuing on to Evesham. Alternatively it's possible to get a Chiltern Railways train to Stratford-upon-Avon from London Marylebone.

Johnsons Nos 21 and 22 **buses** stop here en route between Stratford-upon-Avon and Moreton-in-Marsh. On a Sunday, when there are no buses, you would need to organise a **taxi** (approx £20 one way from Moreton-in-Marsh, or £28 from Stratford-upon-Avon) for the final leg of the journey. Taxi firms include Chipping Campden Cars

❑ **Arts and Crafts movement**
The Arts and Crafts movement was founded in late Victorian Britain, born of a backlash against the uniformity which resulted from the Industrial Revolution. Its proponents – practical architects and designers as well as theorists – were largely concerned with restoring a sense of individuality and cohesion to an increasingly fragmented workplace. There was more than a touch of the romantic in their ideals, which included spiritual harmony and a one-ness with nature. These aims were to be achieved in part through reuniting the fields of art, craft and design, so that the designer would be brought back in touch with the maker. Authenticity was a key principle, for example with houses to be constructed from naturally occurring materials and fitting into their environment. If buildings and furniture were relatively simple, ornamental pieces such as books and needlework were considerably more elaborate, often drawing on influences not only from the past but from external cultures. Ironically, high-minded intentions to improve the lot of the working man proved unrealistic, since individually crafted work was expensive to produce and out of the reach of all but a privileged few.

The major founders of the movement were the writer and critic John Ruskin, and William Morris, who trained as an architect and was variously a designer, Socialist and author. Although the movement was essentially urban, many of its practitioners moved to the country, and some to the Cotswolds. One of these, the architect CR Ashbee, was the founder in 1888 of the **Guild of Handicrafts**, which he moved from London to Chipping Campden's Silk Mill in 1902. When Ashbee went bankrupt eight years later, his workshop was taken over by the silversmith George Hart, whose great-grandson David now runs the business (see p76). The work of Ashbee and eight other craftsmen is featured at **Court Barn Museum** [9] (☎ 01386-841951, 🖳 www.court barn.org.uk; Apr-Sep Tue-Sun and bank hol Mon 10am-5pm, Oct-Mar Tue-Sun & bank hol Mon 10am-4pm, closed 24 Dec-mid Jan; £4), in a converted barn near the church. Other places along the trail that are linked to the movement include the **Gordon Russell Furniture Museum** in Broadway (see p83), Cheltenham's **Art Gallery & Museum** (see p109), inspired by William Morris, both the **Painswick Centre Gallery** in Painswick (see p123), and **All Saints' Church** in Selsley (see p133).

The movement impacted on gardens, too, typified by topiary hedges creating a series of rooms. Such influences were important at both **Owlpen Manor** (see p136) and **Hidcote Manor Gardens** (☎ 01386-438333, 🖳 www.nationaltrust.org.uk; May-Aug daily 10am-6pm, mid Mar-Apr & Sep Mon-Wed & Sat-Sun 10am-6pm, Oct-early Nov to 5pm, mid Feb-early Mar & mid Nov-mid Dec weekends only 11am-4pm; £10, NT members free), a few miles north of Chipping Campden.

ROUTE GUIDE AND MAPS

CHIPPING CAMPDEN

Where to stay
1 Woodborough
2 Wolds End House
3 Staddlestones
4 Bramley House
5 Taplins
6 The Chance
7 Cherry Trees
11 Eight Bells Inn
17 Dragon House
19 Bantam Tea Rooms
21 Badgers Hall
24 Noel Arms
29 The Kings
36 Sandalwood House
38 Old Bakehouse
39 Volunteer Inn
42 Red Lion Inn
43 Cornerways
44 Stonecroft
45 Catbrook House

Where to eat and drink
11 Eight Bells Inn
18 Caminetto
19 Bantam Tea Rooms
21 Badgers Hall Tea Rooms
27 Michael's
29 The Kings

Where to eat and drink (cont'd)
34 Joël's
35 Le Petit Croissant
37 Butty's @ The Old Bakehouse
39 Maharaja and Volunteer Inn
40 Campden Coffee Company
42 Red Lion Inn

Other
8 Campden House
9 Court Barn Museum
10 Almshouses
12 Grevel House
13 Pharmacy (Robscott)
14 Lloyds TSB bank & ATM
15 Maylam's Deli
16 Jaffé & Neale Bookshop
20 Tourist Information Centre
22 Co-operative food
23 Post office
25 Town Hall
26 Market Hall
28 Campden Surgery
30 HSBC bank & ATM
31 Drinkwater's greengrocer
32 La Tradition Bakery
33 One Stop
40 Silk Mill
41 Robert Welch

ROUTE GUIDE AND MAPS

(☎ 01386-840111 or mob ☎ 07751-334696) and Cotswold Private Hire (mob ☎ 07980-857833).

Services

The good **tourist information centre** [20] (☎ 01386-841206, 💻 www.chippingcamp-denonline.org, Apr-mid Nov daily 9.30am-5.30pm, mid Nov-Mar Mon-Thu 9.30am-1pm Fri-Sun 9.30-4pm) has its base in the Old Police Station on the High St. In addition to plenty of brochures and leaflets, there is a town guide for £1.

Those in search of a **bank** will find a branch of HSBC with an ATM [30] on the island in the centre of the High St, and Lloyds TSB further along [14]. The **post office** [23] is across the road, just a few doors down from the tourist office.

Nearby are two small **groceries**: Co-

operative food [22] (Mon-Sat 7am-10pm, Sun 8am-10pm), and the One Stop [33] (daily 7am-10pm), though Drinkwater's **greengrocer** [31] and Maylam's **Deli** [15] (Mon-Sat 9am-5pm, Sun 11am-5pm) are more individual. Recently-opened La Tradition **bakery** [32] has quickly gained an excellent reputation. For those in search of **books**, Jaffé & Neale [16] (☎ 01386-841011, Mon-Fri 10am-5pm, Sat 9.30am-5pm, Sun 11am-5pm) has an interesting stock, including some good art books. Every Friday morning (9-11am) except in January there's an indoor **market** with food and craft stalls in the Town Hall [25].

For something original, don't miss the **Guild** on Sheep St in Silk Mill [40]. Home to several artisans, it boasts a good art gallery, too (daily 10am-5pm), but the real draw is upstairs, where Hart's **silversmith**

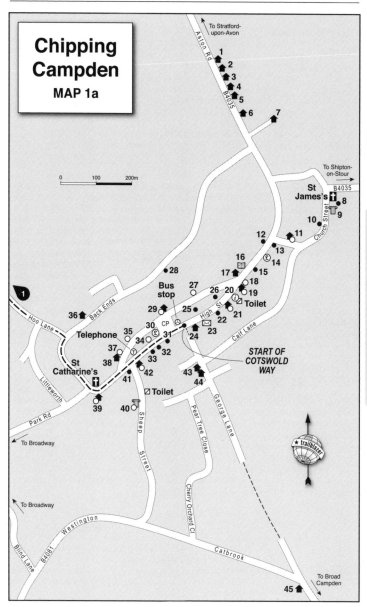

Chipping Campden

MAP 1a

0   100   200m

To Stratford-upon-Avon

To Shipton-on-Stour

B4035

Aston Rd

B4035

St James's

Church Street

1
2
3
4
5
6
7
8
9
10
11
12
13
14
15
16
17
18
19
20
21
22
23
24
25
26
27
28
29
30
31
32
33
34
35
36
37
38
39
40
41
42
43
44
45

Bus stop

CP

Telephone

St Catharine's

Back Ends

Hoo Lane

Littleworth

Park Rd

To Broadway

To Broadway

Blind Lane

B4081

Westington

Sheep Street

Pear Tree Close

Cherry Orchard Cl

George Lane

Catbrook

To Broad Campden

High St

Calf Lane

START OF COTSWOLD WAY

Toilet

Toilet

★ trailblazer

❑ Olimpick Games

Chipping Campden displays its frivolous side in the form of Robert Dover's Olimpick Games (🖳 www.olimpickgames.co.uk), held on Dover's Hill every May on the Friday after the Whitsun Bank Holiday. Dating back to 1612, it's a noisy affair, with bands, cannon fire and fireworks, culminating in a torchlit procession into the town for dancing in the square. If events such as sack races, a tug of war and even shin-kicking would raise an eyebrow at the Olympics, there's also the more conventional shot put, part of the Championship of the Hill, as well as wrestling and cross-country races.

The following day is the **Scuttlebrook Wake**, more of a village fête in style, with a Scuttlebrook Queen, maypole dancing and colourful floats.

(☎ 01386-841100, 🖳 www.hartsilversmiths.co.uk, Mon-Fri 9am-5pm, Sat 9am-noon) has operated since the early 20th century. Commission your own family heirloom, or take time to watch the craftsmen at work. The designs of another silversmith, **Robert Welch** [41] (☎ 01386-840522, 🖳 www.robertwelch.com, Mon-Sat 9.30am-5.30pm, Sun 10am-4pm), are displayed at the shop bearing his name on Lower High St.

Campden Surgery [28] (☎ 01386-841894) is along Back Ends. The **pharmacy**, Robscott [13], is on the corner of the High and Church streets. There are public **toilets** behind the tourist office (though you'll need 20p to access them), and opposite Silk Mill.

Where to stay

Many walkers starting at Chipping Campden will want to stay a night before setting off the following morning, if only to have a chance to see something of the town. There's plenty of choice – though accommodation does get booked up quickly, especially in the summer and at weekends. **Campers**, though, will be out of luck; the nearest campsite is at Hailes (see p94), so you'll have to start straight on the trail or spend the first night in a B&B.

A few **B&Bs** are centrally located among the stone cottages of the High St itself. On Lower High St, rooms at ***The Old Bakehouse*** next to the café [38] (☎ 01386-840979, mob ☎ 07717-330838; 2T or D en suite) cost £75, with single occupancy at £60. Further up the street, two of the tea rooms, ***Badgers Hall*** [21] (☎ 01386-840839, 🖳 www.badgershall.co.uk; 3T or D; WI-FI) and ***Bantam Tea Rooms*** [19] (☎ 01386-840386, 🖳 www.thebantam.co.uk; 1S/1T/2D with ☛), offer B&B in en suite rooms above the premises. In the first, beamed rooms under the eaves come in at £98.50-112 (including a clotted cream tea) for two sharing, with single occupancy rates available on request; there's a minimum stay of two nights. At Bantam you'll be paying £85, or £65 for the single.

Near the Market Hall, ***Dragon House*** [17] (☎ 01386-840734, 🖳 www.dragonhouse-chipping-campden.com; 1T/1D both en suite; WI-FI), dating from medieval times and in a quiet location behind the High St, has rooms from £73, with single occupancy for £57. Guests share a sitting room and are welcome to sit out in the garden.

Behind the High St, ***Sandalwood House*** [36] (☎ 01386-840091; 1D/1F; ☛; WI-FI) is a detached building in a peaceful spot on Back Ends, with the en suite double at £75 (£58 for single occupancy), and £95 for the family room with private bathroom, sleeping three.

At the other end of the town, two modern options with unfussy rooms sit next to each other on George Lane, with footpath access to the High St. ***Stonecroft*** [44] (☎ 01386-840486, 🖳 www.stonecroft-chippingcampden.co.uk; 1T/2D; WI-FI) has a twin and a double with an interconnecting bathroom, and an en suite double. Rates are £75 for two sharing (£63 single occupancy). *Cornerways* [43] (☎ 01386-841307, 🖳 www.cornerways.info; 2F, both en suite WI-FI) charges £70 for two sharing (£90 for three and £110 for four).

On the outskirts of the town, overlooking farmland to the front and rear but still an easy walk from the High St, is *Catbrook House* [45] (☎ 01386-841499, 🖳 www .chippingcampden.co.uk/catbrook.htm; 1T or D en suite/2D). It's a detached stone house, with rooms from £60 with a private shower (single occupancy from £50), or from £78 en suite.

Many of the town's B&Bs lie in the opposite direction, along Aston Rd: solid stone houses with gardens backing on to open countryside. The first, *Cherry Trees* [7] (☎ 01386-840873; www.cherrytrees campden.com; 2D/1T or F; 1 🐶; WI-FI), is slightly elevated along a narrow track about 150m from the road, with views to Broadway Tower. Two rooms are en suite; the other, a double, has private facilities with a bath; both doubles have king-size beds. Rates are £75-85 for two sharing, £110 for three, or £55-65 for single occupancy. Back on Aston Rd itself is *The Chance* [6] (☎ 01386-849079, 🖳 www .the-chance.co.uk, No 1; 3D, all en suite, 🐶; WI-FI), which costs £75 per room (£70 single); in high season, there is usually a two-night minimum stay. Next up is *Taplins* [5] (☎ 01386-840927, 🖳 www.cotswoldstay .co.uk, No 5; 1D/1D or T both en suite, 🐶; WI-FI), under the same ownership as the antiques shop in the town, which perhaps accounts for the Victorian-style roll-top bath in one of the rooms. B&B here costs £75 a night, or from £50 for single occupancy. Continuing on are *Bramley House* [4] (☎ 01386-840066, 🖳 www.bramley house.co.uk, No 6; 2D en suite; WI-FI), at £70-80 a night (£60 single occupancy), who only accept bookings for a minimum of two nights, and *Staddlestones* [3] (☎ 01386-849288, 🖳 www.staddle-stones .com, No 7; 2D/1D or F, all en suite; WI-FI; 🐕), charging £75-85 for a double, or £105-130 for the garden studio, which has its own sitting room and can sleep up to four. At *Wolds End House* [2] (☎ 01386-840956, 🖳 www.woldsendhouse.co.uk;

1T/2D; WI-FI), B&B is £55 (single occupancy £45) for the twin or smaller double, which share a bathroom, or £65 for a king-size double en suite. Finally there's *Woodborough* [1] (☎ 01386-841585, 🖳 www.chippingcampdenbandb.co.uk; 1F en suite; WI-FI), where a family suite incorporates a double room and a sitting room with two sofa beds. Rates vary according to the number of occupants: £74 single, £85 for two sharing a room, or £105-140 for two to four people in separate rooms.

If a **pub** is more your idea of a convivial place to spend the night, Chipping Campden comes up trumps. On Lower High St, almost opposite St Catharine's Church, the 17th-century *Volunteer Inn* [39] (☎ 01386-840688, 🖳 www.thevolunteerinn.net; 5D/4D or T; WI-FI) has two rooms sharing a bathroom, one with a private bathroom, and the rest en suite. B&B is £60-90 (single occupancy £50), though rates may be negotiable if you turn up on spec. Added extras? There's a luggage transfer service and the possibility of parking your car for the duration of the walk; they might even be able to drive it back to you in Bath!

Negotiable rates for walk-in guests may also be possible at the family-run *Red Lion Inn* [42] (☎ 01386-840760, 🖳 www .theredlioninn.org, Lower High St; 1T or D/4D all en suite; WI-FI; 🐕), where B&B is normally from £69 to £85 (single occupancy £59-69). Continuing upmarket brings us to the *Eight Bells Inn* [11] (☎ 01386-840371, 🖳 www.eightbellsinn.co.uk; 1S/ 5D/1D or F; 3D with 🐶; WI-FI), on Church St, a 14th-century hostelry where the rooms, furnished in a sympathetic yet contemporary style, cost £85-125 per night, or for single occupancy, £60-85. Note that at weekends there's a minimum two-night stay.

Smarter still are the hotels, of which *The Kings* [29] (☎ 01386-840256, 🖳 www .kingscampden.co.uk; 4T/13D, en suite; 🐶 in all but 3; WI-FI) has B&B at £115-295, or £97-200 for single occupancy, while the *Noel Arms* [24] (☎ 01386-840317, 🖳 www.noelarmshotel.com; 15T or D/12D, all en suite; 🐶; WI-FI; 🐕 £15) charges £150-220 (deduct £10 for single occupancy).

Where to eat and drink

Top-quality food with prices to match is done well along Chipping Campden's High St, but there's a good range of more accessible fare, especially at lunchtime.

For food on the move, start at *Butty's @ The Old Bakehouse* [37] (☎ 01386-840401; Mon-Fri 7.30am-2.30pm, Sat 8.30am-2pm), where the name says it all: surf the internet while you munch your lunch – with baguettes costing around £3.50. Or try *Le Petit Croissant* [35] (☎ 01386-841861; Mon-Sat 9am-5pm, Sat 8.30am-5pm, Sun 11am-4pm), more of a deli/bakery with sandwiches (including takeaway) and light lunches served in their café with a terrace.

If you'd rather spend time over lunch, try *Joël's* [34] (☎ 01386-840598; Tue-Sat 10.30am-1.45pm, Tue-Thu 6.30-8.45pm, Fri-Sat 6.30-9pm), where a terrace under willow trees makes a popular summer alternative to the restaurant. With pizza and pasta from £7.50 at lunch and in the evening (except Saturday), it won't break the bank; even the traditional European cuisine on the dinner menu is relatively reasonable. For irresistible cakes (and light lunches), *Bantam Tea Rooms* [19] (see p78, Mon-Sat 10am-5pm, Sun 10.30am-5pm, or 4pm in winter) has an enviable selection, as does the friendly *Badgers Hall Tea Rooms* [21] (see p78, daily 10am-4.30pm). For a coffee fix, head straight for the more contemporary *Campden Coffee Company* [40] (☎ 01386-849251; Mon-Fri 9am-5pm, Sat & Sun 10am-5pm) in Silk Mill on Sheep St, where coffee beans are roasted on the premises. There are smoothies, too, as well as soups, jacket potatoes, baguettes and ice creams.

The town has some excellent pubs, too. The *Eight Bells Inn* [11] (see p79; food served Mon-Thu noon-2pm & 6.30-9pm, Fri-Sun noon-2.15pm, Fri-Sat 6.30-9.30pm, Sun 6.30-8.45pm) has been refurbished but not overly so, and retains the atmosphere of a traditional pub. Wherever you eat – in the bar, the restaurant or the courtyard garden – you should eat well, from salads and sandwiches to upmarket bangers and mash or Mediterranean tagliatelle at £12.75.

The atmosphere at the *Red Lion Inn* [42] (see p79; food served Mon-Thu noon-2pm & 6-9pm, Fri-Sun noon-2.30pm & 6-9.30pm) is relaxed and friendly, and there's a courtyard bar if you'd rather be outside with a pint of IPA. The menu is primarily traditional English, with daily specials that reflect seasonal produce: expect to pay from £8.95 for a main course, with lighter bites at lunch costing around £4.95.

There's a brasserie at *The Kings* [29] (see p79; Mon–Fri noon-2.30pm, Sat-Sun noon-3pm, daily 6.30-9.30pm), too, more intimate than its formal restaurant, with a varied and changing menu that features dishes such as linguine with walnut pesto, wild garlic and spinach (£8.25), as well as sandwiches.

The Italian *Caminetto* [18] (☎ 01386-840934; Tue-Sat noon-1.30pm & 7-10pm) is emphatically not a pizza place (think *feggato veneziana* at £17.50, with pasta mains from £8.75), but it does come well recommended. *Michael's* [27] (☎ 01386-840826, 🖳 www.michaelsmediterranean.co.uk; Tue-Sat 11-2.30pm & 7-10pm, Sun noon-3pm) does all things Greek/Mediterranean, albeit at decidedly un-Greek prices. Try *mezedakia* (nine hot/cold hors d'oeuvres for sharing) at £13.50, or moussaka with salad (£10.95 at lunchtime, or £14.75 in the evening).

If you fancy a curry, head for the Indian *Maharaja* [39] (☎ 01386-840688; Sun-Thu 5.30-10pm, Fri-Sat 5.30-10.30pm) at the Volunteer Inn. The pub itself sticks to the beer, which can be savoured in summer in the garden.

CHIPPING CAMPDEN TO BROADWAY   MAPS 1-3

This first **6-mile (9.7km, 3-3¹/₂hrs)** stretch of the Cotswold Way, characterised by agricultural land and open hills, is a great introduction to the trail as a whole. A gradual ascent leads across farmland to **Dover's Hill**, at 738ft (225m) the first of many high points along the walk, affording the first of many superb views.

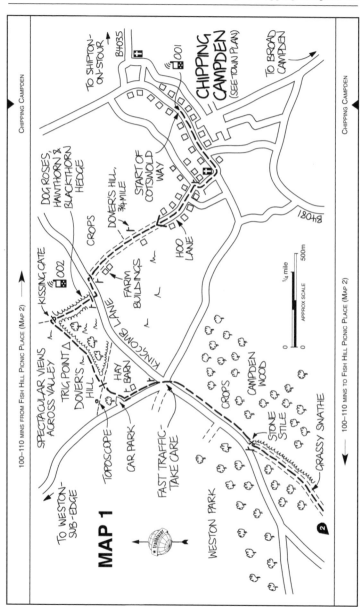

100–110 MINS FROM FISH HILL PICNIC PLACE (MAP 2) →

TO SHIPTON-ON-STOUR

B4035

☗ 001

CHIPPING CAMPDEN
(SEE TOWN PLAN)

TO BROAD CAMPDEN

DOG ROSES, HAWTHORN & BLACKTHORN HEDGE

START OF COTSWOLD WAY

DOVER'S HILL, ¾ MILE

CROPS

KISSING GATE

☗ 002

HOO LANE

FARM BUILDINGS

B4081

SPECTACULAR VIEWS ACROSS VALLEY

TRIG POINT △

DOVER'S HILL

HAY BARN

KINGCOMBE LANE

500m

¼ mile

APPROX SCALE

0

0

TO WESTON-SUB-EDGE

TOPOSCOPE

CAR PARK

FAST TRAFFIC – TAKE CARE

WESTON PARK

MAP 1

CROPS

CAMPDEN WOOD

STONE STILE

GRASSY SWATHE

2

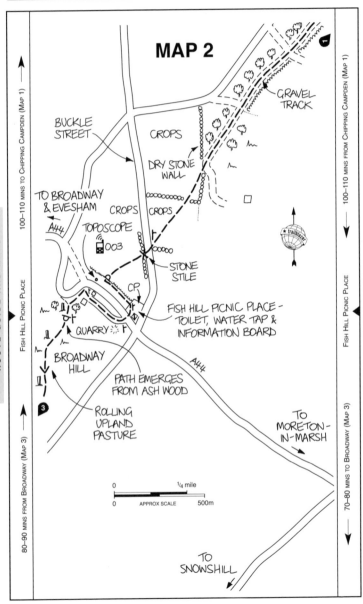

MAP 2

100–110 MINS TO CHIPPING CAMPDEN (MAP 1)

FISH HILL PICNIC PLACE

80–90 MINS FROM BROADWAY (MAP 3)

100–110 MINS FROM CHIPPING CAMPDEN (MAP 1)

FISH HILL PICNIC PLACE

70–80 MINS TO BROADWAY (MAP 3)

GRAVEL TRACK

BUCKLE STREET

CROPS

DRY STONE WALL

TO BROADWAY & EVESHAM

A44

CROPS   CROPS

TOPOSCOPE

003

STONE STILE

CP

trailblazer

FISH HILL PICNIC PLACE –
TOILET, WATER TAP &
INFORMATION BOARD

QUARRY

BROADWAY HILL

PATH EMERGES
FROM ASH WOOD

A44

ROLLING
UPLAND
PASTURE

TO
MORETON-
IN-MARSH

3

0   ¼ mile
0   500m
APPROX SCALE

TO
SNOWSHILL

Get your bearings (and your breath) at **Broadway Tower** (see box below), the second-highest point along the trail, before the steep descent to Broadway.

BROADWAY MAP 3a, p87

Named for its wide central street, once the main road between Worcester and London, Broadway is to many tourists (and there are a lot of them) synonymous with the Cotswolds.

A broad green at one end of the High St sets a somewhat bucolic tone, enhanced by trees lining the road and rows of stone cottages, giving rise to an excess of clichés and tourist shops. And yet, despite the high number of visitors, the town retains a considerable charm, particularly outside the summer months.

Celebrating Broadway's links with the Arts and Crafts movement (see box p75), the **Gordon Russell Furniture Museum** (☎ 01386-854695, 🖳 www.gordonrussell museum.org; Apr-Oct Tue-Sun 11am-5pm, Nov-Dec & Feb-Mar 11am-4pm; entry £4) pays tribute to a man who from 1918 committed his working life on this site to designing and making furniture.

Somewhat unusually, Broadway's original parish church of **St Eadburgha's** is marooned in a serene location well over half a mile (1.25km) to the south, towards Snowshill. Nowadays the role is filled by **St Michael & All Saints**, close to the town and an attractive backdrop to the trail as it leaves Broadway.

Transport

Several **buses** stop in the town between Monday and Saturday. Of these, the most useful for walkers is the 606, run by Castleways, which goes to Cheltenham via Stanton turn ($^1/_2$ mile from village), Winchcombe and Cleeve Hill. Castleways also runs the 559 to Evesham via Broadway, while Johnsons' 21/22 services connect Stratford-upon-Avon with Chipping Campden and Moreton-in-Marsh, with the 21 service stopping in Broadway. See public transport map and table, p46.

Broadway's **taxi** firms include Cotswold Horizons (☎ 01386-858599) and Delta Taxis (mob ☎ 07798-767688).

❑ Broadway Tower Map 3, p84

With its turreted top and walls of oolitic limestone, the tall tower that looms into view as you cross the fields on the outskirts of Broadway is an unlikely sight, apparently protecting only the sheep that graze nearby. Built in 1799 as a folly for Lady Coventry by the 6th Earl of Coventry, it sits atop Beacon Hill which, at 1024ft (312m), is the second highest point in the Cotswolds. In its heyday, it was a lively retreat, attracting several Pre-Raphaelite artists, among them the Socialist and artist William Morris (1834-96), who was a regular visitor from his home at Kelmscott. Rejected by the National Trust in 1949, the tower is now in private hands, and open to the public (☎ 01386-852390, 🖳 www.broadwaytower.co.uk; Apr-Oct daily 10.30am-5pm, Nov-Mar Sat & Sun 10.30am-3pm; admission £4.50).

According to Morris's daughter, May, men used to bathe on the roof of the tower, which was described as 'the most inconvenient and the most delightful place ever seen'. Today's visitors can climb up to the roof, too, but only for the scenery: in good weather there are superb 360° views across 13 counties. The ground floor is given over to a shop, while each of the interim floors showcases a series of small exhibitions covering the history of the tower, and its links with both William Morris and the Royal Observer Corps. Outside, a small enclosure houses a herd of red deer.

The *Rookery Barn* restaurant in the grounds was closed in late 2011. Should it reopen, you can expect a welcoming wood-burning stove on a cold day, and a menu that ranges from lunches to cream teas.

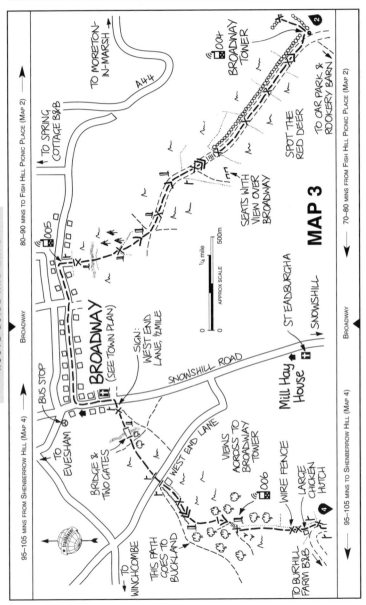

95–105 MINS FROM SHENBERROW HILL (MAP 4) ◀ ▶ BROADWAY

80–90 MINS TO FISH HILL PICNIC PLACE (MAP 2) ▶

95–105 MINS TO SHENBERROW HILL (MAP 4) ◀ ▶ BROADWAY ◀ 70–80 MINS FROM FISH HILL PICNIC PLACE (MAP 2)

MAP 3

TO MORETON-IN-MARSH

A44

TO SPRING COTTAGE B&B

004 BROADWAY TOWER

TO CAR PARK & ROOKERY BARN (MAP 2)

SPOT THE RED DEER

SEATS WITH VIEW OVER BROADWAY

005

BROADWAY
(SEE TOWN PLAN)

BUS STOP

SIGN: WEST END LANE, ½ MILE

TO EVESHAM

BRIDGE & TWO GATES

WEST END LANE

SNOWSHILL ROAD

Mill Hay House

ST EADBURGHA

SNOWSHILL

¼ mile
APPROX SCALE
500m

VIEWS ACROSS TO BROADWAY TOWER

006

WIRE FENCE

LARGE CHICKEN HUTCH

TO WINCHCOMBE

THIS PATH GOES TO BUCKLAND

TO BURHILL FARM B&B

Services

Almost everything in Broadway happens on the High St, though the smart **tourist information centre** (☎ 01386-852937, 🖳 www.beautifulbroadway.com; mid Feb-Oct Mon-Sat 10am-5pm, Sun 2-5pm, Nov-Dec, Mon-Sat 10am-4pm) is set back behind the **supermarket**, Budgens (daily 8am-9pm). On the High St itself, near The Green, is the more personal and very well-stocked Broadway Deli (Mon-Sat 8am-5pm), with fresh fruit and veg, bakery bread and all sorts of goodies.

On the other side of the road, Blandford Books (☎ 01386-858588; Mon-Sat 9.30am-5.30pm, Sun 10.30am-5.30pm) stocks a good range of **books**, and is particularly strong on local titles. Those browsing for **antiques** will find plenty to delay them, too.

More practically, the **post office** is on the High St, as are branches of both HSBC & Lloyds TSB **banks**, both with ATMs; there's another ATM at Budgens.

For **medical** matters, contact Barn Close Surgery (☎ 01386-853651) opposite the post office, or the nearby Lloyds **pharmacy**. A footpath from the High St leads through to the public **toilets** in the car park on Church Close.

Where to stay

There's no shortage of places to stay in this picture-postcard village that draws American visitors in their droves. Finding something within a tight budget is much harder – and unless you're planning to walk in the depths of winter, you'd be well advised to book ahead.

A couple of **pubs** offer accommodation. At the traditional *Horse and Hound* (☎ 01386-852287; 4D/1F, all en suite, ➡; WI-FI; 🐾 £10) at the top of the High St, a room above the pub is from £60 for single occupancy in the winter to £120 for the family room in summer. Rates at the 17th-century *Crown & Trumpet* (☎ 01386-853 202, 🖳 www.cotswoldholidays.co.uk; 1T/3D all en suite, ➡; WI-FI), which have regular live music, are from £65 for two sharing, depending on the day and time of year; at weekends there is a two-night minimum stay. There are several more traditional

B&Bs in and around the centre. The Cotswold Way runs right past the gate of *Cowley House* (☎ 01386-858148, 🖳 www.cowleyhouse-broadway.co.uk, Church St; 3D/4T or D/1T, D or F; ➡; 🐾 £10; WI-FI), which is part 17th-century. Just off The Green, so peaceful but central, it has rooms with private or en suite facilities for £75-105 (£60-70 single occupancy), the higher rate coming with a four-poster bed. Small dogs can be accommodated in one room, which has a private garden. Packed lunches (£7) are available on request, and for £7.50 a load they'll even do your laundry.

At the far end of the High St, away from any traffic but also on the Cotswold Way, is the award-winning *Olive Branch* (☎ 01386-853440, 🖳 www.theolive branch-broadway.com; 1S/3D/3T or D/2T, D or F; ➡; WI-FI; 🐾 1 room only £5), built in 1592 and offering B&B for over 50 years. Today, rooms are fitted out in an elegant but cottagey style, with en suite facilities (three with bath) and a range of extras. Rates are £85-95 for two sharing, £58-68 in the single room (with private bathroom), and £65-75 for single occupancy of a twin/double room. Packed lunches can be supplied on request at £15. New on the scene, on the opposite side of the road, is the small 18th-century *Half Penny Cottage* (☎ 01386-854723, 🖳 halfpennybb@gmail .com; 2D; ➡; WI-FI). As the rooms share a private bathroom, only one is let at a time, except to a family or group of friends. You'll pay £85 for the double alone or £150 for both rooms.

Further down, set back in a courtyard next to the Lygon Arms, *Small Talk Lodge* (☎ 01386-858953, 🖳 www.smalltalk lodge.co.uk; 2T/4D/1F, all en suite, ➡; WI-FI) has rooms for £65-68 (single occupancy £45-50), or £68-73 with a four-poster bed.

Still very central, on Leamington Rd just off the High St, is *Hadley House* (☎ 01386-853486, 🖳 hadley.house@virgin .net, 🖳 www.cotswolds.info; 2T/3D, all en suite; WI-FI; 🐾), where B&B costs £70-75 (£55 single occupancy). Just off this road, on the corner of Colletts Fields and the footpath from Upper High St, is *Dove Cottage* (☎ 01386-859085, 🖳 www.broad

way-cotswolds.co.uk; 1T/1D, ☛, both en suite; WI-FI), charging from £75/80 for the twin/double (single occupancy from £50).

To the west of town, there's a cluster of good-sized B&Bs lining Station Rd. First up, less than quarter of a mile (0.3km) from the trail, is *Whiteacres* (☎ 01386-852320, ☐ www.broadwaybandb.com; 1T/4D, all en suite; WI-FI; 🐾), with B&B at £70-75, or £55-60 for single occupancy. The neighbouring *Windrush House* (☎ 01386-853577, ☐ www.windrushhouse.com; 3D/2T, all en suite; WI-FI) offers a more contemporary décor in the rooms which is reflected in the higher price (from £90 a night, and £75 for single occupancy). Next door again, walkers are particularly welcome at *Southwold House* (☎ 01386-853681, ☐ www.cotswolds-broadway-southwold.co.uk; 1S/2T or D/4D/1F, all en suite, ☛; WI-FI), with a bath in one of the pretty double rooms (some with king-size beds), a drying cupboard for wet clothes, and packed lunches on request at around £6.50. B&B here costs £40-55 single, £70-85 double/twin, and £90-120 for the family room. A similar distance further up the road is *Brook House* (☎ 01386-852313, ☐ www.brookhousebandb.co.uk; 1S/1T/2D/1F; WI-FI; 🐾), where three of the rooms are en suite and the others share a bathroom, ☛; rates start from £35 per person. Last of the bunch, about half a mile (0.8km) from the trail, is *The Old Stationhouse* (☎ 01386-852659, ☐ www.broadwaybedandbreak fast.com; 2T or D/3D, all en suite, ☛; WI-FI), occupying the old stationmaster's lodgings down a private drive between the railway bridge and the Murco garage. With new owners comes a full refurbishment for early 2012, when B&B will be from £90 for two sharing.

In the opposite direction lies *Spring Cottage* (off map 3; ☎ 01386-852920, ☐ juneruddy@googlemail.com; 2D en suite, ☛; WI-FI), backing onto farmland on the quiet Bibsworth Lane. To find it, head east from the trail along Upper High St for about quarter of a mile (0.4km), then turn left at East House and continue for a similar distance; it's the last house on the right, and one of the rooms is detached, with its own fridge and microwave. B&B here costs £70, or £60 for single occupancy.

For most walkers, the renowned *Lygon Arms* (☎ 01386-852255, ☐ www.barcelo hotels.co.uk, 78 rooms; ☛; WI-FI; 🐾 £15) at £139-250 a night is likely to remain firmly off limits, but at least it puts other places in perspective. And if you fancy being truly decadent, you could swap your boots for Queen Anne-style splendour at *Mill Hay House* (see Map 3, p84; ☎ 01386-852498, ☐ www.millhay.co.uk; 3D, all en suite, ☛; WI-FI) where, from a mere £160 a night (single occupancy from £120), Annetta Gorton offers 'gourmet B&B'. It lies on Snowshill Rd less than half a mile (0.65km) south of the trail.

Where to eat and drink

A popular option for lunch or dinner is *The Swan* (☎ 01386-852278, ☐ www.theswan-broadway.co.uk; Mon-Fri noon-9.30pm, Sat 11am-10pm, Sun 11am-9.30pm), opposite The Green, where comfy chairs & heavy wooden tables feel right at home in the old building. Relaxed and informal, it offers a varied menu, with the likes of sausage and mash at lunch (£7.95), and slow cooked pork belly glazed in maple syrup (£12.95) from the dinner menu. Do book if you want to be sure of a table.

The rather more traditional *Horse and Hound* (see p85; daily noon-3pm & 6-9pm) has a standard lunch menu including soup (£4.95) as well as more substantial fare from £7.50-14.25. They serve the occasional guest ale, too. More lively is the *Crown & Trumpet* (see p85; Mon-Fri noon-2.30pm & 6-9.15pm, Sat-Sun noon-9.15pm) on Snowshill Rd, where there's jazz and blues most Thursday evenings, and contemporary live music on Saturday. Their Sunday roast costs from £8.95 and they have ales from Stanway Brewery (four brewed exclusively for them), Stroud Brewery and Cotswold Spring.

Part of the Lygon Arms, but in a separate building, is the not-inaccessible, *Goblets* (☎ 01386-852255; daily 10-4pm, Tue-Sun 6.30-9pm). A coffee shop during the day, serving the likes of lunchtime baguettes, it morphs into a bistro restaurant

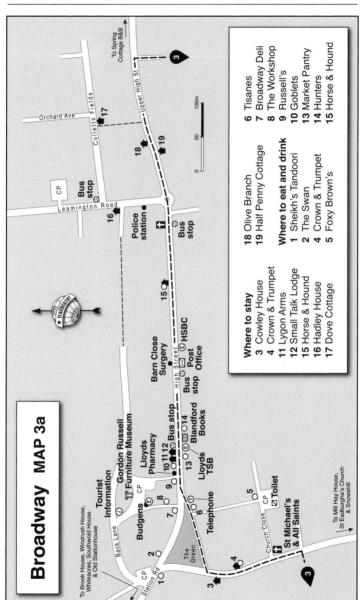

Broadway MAP 3a

To Spring
Cottage B&B

3

Orchard Ave

Colletts Fields

17

Upper High St

0   50   100m

18

19

Bus
stop

CP

Leamington Road

16

Police
station

Bus
stop

15

Barn Close
Surgery

High Street

HSBC

Post
Office

Bus
stop

Gordon Russell
Furniture Museum

Lloyds
Pharmacy

Bus stop

10 11 12   14

13   Blandford
            Books

Lloyds
TSB

Tourist
Information

CP

Budgens

8   9

7   6

Telephone

Back Lane

2

CP

The
Green

Station Rd

1

To Brook House, Windrush House,
Whiteacres, Southwold House
& Old Stationhouse

5

Toilet

CP

Church Close

St Michael's
& All Saints

4

3

3

To Mill Hay House,
St Eadburgha's Church
& Snowshill

trailblazer

Where to stay
3 Cowley House
4 Crown & Trumpet
11 Lygon Arms
12 Small Talk Lodge
15 Horse & Hound
16 Hadley House
17 Dove Cottage

6 Tisanes
7 Broadway Deli
8 The Workshop
9 Russell's
10 Goblets
13 Market Pantry
14 Hunters
15 Horse & Hound

18 Olive Branch
19 Half Penny Cottage

Where to eat and drink
1 Sheikh's Tandoori
2 The Swan
4 Crown & Trumpet
5 Foxy Brown's

ROUTE GUIDE AND MAPS

in the evening, with mains at around £15.

Along a passageway leading from the High St, *The Workshop* (☎ 01386-858435; daily noon-2.30pm, 3-5pm & 6-9pm), is the relaxed sibling of Russell's, offering bistro-style food, afternoon tea, and – from 6pm to 7pm during the week – supper specials such as roast chicken or fish and chips at £8-9.50.

Continuing upmarket, *Russell's* itself (☎ 01386-853555; 🖥 www.russellsofbroadway.co.uk; daily noon-2.30pm, Mon-Fri 6-9.30pm, Sat 6.30-9.30pm) offers a fixed-price lunch or early dinner menu at £12.95-15.95. There's an à la carte menu, too, albeit best kept for very special occasions.

If that lot doesn't appeal, or you can't face life without a curry, don't panic: the tandoori restaurant *Sheikh's* (☎ 01386-858546; daily noon-2pm & 6-10.30pm), just off The Green, has a good reputation locally.

Not surprisingly, with so many tourists around, tea is high on the agenda here. Try *Tisanes* (☎ 01386-853296; daily 10am-5pm) on The Green, its bow window neatly fitting the archetypal image of an English tea shop – and offering gluten-free dishes, too. Further up, on the High St, the *Market Pantry* (☎ 01386-858318; Mon-Fri 9am-5pm, Sat 9.30am-5pm, Sun 10am-5pm) promises 'Great Food', which comes up at breakfast, lunch and tea, to include toasties at £5.50 and some original tartines (£6.25). The nearby *Hunters* (☎ 01386-858522; Mon-Fri 10am-4.30pm, Sat-Sun 10am-5pm) falls into a similar category, but also does takeaway sandwiches from £2.30.

Tempting smells emanate from the pies and fresh bread at the equally central *Broadway Deli* (see p85, 🖥 www.broadwaydeli .co.uk), which has its own simple café. Then there's the bright and efficient *Foxy Brown's* (☎ 01386-852155, daily 9.30am-5.30pm), in the precinct leading to the car park, serving the likes of warm chicken salad (£7.25) as well as coffee and cakes.

BROADWAY TO WINCHCOMBE   MAPS 3-8

This **12-mile (19.3km, 6-7hrs)** stretch should fulfil the expectations of anyone who has leafed through glossy coffee-table books on the Cotswolds. Here are the rolling hills, the fine views and the cottages of time-weathered stone. This is rural England at its best, with **Stanton** the quintessential Cotswold village. Some steep ups and downs bring in several cultural highlights, too: **Stanway House** (see p92); the site of the Iron-Age **Beckbury Camp**, where a stone monument known locally as 'Cromwell's seat' is reputed to mark where Thomas Cromwell watched Hailes Abbey burn; and the ruins of **Hailes Abbey** itself (see box p94) – which are well worth exploring. From here it's an easy and pleasant walk to the fine old wool town of Winchcombe.

BUCKLAND   off MAP 3, p84

Just 250m off the trail, *Burhill Farm* (☎ 01386-858171, 🖥 www.burhillfarm.co.uk; 2D, both en suite; WI-FI) lies in rural isolation in a deep, sheltered valley. B&B costs £37.50 per person sharing, or £45 for single occupancy. If booked in advance the owner will prepare a light supper, such as an omelette, for walkers, who otherwise face quite a trek at the end of a walking day to get something to eat. Alternatively, stop in Broadway on your way here.

❏ **Important note – walking times**
Unless otherwise specified, **all times in this book refer only to the time spent walking**. You will need to add 20-30% to allow for rests, photography, checking the map, drinking water etc. When planning the day's hike count on 5-7 hours' actual walking.

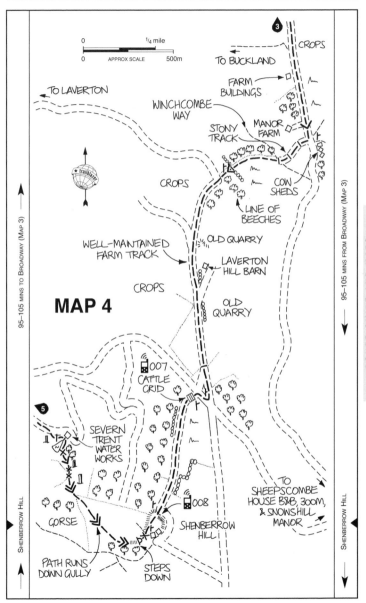

MAP 4

TO LAVERTON

TO BUCKLAND

CROPS

FARM BUILDINGS

WINCHCOMBE WAY

STONY TRACK

MANOR FARM

COW SHEDS

LINE OF BEECHES

CROPS

OLD QUARRY

WELL-MAINTAINED FARM TRACK

LAVERTON HILL BARN

CROPS

OLD QUARRY

007 CATTLE GRID

SEVERN TRENT WATER WORKS

008

SHENBERROW HILL

TO SHEEPSCOMBE HOUSE B&B, 300m, & SNOWSHILL MANOR

GORSE

PATH RUNS DOWN GULLY

STEPS DOWN

0   1/4 mile

0   APPROX SCALE   500m

★ trailblazer

95-105 MINS TO BROADWAY (MAP 3)

95-105 MINS FROM BROADWAY (MAP 3)

SHENBERROW HILL

SHENBERROW HILL

❏ **Snowshill Manor**   **off Map 4, p89**
Even those least interested in museums will find something appealing about a man
who amassed a collection that ranged from Samurai armour to stringed instruments
to boneshaker bicycles. Charles Paget Wade was just such a collector, cramming his
house, 2^1/$_2$ miles (4km) south of Broadway, with a seemingly random range of over
22,000 items. Even the gardens, with their terraces, ponds and outdoor rooms, were
the subject of his apparently boundless enthusiasm.

Today, Snowshill Manor (☎ 01386-852410, www.nationaltrust.org.uk; Apr-Jul
& Sep-Oct Wed-Sun & bank hols manor noon-5pm, garden 11am-5.30pm; Jul-Aug
Wed-Mon manor 11.30am-4.30pm, garden 11am-5pm, grounds also Nov noon-4pm,
last entry 1hr before closing; admission £9.70, gardens only £5.40, NT members free)
is in the hands of the National Trust, which struggles to keep pace with the number
of visitors to what is a relatively small house. For walkers along the Cotswold Way,
the house is best approached along the footpaths leading east from Shenberrow Farm;
it's a distance of around ^{3}/$_4$ mile (1.2km). The restaurant in the grounds makes a
detour around lunchtime particularly appealing, but with timed tickets to visit the
house, it may be best to go at a quieter time of day to avoid disappointment.

SNOWSHILL   off MAP 4, p89
Snowshill lies a good mile (1.5km) south of
Broadway, but is more easily approached
from Shenberrow Hill.

Much nearer to the trail than the village itself is **Sheepscombe House** (☎
01386-853769, 🖳 www.broadway-cots
wolds.co.uk/sheepscombe.html; 2T or D/
1D with ➥; WI-FI), with one room in the
main house and the others in an annexe;

two can offer family accommodation. B&B
with a view and en suite facilities or a private bathroom is from £95 for two sharing
(single occupancy from £60). Sheepscombe
can also provide a luggage transfer for
guests. Dinner can be taken at the
Snowshill Arms (☎ 01386-852653; daily
noon-2pm & 6.30-9pm), a 5- to 10-minute
walk from the house.

STANTON   MAP 5
Broadway may attract the tourists, but for
true Cotswold beauty Stanton is hard to
beat. At its heart is the church of St Michael
& All Angels, its tall spire clearly visible in
the valley from the surrounding hills.

Castleways' 606 **bus** between
Broadway and Cheltenham stops at Stanton
turn (about ^{1}/$_2$ mile from the village), on its
way to Winchcombe; see public transport
map and table, p46.

There are a few **B&Bs** in the village,
all on the trail, and all benefiting from the
excellent **pub**, **The Mount Inn** (☎ 01386-
584316, 🖳 www.themountinn.co.uk; daily
noon-2pm, Mon-Sat 6-9pm). Up a steep
hill, yet only a stone's throw from the trail, it
boasts an inglenook fireplace, Donnington

beers and superb views; evening reserva-
tions are strongly recommended. The menu
ranges from tapas and baguettes to the likes
of vegetable crumble (£10) and specials such
as pan-seared venison with barley and wild
mushroom jus (£14).

Within just 200m of the pub is
Shenberrow Hill (☎ 01386-584468, 🖳
www.broadway-cotswolds.co.uk/shenber-
rowhillbb.html; 1T/2D, all en suite, ➥; WI-
FI), not to be confused with the complex of
buildings at the top of Shenberrow Hill.
Two rooms in the main house and one in the
annexe are available at £78 for two sharing
(£48 single occupancy). Right in the heart
of the village, **The Vine** (☎ 01386-584777,
🖳 www.broadwaycotswolds.co.uk/vine

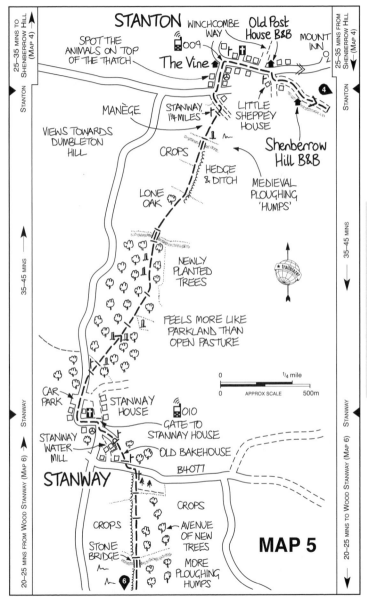

STANTON

WINCHCOMBE WAY

Old Post House B&B

MOUNT INN

SPOT THE ANIMALS ON TOP OF THE THATCH

009

The Vine

25-35 MINS TO SHENBERROW HILL (MAP 4)

25-35 MINS FROM SHENBERROW HILL (MAP 4)

STANTON

STANTON

MANÈGE

STANWAY 1¼ MILES

LITTLE SHEPPEY HOUSE

VIEWS TOWARDS DUMBLETON HILL

CROPS

HEDGE & DITCH

Shenberrow Hill B&B

4

LONE OAK

MEDIEVAL PLOUGHING 'HUMPS'

35-45 MINS

NEWLY PLANTED TREES

35-45 MINS

★ trailblazer

FEELS MORE LIKE PARKLAND THAN OPEN PASTURE

0   ¼ mile

0   500m

APPROX SCALE

CAR PARK

STANWAY HOUSE

010

GATE TO STANWAY HOUSE

STANWAY WATER MILL

OLD BAKEHOUSE

B4077

STANWAY

20-25 MINS FROM WOOD STANWAY (MAP 6)

STANWAY

STANWAY

20-25 MINS TO WOOD STANWAY (MAP 6)

CROPS

CROPS

AVENUE OF NEW TREES

STONE BRIDGE

6

MORE PLOUGHING HUMPS

MAP 5

ROUTE GUIDE AND MAPS

.html; 4T or D/1F; ●) offers B&B for £75 (single occupancy £55 Mon-Thu only) in rooms with their own shower and wash-basin, but sharing a toilet, or £100 in the en-suite family room (up to three people). The owner specialises in horseriding (☎ 01386-584250).

Equally central is the *Old Post House*

(☎ 01386-584398, ▣ www.broadway-cotswolds.co.uk/oldposthouse.html; 1T en suite), its gate tucked behind the scarlet phone kiosk that now serves as an informa-tion post. Conversion of the old telephone exchange has resulted in a traditional but tasteful room, which costs £75 for two peo-ple sharing or £45 for single occupancy.

STANWAY   MAP 5, p91

If you're passing through in June, July or August on a Tuesday or Thursday between 2pm and 5pm, you could visit the Jacobean **Stanway House** (☎ 01386-584469, ▣ www.stanwayfountain.co.uk; fountain £4.50, house & fountain £7), set in a restored 18th-century water garden with what is claimed to be the tallest gravity fountain in the world. At 300ft (91m), it's certainly impressive. The fountain 'plays' at 2.45pm and 4pm. At other times you'll have to be content with the sight of the imposing gatehouse and the neighbouring

church. A second attraction on the Stanway estate is the restored **Stanway Watermill** (☎ 01386-584446, ▣ www.stanwaymill.co .uk; £3; phone for combined ticket with the house), which opens to visitors at the same times as the house, plus 10am-noon on Thursday all year. An added bonus is the *Old Bakehouse* (☎ 01386-584204, ▣ www.oldbakehousestanway.co.uk; Tue, Thu & Sun 2-4.45pm), just a few steps up from the watermill, which serves cakes and cream teas in the summer months only.

WOOD STANWAY   MAP 6

Blink and you could miss the sleepy hamlet of Wood Stanway, but it does offer a couple of **B&B** options. The 17th-century *Wood Stanway Farmhouse* (☎ 01386-584318, ▣ www.woodstanwayfarmhouse.co.uk; 1D/1T/2F, ●; WI-FI), 30 yards down the road to the right as you come through the gate, has open views across farmland and the hills. B&B costs £65 for two people (single £40) or from £65 in the family rooms (one shar-ing a bathroom), which sleep up to four. The nearest pub is 1¼ miles (2km) away in Toddington, but a three-course evening

meal at £17 per person can be prebooked, and you can get a packed lunch for £3.50.

Smaller but built of similarly age-soft-ened stone, *Orchard Cottage* (☎ 01386-584752, ▣ www.woodstanway.co.uk; 1D/1T, en suite, ●) is just a stone's throw away, with B&B for £35 per person (single occupancy £40). An evening meal can be provided at £21.50 if booked in advance, and a packed lunch at £5. Horseriding can be arranged through the owner's daughter, who runs a stable at Glebe Farm.

NORTH FARMCOTE   MAP 6

One of the few working farms offering B&B within reasonable reach of the Cotswold Way is *North Farmcote* (☎ 01242-602304, ▣ www.northfarmcote.co .uk; 2T/1D or F; ●; WI-FI; 🐾), in a glorious location just over quarter of a mile (0.2km) from the trail (see Map 7 for access, and follow the sign for Farmcote Herbs). One

twin and the double are en suite; the other twin has a private bathroom. Each costs £70-80, or £50 for single occupancy, and £90 for three sharing.

The nearest pub for an evening meal is a couple of miles away at Ford; if the own-ers aren't busy they are prepared to drive guests to the pub.

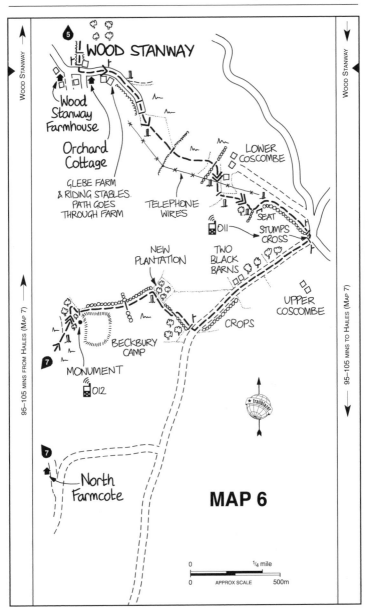

WOOD STANWAY

Wood Stanway Farmhouse

Orchard Cottage

GLEBE FARM & RIDING STABLES. PATH GOES THROUGH FARM

TELEPHONE WIRES

LOWER COSCOMBE

011

SEAT
STUMPS CROSS

NEW PLANTATION

TWO BLACK BARNS

UPPER COSCOMBE

CROPS

BECKBURY CAMP

MONUMENT

012

North Farmcote

MAP 6

0   ¼ mile

0   500m
APPROX SCALE

WOOD STANWAY

WOOD STANWAY

95–105 MINS FROM HAILES (MAP 7)

95–105 MINS TO HAILES (MAP 7)

ROUTE GUIDE AND MAPS

HAILES   MAP 7

Hailes (or Hayles, or Hales) – which really does have three spellings – takes its name from the abbey (see box below).

The trail descends parallel to the orchards of *Hayles Fruit Farm* (☎ 01242-602123, 💻 www.hayles-fruit-farm.co.uk). This has one of the few **campsites** along the entire Cotswold Way that is actually on the trail, so make the most of it. It's a large, level, grassy site, where you can pitch a tent for £6 per person per night. Just up the hill is their excellent **farm shop** (daily 9am-5pm), where you can buy good cakes and delicious apple juice, as well as fresh bread and the makings for a substantial breakfast. There's also a welcoming **tea room and restaurant** (daily

9am-5pm; hot food served noon-3pm); sit by the window to combine your meal with a spot of birdwatching!

If you'd prefer a **B&B**, *Ireley Farm* (Map 7, opposite; ☎ 01242-602445; 1T/3D; 1 🛌) could fit the bill, with en-suite double rooms and a twin with a private bathroom. You'll pay from £30 per person sharing, with a simple meal available from about £7.50 a head. Access is via a footpath from Hailes of just over half a mile (0.8km), and the farm is also within walking distance of Winchcombe Pottery (see p98).

Castleways' 606 **bus** stops on the main B4632, en route between Broadway and Cheltenham, via Winchcombe; see public transport map and table, p46.

❏ Hailes Abbey   Map 7

Hailes Abbey (☎ 01242-602398, 💻 www.english-heritage.org.uk; daily Apr-Jun & Sep 10am-5pm, Jul-Aug 10am-6pm, Oct 10am-4pm; admission £4.20, National Trust and English Heritage members free) dates back to the 13th century. It owes its construction to a vow made by Richard, Earl of Cornwall (1209-72), should he survive a storm at sea during his return from a military campaign. The ship returned safely to harbour, and the earl, son of King John and brother of Henry III (who was responsible for the construction of Westminster Abbey), founded the abbey in 1246.

The site, that of an existing settlement, was chosen carefully. Limestone was readily available for building, there was good grazing for sheep, and a reliable water supply, with which the monks created a series of fishponds. The building itself was an elaborate affair, in contrast with the traditional simplicity of the Cistercian brotherhood – and indeed with the austerity of the earlier parish church, which lies across the road, and is still in use. The importance and grandeur of the abbey lay largely in its possession of the Holy Blood relic, which was housed in its own specially designed shrine, and which brought considerable income into the abbey's coffers.

Initially, the population at the new abbey comprised a prior, 20 monks and ten lay brothers, who moved here from Beaulieu Abbey in Hampshire, but much of the community died in 1361 during a recurrence of the Black Death. The monastery was dissolved in 1539, one of the last to be closed on Henry VIII's orders, and the abbey destroyed. The remainder of the estate was given by the king to Katherine Parr. Later, the buildings were adapted as a country house, but by 1794 that, too, lay in ruins. Today, it is the ruined cloisters that most vividly conjure up some sense of the ordered life once led by the monks. All that remains of the abbey are the footings, yet these – together with artefacts found on the site, on display in the excellent visitor centre – give a powerful indication of the scale and drama of the original building. In the words of St Bernard, *Bonum est nos hic esse*: 'It is good for us to be here.'

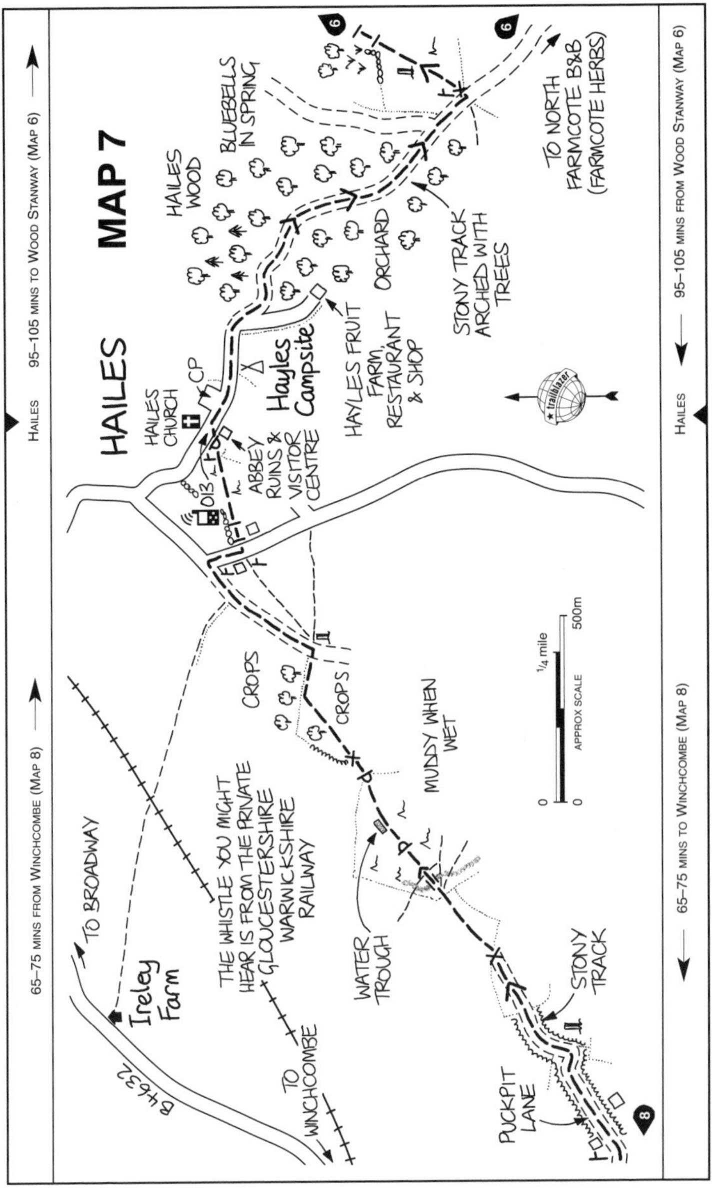

MAP 7
HAILES
Hailes 95–105 mins to Wood Stanway (Map 6)
65–75 mins from Winchcombe (Map 8)
HAILES CHURCH
CP
HAILES WOOD
BLUEBELLS IN SPRING
Hayles Campsite
ABBEY RUINS & VISITOR CENTRE
013
HAYLES FRUIT FARM, RESTAURANT & SHOP
ORCHARD
STONY TRACK ARCHED WITH TREES
TO NORTH FARMCOTE B&B (FARMCOTE HERBS)
6
TO BROADWAY
Ireley Farm
B4632
THE WHISTLE YOU MIGHT HEAR IS FROM THE PRIVATE GLOUCESTERSHIRE WARWICKSHIRE RAILWAY
TO WINCHCOMBE
CROPS
CROPS
MUDDY WHEN WET
WATER TROUGH
STONY TRACK
PUCKPIT LANE
8
APPROX SCALE
0
1/4 mile
0
500m
trailblazer
Hailes 95–105 mins from Wood Stanway (Map 6)
65–75 mins to Winchcombe (Map 8)

ROUTE GUIDE AND MAPS

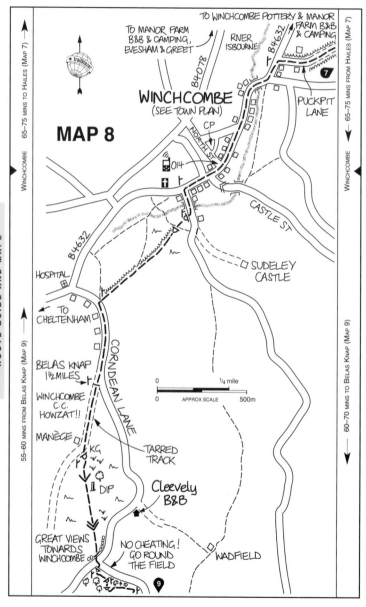

MAP 8

WINCHCOMBE
(SEE TOWN PLAN)

TO MANOR FARM
B&B & CAMPING,
EVESHAM & GREET

TO WINCHCOMBE POTTERY & MANOR
FARM B&B
& CAMPING

RIVER
ISBOURNE

B4078

B4632

PUCKPIT
LANE

7

CP

NORTH ST

☎ 014

✝ ✝

CASTLE ST

SUDELEY
CASTLE

HOSPITAL

B4632

TO
CHELTENHAM

CORNDEAN LANE

BELAS KNAP
1½ MILES

WINCHCOMBE
C.C.
HOWZAT!!

MANÈGE

KG

DIP

TARRED
TRACK

Cleevely
B&B

GREAT VIEWS
TOWARDS
WINCHCOMBE

NO CHEATING!
GO ROUND
THE FIELD

WADFIELD

9

0   ¼ mile
0   500m
APPROX SCALE

65–75 MINS TO HALES (MAP 7)

WINCHCOMBE

65–75 MINS FROM HALES (MAP 7)

WINCHCOMBE

60–70 MINS TO BELAS KNAP (MAP 9)

55–60 MINS FROM BELAS KNAP (MAP 9)

ROUTE GUIDE AND MAPS

WINCHCOMBE   MAP 8a, p99

The ancient Saxon borough of Winchcombe, one-time capital of the kingdom of Mercia, later enjoyed status as a focal point for pilgrims. Its abbey has long since gone, but the town – emphatically not a village – of Winchcombe remains a significant presence in the Cotswolds. For walkers along the Cotswold Way, it's an ideal place to stay, or stop for a bite to eat at one of a number of pubs, restaurants and tea rooms. Even if you're short of time, it's worth taking a look inside the wool church of **St Peter's**.

If you've longer to spare, you might want to check out **Sudeley Castle** (see below), or one of two small museums. Next to the **old stocks** and the tourist information office (see p98), at **Winchcombe Folk and Police Museum** (☎ 01242-609151, 🖳 www.sunloch.me.uk/museum/index.html; Apr-Oct Mon-Sat 10am-1pm & 2-5pm; £1.50), exhibits about the town's history rub shoulders with a collection of police paraphernalia. Those with a nostalgic bent might prefer the hands-on **Winchcombe Railway Museum** (☎ 01242-609305; Good Friday-end Sep Wed-Sun 10.30-5pm, daily during school summer holidays; Gloucester St; £2.50), where behind an unassuming private house there are signals to be moved, tickets to clip and points

aligned – as well as a Victorian garden. The railway line, which skirts the town to the west, was axed by Beeching in the 1960s but was bought in 1981 by **Gloucestershire Warwickshire Steam Railway** (☎ 01242-621405, 🖳 www.gwsr.com) and restored. Steam trains, run by volunteers, continue to attract enthusiasts: trains run between Toddington and Cheltenham Racecourse. For timetables and special events, see the website or give them a ring.

The Cotswold Voluntary Wardens lead a heavily oversubscribed annual series of **11 consecutive walks** for up to 23 participants who would like to complete the whole trail. Each walk takes place on the first Wednesday of the month, starting in May in Bath, and finishing at Chipping Campden the following March. A coach (for which there is a charge) takes walkers from Winchcombe to the starting point, meets them for a pre-planned pub for lunch and collects them at the end. Find out more by calling ☎ 01242-820192.

Transport

Winchcombe is well placed on a north–south **bus** route running through the Cotswolds. The 606, operated by Castleways, links Broadway with Cheltenham, stopping at Stanton turn (^{1}/2

❏ Sudeley Castle   Map 8

The history of Sudeley Castle (☎ 01242-602308, 🖳 www.sudeleycastle.co.uk; Apr-Oct daily 10.30am-5pm; entry £8.50) can be traced back as far as King Ethelred, in the 10th century. Although nothing of his manor house remains, the estate's royal connections run like a thread through its chequered past, from Edward IV to Queen Elizabeth I. The buildings visible today, including the Dungeon Tower and St Mary's Church, were constructed by Baron Sudeley from the mid-15th century. It is in the church that Katherine Parr, the sixth of Henry VIII's wives, is buried, having lived at Sudeley following the king's death. A century later, the castle fell into disuse, becoming increasingly dilapidated until it was bought and restored during Victoria's reign by members of the Dent family. The castle today is the private home of their descendants.

Visitors can look round the church and tour the estate, with its beautiful rose gardens, a pheasantry, and a wonderful wooden fort that will make you wish you were ten years old again. There is also a series of exhibitions and a coffee shop. If you want to go round the castle, you'll have to book a connoisseur tour (Tue, Wed & Thu at 11am, 1pm & 3pm); the cost of £13 includes the entrance fee.

mile from village), Winchcombe and Cleeve Hill. For details, see the public transport map and table, p46.

A reliable **taxi** service is run by Taylor's (☎ 01242-603651, mob ☎ 07814-570876).

Services

There's a small **tourist information centre** (☎ 01242-602925; Apr-Oct Mon-Sat 10am-5pm, Sun 10am-4pm, Nov-Mar Sat/Sun 10am-4pm, closed daily 1-2pm) in the old Town Hall, on the corner of North St.

Lloyds TSB **bank** has a branch with an ATM on the High St, but most other tourist amenities are found along North St, which lies at right angles to the trail from the tourist information office. This is where you'll find the **post office**, as well as the town's **supermarket**, the Co-op (Mon-Sat 7am-10pm, Sun 8am-10pm), and several independent shops. Try North's **bakery** for fresh rolls and sandwiches, or the excellent **delicatessen** Food Fanatics (Mon-Fri 8am-7pm, Sat 8am-6pm, Sun 10am-5pm), where sandwiches are made to order or to eat in.

Just over half a mile (1km) north of Puckpit Lane on the B4632, to the left just after the railway bridge, you'll find **Winchcombe Pottery** (off Map 8, p96; ☎ 01242-602462, ☐ www.winchcombepottery.co.uk; Mon-Fri 9am-5pm, Sat 10am-4pm, May-Sep Sun noon-4pm), where pots are still turned, fired and sold on the premises. There's a **shoe repairer** (☎ 01242-604602; Mon-Fri 9am-1pm, Mon, Tue, Wed & Fri 2.15-4.30pm) here, too, so if your boots need some attention it's worth going out of your way. In the centre of town, along Hailes St, there's a **newsagent**, which sells drinks and snacks, and a **launderette** (Mon-Sat 9am-5pm).

Winchcombe **medical centre** (☎ 01242-602307) is about a quarter of a mile (0.4km) north of the town, along Greet Rd, and there's a branch of Lloyds **pharmacy** on the High St.

Where to stay

Winchcombe has a good assortment of small pubs and inns and a few B&Bs, most of them fairly central. **Campers**, though,

will need to walk some three-quarters of a mile (1.2km) from the trail to **Manor Farm** (off map 8; ☎ 01242-602423; 1T/2D, all en suite, ☞) where you'll pay £6 per person, per night. There's **B&B** here, too, at £75 (single occupancy £50). To get there from the Cotswold Way, turn right at the end of Puckpit Lane, go under the railway bridge and turn immediately left (past the pottery) to **Greet**. Just before the Harvest Home pub, turn right; the farm is about a quarter of a mile (0.4km) up that road on the left-hand side.

Quietly situated parallel to the main road is *One Silk Mill Lane* (☎ 01242-603952, ☐ jenny.cheshire@virgin.net; 2D or T, en suite, ☞; WI-FI), where you'll pay £70 for two sharing (single occupancy £40).

At right angles to the Cotswold Way is North St, which becomes Gretton Rd. Here, *Oaklands* (☎ 01242-602272, ☐ www.band batoaklands.co.uk, No 16; 2T/1D, en suite, ☞; WI-FI; ✿) charges £45 per person B&B. On the opposite side of the road is *Blair House* (☎ 01242-603626, ☐ www.blairhousewinchcombe.co.uk, No 41; 2S or D/1T/1D; ☞; WI-FI; ✿), which has an en suite double for £68 B&B (single occupancy £48). The other rooms share a bathroom, with bath, and come in at £62 for the double, or £64 for the twin; single occupancy of these rooms is £44.

For those seeking a more rural setting, the half-timbered *Cleevely* (see Map 8, p96; ☎ 01242-602059; 1T en suite/1F private bathroom ☞), on Corndean Lane, could fit the bill. Just off the trail (and ¾ mile – 1.2km – from the nearest pub, in Winchcombe), it is surrounded by farmland and enjoys glorious views. B&B here is from £32 per person sharing, or £36 for single occupancy.

Of the **pubs** and inns, the *The White Hart Inn* (☎ 01242-602359, ☐ www.white hartwinchcombe.co.uk; 4T/3T or D/4D; ☞; WI-FI; ✿) on High St is right on the trail and ideal for walkers, with three designated ramblers' rooms (2T/1D). These share a bathroom and cost £40-80, depending on the time of year and availability. The other, en suite rooms (1T/3T or D/4D, 6 with ☞) are divided into standard (£60-100) and

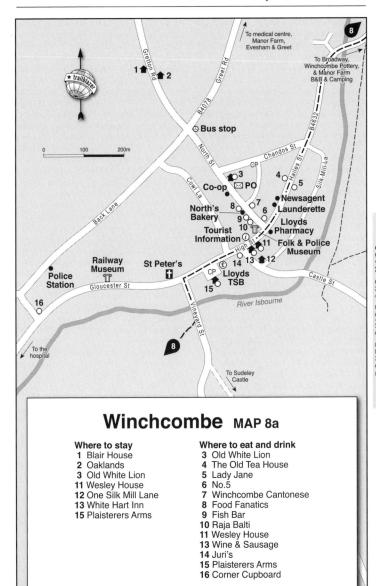

Winchcombe MAP 8a

Where to stay
1 Blair House
2 Oaklands
3 Old White Lion
11 Wesley House
12 One Silk Mill Lane
13 White Hart Inn
15 Plaisterers Arms

Where to eat and drink
3 Old White Lion
4 The Old Tea House
5 Lady Jane
6 No.5
7 Winchcombe Cantonese
8 Food Fanatics
9 Fish Bar
10 Raja Balti
11 Wesley House
13 Wine & Sausage
14 Juri's
15 Plaisterers Arms
16 Corner Cupboard

ROUTE GUIDE AND MAPS

superior (£70-120). Single occupancy of any room brings a £10 discount.

Right next door is the smartly gabled *Wesley House* (☎ 01242-602366, 🖥 www.wesleyhouse.co.uk; 4D/1T; WI-FI), more of a restaurant with rooms, charging £90 for a double from Monday to Friday. On Saturday, rooms may be booked only as part of a dinner, bed and breakfast package, at £185 for two people sharing.

Set back from the main road on Abbey Terrace, near Lloyds TSB, *The Plaisterers Arms* (☎ 01242-602358; 2T/3D all en suite; 🛁 in 1 twin; WI-FI; 🐾) has B&B for £60 for two sharing, or £40 for single occupancy. Back on North St, new management has taken over at the *Old White Lion* (☎ 01242-603300; 2T/4D, all en suite, 🛁; WI-FI; 🐾), where B&B is now £55-110 per room, depending on its size and standard.

Where to eat and drink

If the Cotswolds without an English tea is unthinkable, head straight for the award-winning *Juri's Tea Rooms* (☎ 01242-602469, 🖥 www.juris-tearoom.co.uk, High St; 10am-5pm Thu/Fri, 10.30am-5pm Sat, 11am-5pm Sun), on the corner of Castle St, opposite the White Hart. Although Japanese owned and run, it feels as English as they come, with 15 types of tea and plenty of home-made cakes. Further down Hailes St, sandwiches and Fairtrade hot drinks are the order of the day at the *Old Tea House* (☎ 01242-604363; Mon & Thu-Sat 9.30am-4.30pm, Sun 10am-4.30pm), which you'll pass on your way into town from the north. Vying for custom opposite is the *Lady Jane* (☎ 01242-603578, Sat-Wed 10am-5pm), an olde-worlde place

where the menu extends to the likes of cottage pie, or soup and a sandwich for £7.15. New on the scene is the informal café at the deli, *Food Fanatics* (see p98, ☎ 01242-604466), with a range of sandwiches, quiches and cakes.

For more hearty fare, try one of the pubs. On the main street are *The Plaisterers Arms* (see above; daily noon-2.30pm – or 3pm Sun, & 6-9pm) and *The Corner Cupboard* (☎ 01242-602303; Mon-Sat noon-2.30pm, 6-8.30pm, Sun 12-8pm). The *Old White Lion* (see above; daily noon-3pm, Fri/Sat 6-9pm) serves doorstep sandwiches from £4.95 alongside staples such as steak and ale pie (£7.95).

The restaurant at The White Hart Inn (see above), the *Wine and Sausage* (🖥 www.wineandsausage.co.uk; daily 8am-9pm), speaks for itself: come for a range of local sausages (and other fare), washed down with wine – or beer, or cider. They serve breakfast, coffee and afternoon teas, too. For a special occasion, try *Wesley House* (see above; daily noon-2pm, 7-9.30pm), or the Michelin-starred *No 5* (☎ 01242-604566, 🖥 www.5northstreetrestaurant.co.uk; Wed-Sun 12.30-1.30pm, Tue-Sat 7-9pm).

If none of these appeals, Winchcombe has the usual selection of takeaways, all along North St: *Raja Balti* (☎ 01242-604194; Sun-Thu 5.30-11pm, Fri & Sat 5.30pm-midnight), which also has a restaurant area; the *Fish Bar* (☎ 01242-603080; Tue-Sat 11.30am-2pm, Mon-Thu 4.30-9.30pm, Fri/Sat 4.30-10pm); and *Winchcombe Cantonese Chinese Takeaway* (☎ 01242-602116; Wed-Mon 5-11pm).

WINCHCOMBE TO CLEEVE HILL   MAPS 8-10

The next **6 miles (9.7km, 3-3¹/₂hrs)** take in one of the highlights of the entire trail: **Cleeve Hill Common**, passing the ancient long barrow of **Belas Knap** (see box, opposite). A change of routing in 2009 has replaced some of the former open walking with woodland, but the common remains the ultimate goal. Considered to be the largest single area of unimproved limestone grassland in Gloucestershire, it rises to the highest point on the trail at 1066ft (325m). Sheep, golfers and walkers share the closely cropped turf, but it's a successful partnership; there is plenty of space for all.

Much of the trail at this point runs along the edge of the Cotswold escarpment, with a grandstand view of **Cheltenham Racecourse** on the plains below. If visibility is poor, take especial care along this stretch; it would be all too easy to stray too close to the edge.

POSTLIP   MAP 9a, p103

The Cotswold Way neatly sidesteps the hamlet of Postlip, but the section between Belas Knap and Cleeve Hill Common does skirt around the edge of the privately-owned Postlip Hall. There's a perfectly positioned B&B right on the trail here at *Postlip Hall Farm* (☎ 01242-603351, 🖵 www.smoothhound.co.uk/hotels/postlip; 1T or D/1D), but with no evening meal available you may have to consider a taxi to the nearest pub in Winchcombe (see opposite). The house itself is built of stone and sheltered behind high hedges on a working farm. En suite rooms cost £75 for a one-night stay, or £55 for single occupancy.

❑ Belas Knap   Map 9, p102

Sheltering in the corner of a field, at the edge of the woods, the ancient long barrow (see box p134), or burial ground, of Belas Knap rises up from the ground rather like a beached whale, some 180ft (55m) long and 18ft (5.5m) high. Dating back to around 2500BC, it was used for successive burials, possibly over several centuries, until it was deliberately blocked. Archaeologists have uncovered the remains of 38 human skeletons, as well as animal bones, flints and pottery. At the northern end, an apparent entrance in fact leads nowhere, but the reason for this is unclear.

The grass-covered mound – for such is its appearance today – is dotted with cowslips and daisies, but you can clearly see the thin layers of stone, neatly stacked like sheaves of paper, that were used in its construction.

CLEEVE HILL   MAP 10, p104

Right by the trail, and up on Cleeve Hill itself, the bar at *Cleeve Hill Golf Club* (☎ 01242-672025, 🖵 www.cleevehillgolfcourse.co.uk; daily 8am-4pm) is open to non-members for tea, coffee and light lunch. You can eat in the clubhouse, on the veranda or on the grass looking up to Cleeve Hill and the golf course, choosing from a menu that's available from midday and includes everything from baguettes for £4.10 to a range of pies and pasta dishes at around £7.20.

All three hotels on Cleeve Hill are clustered fairly close together about a quarter of a mile (0.4km) down the hill from the trail, along the busy B4632 but with views across to the Malvern Hills. First up is the elegant *Cleeve Hill Hotel* (☎ 01242-672052, 🖵 www.cleevehill-hotel.co.uk; 1S/6D/3D or T, all en suite or with private facilities; 🖵; WI-FI), where you'll need sufficient energy in reserve for the steep steps up to the front door. Assuming you're not after a four-poster bed or a suite, a room here will cost £95 for a double B&B, and £97.50 for a twin, with the single at £50, or single occupancy of a larger room from £65. Slightly further down the hill, the *Malvern View* (☎ 01242-672017, 🖵 www.malvernview.com; 1T or D/5D, 🖵; WI-FI) has rooms of varying styles, with all en suite except the twin, which has a private bathroom. Rates are £90-115 for B&B (less £25 for single occupancy). The hotel has its own smart restaurant (Tue-Sat noon-2pm & 7-9pm), including a set dinner menu from Tuesday to Thursday at £19.50 for two courses, or £24.50 for three. For walkers on the northern half of the Cotswold Way, between Chipping Campden and Painswick, they offer an all-inclusive pack-

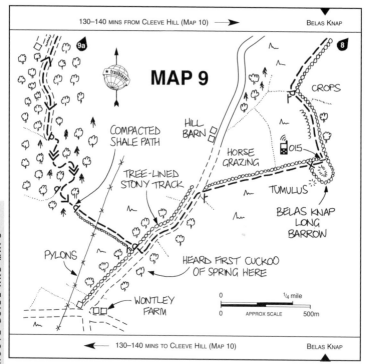

MAP 9

COMPACTED SHALE PATH

HILL BARN

HORSE GRAZING

O15

CROPS

TREE-LINED STONY TRACK

TUMULUS

BELAS KNAP LONG BARROW

PYLONS

HEARD FIRST CUCKOO OF SPRING HERE

WONTLEY FARM

0   ¼ mile
0   APPROX SCALE   500m

age of dinner, bed and breakfast, plus a packed lunch and transfers to and from the trail each day. The cost for a double or twin room for two nights is £320.

Finally, just a couple of hundred yards further down, there's the rather larger ***Rising Sun*** (☎ 01242-676281, 🖥 www.ris ingsunhotel.com; 3S/4T/15D/2F, all en suite with 🛁; WI-FI; 🐾 £10). B&B rates are complex, but a single comes in at £55-70, a double or twin £65-85, and a family room for three people £80-95. Dining (Mon-Fri 7-10am, Sat/Sun 8-10am, daily noon-9.30pm) is pretty relaxed, whether in the restaurant or bar, outside on the terrace, or in the steep hillside garden – where there's a superb view to distract from the traffic, but you may struggle to keep the plates on the table! As well as lunchtime favourites there's a comprehensive menu with mains

averaging £8-12, and a daily specials board. Sunday night is live music night.

Back on the hills, and about ¹/₂ mile (0.8km) from the trail as it heads south of the common through Bill Smyllie Reserve (part of Prestbury Hill Reserve), is the exceptionally welcoming ***Upper Hill Farm*** (Map 11, ☎ 01242-235128, 🖥 www.upper-hillfarm.co.uk; 1T/2D; 🛁; WI-FI; 🐾 by arrangement). Sympathetically restored, it has an elegant guests' lounge, and spacious rooms with modern décor. These cost £70 for two en suite (single occupancy £60); or two couples travelling together can take two doubles sharing a bathroom at £60 per room. In the evening, the owner will drive walkers to a pub for dinner.

Castleways' **bus** 606 between Broad-way and Cheltenham stops on Cleeve Hill; see the public transport map and table, p46.

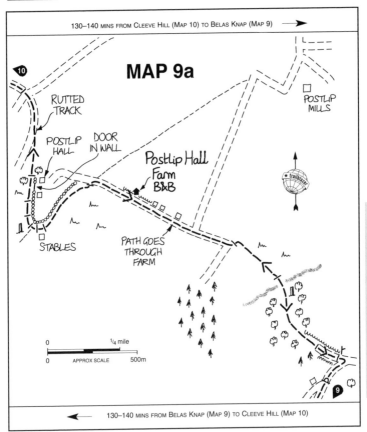

MAP 9a

RUTTED TRACK

POSTLIP HALL

DOOR IN WALL

Postlip Hall Farm B&B

POSTLIP MILLS

STABLES

PATH GOES THROUGH FARM

trailblazer

| 0 | ¼ mile |
| 0 | APPROX SCALE | 500m |

ROUTE GUIDE AND MAPS

CLEEVE HILL TO LECKHAMPTON HILL

MAPS 10-15

The **9½-mile (15km)** section of the trail that skirts around Cheltenham takes about **4¾ to 5½ hours** to complete. If it seems as though the town goes on forever, at least the views are rewarding, and there is plenty to enjoy en route. Those interested in natural history are in for a treat, with ancient beeches and limes in **Lineover Wood** (the word means 'lime bank'), and the protected areas of **Prestbury Hill Reserve** (incorporating both Masts Field and the Bill Smyllie Reserve), **Charlton Kings Common** and **Leckhampton Hill**, each sheltering several rare flowers and butterflies.

Leckhampton Hill itself is the site of one of the many hill forts (see box, p121) that line the escarpment, and of the much-photographed **Devil's**

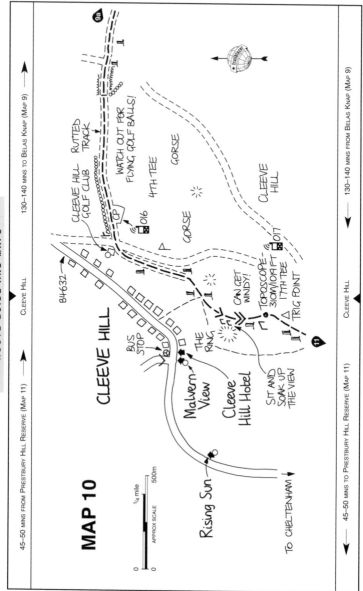

MAP 10

9a

Trailblazer

CLEEVE HILL GOLF CLUB

RUTTED TRACK

WATCH OUT FOR FLYING GOLF BALLS!

4TH TEE

GORSE

GORSE

016

CP

GORSE

CLEEVE HILL

017

TOPOSCOPE 310M/1017FT

17TH TEE

TRIG POINT

CAN GET WINDY!

B4632

CLEEVE HILL

BUS STOP

THE RING

Malvern View

Cleeve Hill Hotel

SIT AND SOAK UP THE VIEW

11

Rising Sun

¼ mile 500m

APPROX SCALE

TO CHELTENHAM

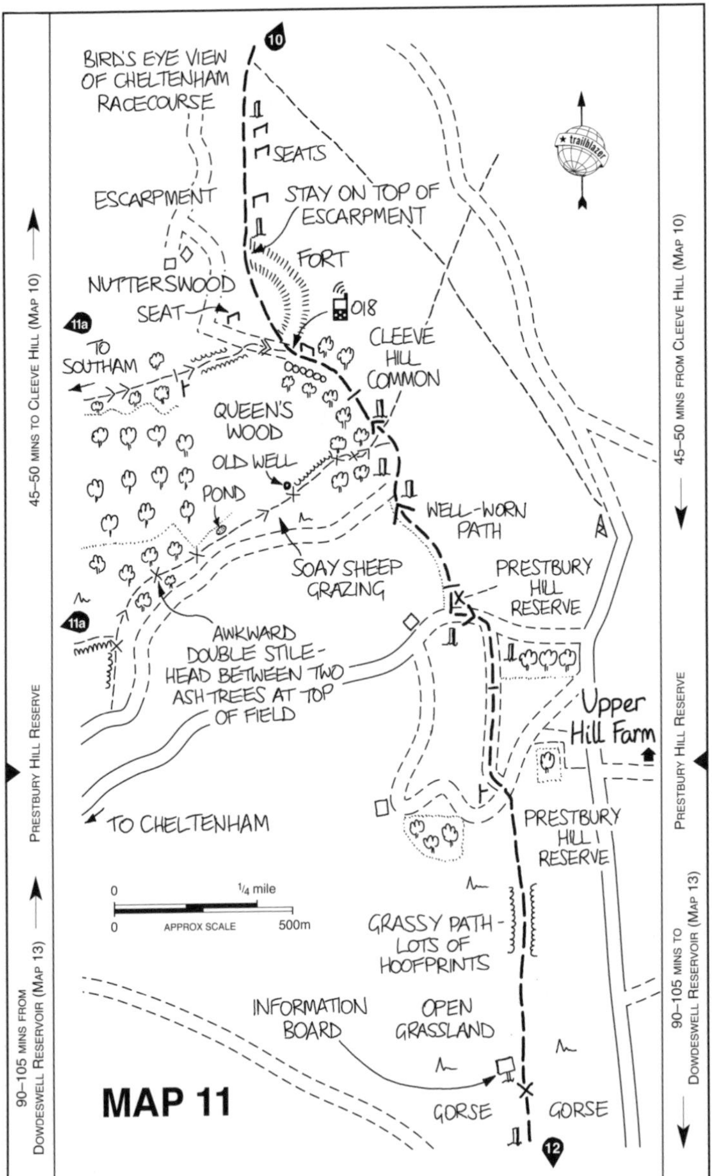

BIRD'S EYE VIEW
OF CHELTENHAM
RACECOURSE

SEATS

STAY ON TOP OF
ESCARPMENT

ESCARPMENT

FORT

NUTTERSWOOD
SEAT

018

TO
SOUTHAM

CLEEVE
HILL
COMMON

QUEEN'S
WOOD

OLD WELL

POND

WELL-WORN
PATH

SOAY SHEEP
GRAZING

PRESTBURY
HILL
RESERVE

AWKWARD
DOUBLE STILE-
HEAD BETWEEN TWO
ASH TREES AT TOP
OF FIELD

TO CHELTENHAM

Upper
Hill Farm

PRESTBURY
HILL
RESERVE

0   ¼ mile

0   500m
APPROX SCALE

GRASSY PATH -
LOTS OF
HOOFPRINTS

INFORMATION
BOARD

OPEN
GRASSLAND

MAP 11

GORSE   GORSE

45–50 MINS TO CLEEVE HILL (MAP 10) →

← 45–50 MINS FROM CLEEVE HILL (MAP 10)

◄ PRESTBURY HILL RESERVE

PRESTBURY HILL RESERVE ►

90–105 MINS FROM DOWDESWELL RESERVOIR (MAP 13) →

90–105 MINS TO DOWDESWELL RESERVOIR (MAP 13) →

ROUTE GUIDE AND MAPS

10

11a

11a

12

Chimney. This tall outcrop of rock towers over a disused quarry, giving rise to a legend involving the Devil hurling stones from this spot at worshippers as they made their way to church on a Sunday. More prosaic suggestions as to its provenance include erosion (somewhat unlikely), and the attractive possibility that it was created as a bawdy joke by 18th-century quarry workers. Whatever its history, the chimney has been regularly climbed by local youngsters over the years and even survived an earthquake in the 1920s. Today, it is securely fenced to help protect it from (very real) erosion.

❏ **Walking between the Cotswold Way and Cheltenham**   **Map 11a**
While the most direct route from Cheltenham to the Cotswold Way is probably along London Rd, this is hardly attractive walking territory. Far more interesting is to head north out of town through the park towards the racecourse, from where a network of footpaths along the edge of Queen's Wood leads up to Cleeve Hill Common – some of it coinciding with the Gustav Holst Way (see p109). If you fancy returning a different way, you can descend along the woodland path to Southam and thence back to the racecourse.

CHELTENHAM   MAP 11b, p108

Cheltenham was swept into the popular consciousness by George III, who first came to take the waters in 1788. Its Regency architecture, with whitewashed houses rather than the natural dressed stone typical of Georgian Bath, continues to attract visitors, but today the town's primary attractions are considerably broader than its architecture or spa waters.

Although Cheltenham is some distance from the trail, many visitors will want to sample at least a section of the Cotswold Way, while some walkers along the trail may wish to work the town into their trip in some way, so the information given here is intended as a starting point.

Details of accommodation in Cheltenham can be obtained from the **tourist information office** (☎ 01242-522878; 🖳 www.visitcheltenham .com; Mon-Sat 9.30am-5.15pm, Wed 10am-5.15pm, bank holiday 10am-1.30pm). Based at 77 The Promenade, it will be moving to new premises at the Art Gallery and Museum when it reopens in 2013. The town is home to several festivals (see p16), and regularly hosts live concerts. For more information, see also 🖳 www.cheltenham-townhall.org.uk.

Transport

Cheltenham is well served by both trains and buses. By **train**, First Great Western links Cheltenham with London Paddington; to go from Cheltenham to Bath usually requires one change. The town is also on the Cross Country Trains route between Newcastle-upon-Tyne and Plymouth, with additional services linking in to other destinations. The station is about a mile (1.6km) west of the town centre, with the D bus service operating frequently between the two: this bus also serves the park and ride at the racecourse.

Of the other **buses**, Castleways' 606 service to Winchcombe and Broadway is of greatest use to walkers. Stagecoach's No 46 provides a frequent service to Painswick. For longer distances, National Express has around nine **coaches** a day between London Victoria and Cheltenham. The terminus for all services is the Royal Well bus station behind the Promenade.

For details of all these services, see the public transport map and table, p46.

Where to eat and drink

While it is beyond the scope of this guide to cover Cheltenham's restaurants in detail, a

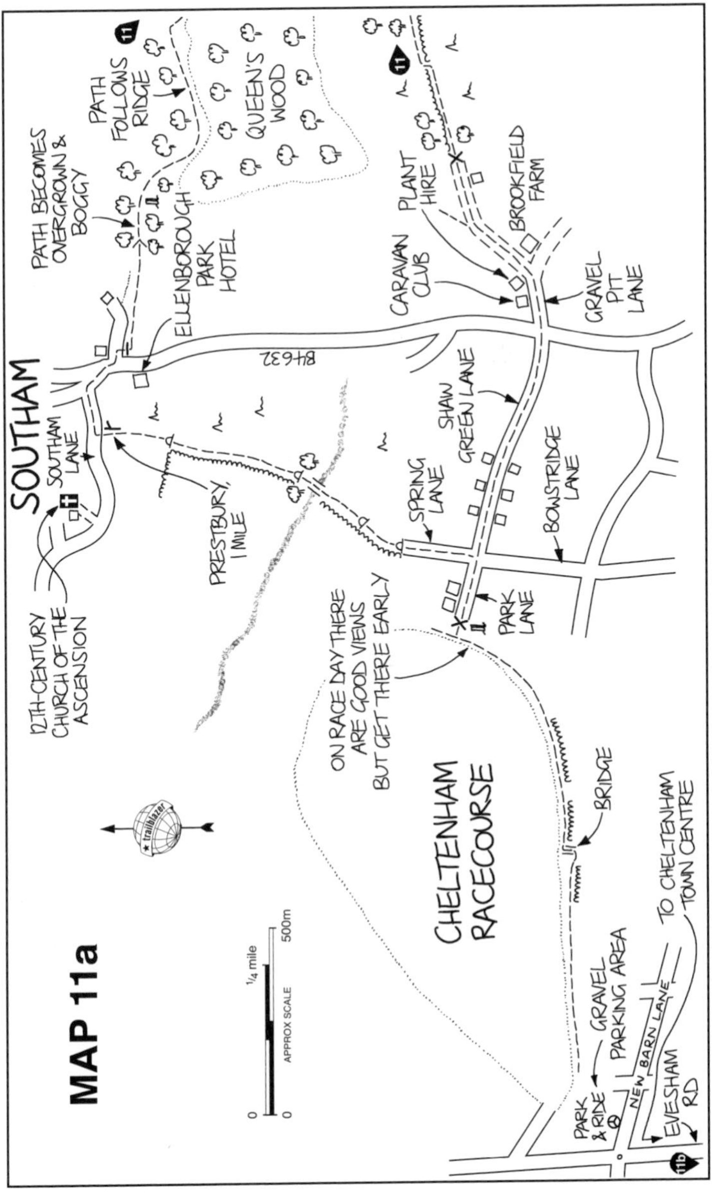

MAP 11a

¼ mile
500m
APPROX SCALE
0
0

SOUTHAM

12TH-CENTURY CHURCH OF THE ASCENSION

SOUTHAM LANE

PRESTBURY, 1 MILE

B4632

PATH BECOMES OVERGROWN & BOGGY

PATH FOLLOWS RIDGE

QUEEN'S WOOD

ELLENBOROUGH PARK HOTEL

PLANT HIRE

CARAVAN CLUB

BROOKFIELD FARM

GRAVEL PIT LANE

SPRING LANE

SHAW GREEN LANE

BOWSTRIDGE LANE

PARK LANE

ON RACE DAY THERE ARE GOOD VIEWS BUT GET THERE EARLY

CHELTENHAM RACECOURSE

BRIDGE

PARK & RIDE

GRAVEL PARKING AREA

NEW BARN LANE

TO CHELTENHAM TOWN CENTRE

EVESHAM RD

ROUTE GUIDE AND MAPS

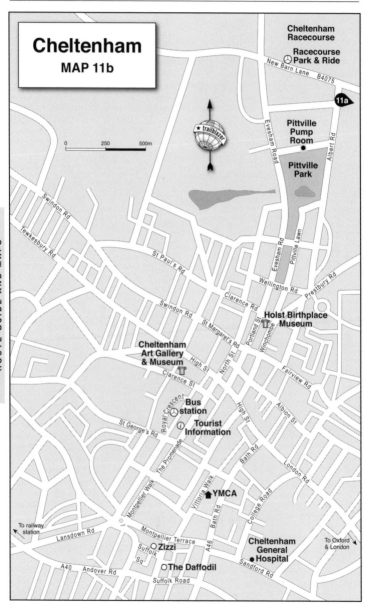

ROUTE GUIDE AND MAPS

couple of places in the attractive Montpellier district should point you in the right direction. A good start might be *Zizzi* (☎ 01242-252493, 🖳 www.zizzi.co.uk, 3 Suffolk Sq; daily noon-10pm). It's part of the relatively predictable pizza/pasta chain, but the star is the setting: a large converted church with stained-glass windows looking down on an outsize pizza oven in place of the altar. A piano in the gallery is played on Friday and Saturday evenings.

Another restaurant with a twist is *The Daffodil* (☎ 01242-700055, 🖳 www.the daffodil.com, Suffolk Parade; Mon-Sat noon-2pm, Mon-Fri 6.30-10pm, Sat 6-10.30pm), grandly located in the old Art Deco cinema. Where once the audience sat enthralled by the big screen, today's visitors dine in contemporary style, with live jazz on Monday evenings. They serve bar snacks all day, too, as well as afternoon tea – and their lunchtime 'Daffodeal' offers a main course sandwiched between a tasty starter and similar pudding for £10. There's also a fixed-price menu (£13.50/15.50 for two/three courses) at lunch and in the early evening (except Monday). Booking is advised in the evenings.

What to see and do

Cheltenham was built with pleasure in mind, laid out with wide promenades, formal gardens and elegant houses fronted by intricate metal balconies. The town's Regency architecture can best be viewed by walking in the Montpellier district then on through the central area and north alongside Pittville Park. Significant among the buildings is **Pittville Pump Room** which, with its distinctive columns and decorated dome, stands at the head of the park. Completed in 1830, it was restored in 1960, and today remains in regular use for functions. Events permitting, visitors can look around the building and take the spa waters from Wednesday to Sunday, 10am to 4pm.

The town's **Art Gallery & Museum** (☎ 01242-237431, 🖳 www.cheltenhammuseum.org.uk) on Clarence St was closed for significant development in 2011, with plans to reopen in 2013. Of major importance is the exhibition of furniture, together with silver, textiles, ceramics and paintings, from the Arts and Crafts movement. Don't miss the remarkably intricate piano created by CR Ashbee for his wife. Other artefacts span the period from ancient Egypt to the 20th century, with a small exhibition dedicated to Edward Wilson of Antarctic fame, who was born in the town.

Further north, **Holst Birthplace Museum** (☎ 01242-524846, 🖳 www.holst-museum.org.uk, 4 Clarence Rd; mid Feb-mid Dec Tue-Sat & bank holiday Mon 10am-4pm; entry £4.50) is set in a small Regency townhouse, displaying a drawing room of that period and a Victorian kitchen. It celebrates the life of the composer Gustav Holst, internationally renowned for his *Planets* suite, which was first performed in London in 1918. Holst was born in this house in 1874, was educated in the town, and returned in the late 1920s, remaining until his death in 1934. The composer's love of his native countryside is celebrated in the waymarked 35-mile (56km) Gustav Holst Way, from Cranham to Wyck Rissington, which in parts runs parallel to the Cotswold Way.

Prestbury Park just north of the town has been home to **Cheltenham Racecourse** (☎ 0844-579 3003, 🖳 www.cheltenham .co.uk) since 1831. Before that, race meetings were held on Cleeve Hill, where horses are still regularly exercised. The course hosts around 14 meetings a year, with the highlight being the four-day National Hunt Festival in March (see p15). A footpath alongside the course affords a close-up view of the races, though be warned: it's a popular spot!

ROUTE GUIDE AND MAPS

WHERE TO STAY AND EAT AROUND CHELTENHAM   MAPS 11-15

Campers and hostellers will be largely disappointed in this area, but in the town itself there is *Cheltenham YMCA* (Map 11b; ☎ 01242-524024, 🖳 www.cheltenhamymca.com, 6 Vittoria Walk; 24S/3 dorms), though staying here will entail a considerable detour off the route. Single rooms cost £21 a night, or you can stay in a single-sex 4- or 6-bed dorm for £16; both rates exclude breakfast.

HAM HILL MAP 12

Clearly signposted 400 yards' (360m) level walk west of the trail, ***Ham Hill Farm*** (☎ 01242-584415, 🖳 www.hamhillfarm.co.uk; 4D or T/1T or F all en suite 1D with private 🛁; WI-FI) offers B&B for £70 (£40 single occupancy), or £78-120 for two to four people in the family room. They'll prepare a packed lunch at £4.50, and for £4 will drive walkers to a pub for an evening meal, though you'll have to get a taxi back.

A little further along the same lane is Ham Hill Farm South, where ***Old Stable Cottage*** (☎ 01242-227003, 🖳 www.al tourism.com/uk/old-stable.html; 2T en suite) charges £85 for two sharing, or £50 for single occupancy. In the evening, the owner is happy to drop walkers down to Charlton Kings for a meal.

CHARLTON KINGS off MAP 13, p112

A couple of places on London Rd offer B&B within less than a mile (1.6km) of the trail. Closest is ***Charlton Kings Hotel*** (☎ 01242-231061, 🖳 www.charltonkingshotel.co.uk; 2S/2T/3D or T/5D, 1F all en suite most with 🛁; WI-FI; 🐕), some three-quarters of a mile (1.2km) to the west. Rates vary, but walkers can expect to pay £89-105 for two sharing B&B (single occupancy £69), £57 for a single and £125 for the family room with three single beds. The **restaurant** is open all day, every day, though hot food is available only in the evening from 6.30pm.

Almost opposite, a narrow lane leads across the River Chelt to ***Detmore House*** (☎ 01242-582868, 🖳 www.detmorehouse.com; 1T/2D/1F, all en suite; 🛁 except in twin room, WI-FI), set amid fields and an orchard and refurbished in 2008. B&B here costs from £95 for two people sharing, rising to £130 for four, with single occupancy from £65.

NEAR DOWDESWELL RESERVOIR MAP 13, p112

If you don't mind a short walk down from the trail, you'll be richly rewarded at ***California Farm*** (☎ 01242-244746, 🖳 www.californiafarm.co.uk; 2T en suite 1 🛁 1 shower /2D en suite, 1 with 🛁; WI-FI), where plenty of thought has gone into welcoming walkers. To get there, take the footpath west of Old Dole Farm to a track, then turn left. Alternatively, you could follow Capel Lane from near Koloshi restaurant (see opp) but then you miss a lovely part of the trail. Rooms, at £95 for two B&B (£55 single occupancy), are well finished and guests have a superb sitting room. If requested in advance, the owner will cook a two/three-course dinner for £19.50/24.50 per person and prepare a packed lunch (£4.50).

At the foot of the hill leading down towards the reservoir, welcoming hot and cold **drinks and snacks** (50p-£1) await the weary at the former B&B, Langett. The old Reservoir Inn on London Rd, however, recently reopened as an Indian restaurant, ***Koloshi*** (☎ 01242-516400, 🖳 www.koloshi.co.uk). They plan to also offer B&B soon.

Pulhams Coaches' 801 **bus** from Cheltenham to Bourton-on-the-Water or Moreton-in-Marsh usually stops outside the restaurant on request. There is no official bus stop here, so be sure to stand somewhere conspicuous where it can safely pull over – just outside the restaurant car park is best. For details, see the public transport map and table, p46.

Symbols used in text 🐕 Dogs allowed with prior notice 🛁 Bathtub in some rooms

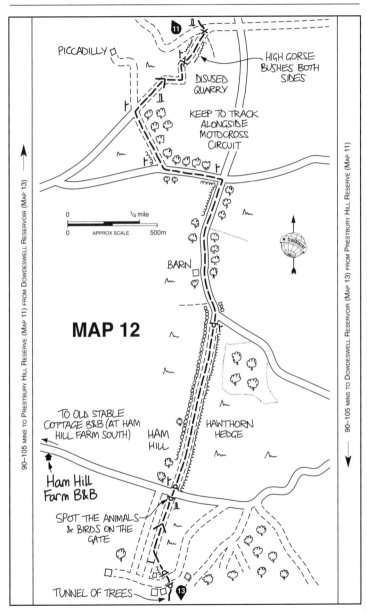

PICCADILLY

HIGH GORSE BUSHES BOTH SIDES

DISUSED QUARRY

KEEP TO TRACK ALONGSIDE MOTOCROSS CIRCUIT

★ trailblazer

BARN

MAP 12

0   ¼ mile
0   APPROX SCALE   500m

TO OLD STABLE COTTAGE B&B (AT HAM HILL FARM SOUTH)

HAM HILL

HAWTHORN HEDGE

Ham Hill Farm B&B

SPOT THE ANIMALS & BIRDS ON THE GATE

TUNNEL OF TREES

90–105 MINS TO PRESTBURY HILL RESERVE (MAP 11) FROM DOWDESWELL RESERVOIR (MAP 13)

90–105 MINS TO DOWDESWELL RESERVOIR (MAP 13) FROM PRESTBURY HILL RESERVE (MAP 11)

ROUTE GUIDE AND MAPS

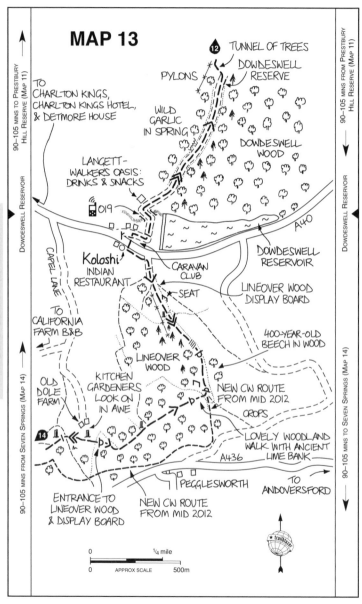

MAP 13

12 TUNNEL OF TREES

PYLONS

DOWDESWELL RESERVE

TO CHARLTON KINGS, CHARLTON KINGS HOTEL, & DETMORE HOUSE

WILD GARLIC IN SPRING

DOWDESWELL WOOD

90–105 MINS TO PRESTBURY HILL RESERVE (MAP 11)

90–105 MINS FROM PRESTBURY HILL RESERVE (MAP 11)

LANGETT-WALKERS OASIS: DRINKS & SNACKS

019

DOWDESWELL RESERVOIR

DOWDESWELL RESERVOIR

A40

Koloshi INDIAN RESTAURANT

CARAVAN CLUB

DOWDESWELL RESERVOIR

SEAT

LINEOVER WOOD DISPLAY BOARD

CAPEL LANE

TO CALIFORNIA FARM B&B

400-YEAR-OLD BEECH IN WOOD

LINEOVER WOOD

KITCHEN GARDENERS LOOK ON IN AWE

NEW CW ROUTE FROM MID 2012

OLD DOLE FARM

CROPS

90–105 MINS FROM SEVEN SPRINGS (MAP 14)

90–105 MINS TO SEVEN SPRINGS (MAP 14)

14

LOVELY WOODLAND WALK WITH ANCIENT LIME BANK

A436

ENTRANCE TO LINEOVER WOOD & DISPLAY BOARD

NEW CW ROUTE FROM MID 2012

PEGGLESWORTH

TO ANDOVERSFORD

0   ¼ mile
0   APPROX SCALE   500m

★ trailblazer

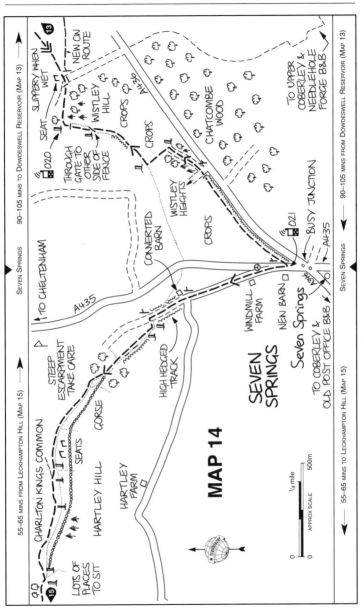

90–105 MINS TO DOWDESWELL RESERVOIR (MAP 13)

← TO DOWDESWELL RESERVOIR (MAP 13)

SEVEN SPRINGS

90–105 MINS FROM DOWDESWELL RESERVOIR (MAP 13) →

13

NEW ON ROUTE

SLIPPERY WHEN WET

SEAT

O20

WISTLEY HILL

CROPS

CHATCOMBE WOOD

TO UPPER COBERLEY & NEEDLEHOLE FORGE B&B

THROUGH GATE TO OTHER SIDE OF FENCE

WISTLEY HEIGHTS

CROPS

CONVERTED BARN

CROPS

O21

BUSY JUNCTION

A435

A436

TO CHELTENHAM

A435

WINDMILL FARM

NEW BARN

Seven Springs

SEVEN SPRINGS

STEEP ESCARPMENT TAKE CARE

HIGH HEDGED TRACK

SEVEN SPRINGS

TO COBERLEY & OLD POST OFFICE B&B

CHARLTON KINGS COMMON

SEATS

GORSE

HARTLEY HILL

HARTLEY FARM

MAP 14

¼ mile   500m

APPROX SCALE

0

15

LOTS OF PLACES TO SIT

55–65 MINS FROM LECKHAMPTON HILL (MAP 15) →

← 55–65 MINS TO LECKHAMPTON HILL (MAP 15)

ROUTE GUIDE AND MAPS

UPPER COBERLEY off MAP 14, p113

Getting away from it all is guaranteed at *Needlehole Forge* (☎ 01242-870531, ☐ www.needleholeforge.co.uk; 1S/2T/2T or D, all en suite or private bathroom; WI-FI; 🐕 £5), albeit some 1¼ miles (2km) from the trail. B&B costs £40 per person, with plenty of room choice – though they don't use all the rooms at once! Their three-course evening meal (£22.50 per person) is a welcome alternative to a four-mile round trip to the pub. The best way to approach it is to take the footpath that skirts the eastern edge of Chatcombe Wood until it meets the Gloucestershire Way, where you turn left; from here the B&B is a further 300 yards (270m) on the left.

SEVEN SPRINGS   MAP 14, p113

There is really little more than a bus stop and a pub at this junction, from where Stagecoach's **bus** 151 operates a frequent service to Cheltenham, Monday to Saturday.

Part of the Hungry Horse chain, the *Seven Springs* (☎ 01242-870219; Mon-Sat 11am-9.30pm, Sun 11am-9pm) offers a huge menu at bargain prices, with glossy pictures to match; finesse is not the order of the day. Alongside the likes of fish and chips in two portion sizes (£4.99-6.49), they do sandwiches and baked potatoes, too.

COBERLEY   off MAP 14, p113

About ¾ mile (1.2km) off the Cotswold Way, the *Old Post Office* (☎ 01242-870694, ☐ www.cotswoldbb.co.uk; 1T or D/1D; 🐕; WI-FI) is now a B&B, idyllically situated close to the village school with views across fields. The double room (£50) has a private bathroom; the other is en suite at £60; for single occupancy, deduct £10. To get here, follow the A436 west from Seven Springs for 300 yards (270m), then turn left on to a footpath and continue on this for about two-thirds of a mile (1km) until you reach the school – and the B&B beyond. In the evening the owner will give walkers a lift to the local pub for a meal.

LECKHAMPTON   MAP 15

Although Leckhampton is quite a way off the trail, a series of footpaths leading down from Leckhampton Hill make *47 Collum End Rise* (☎ 01242-576574, ☐ shelagh_hallaway@yahoo.co.uk; 1S/1T/1D or F; shared bathroom 🐕; WI-FI) reasonably accessible. That said, the footpaths can be confusing, so the owner recommends following the road and will send directions to guests. B&B costs £28 per person, they have drying facilities, and – with advance notice – they'll cook an evening meal for £10 and prepare a packed lunch for £3.50.

LECKHAMPTON HILL TO BIRDLIP   MAPS 15-17

From Leckhampton Hill it's a fairly straightforward **5¾-mile (9.25km)** walk to Birdlip, taking about **2¾ to 3¼ hours**. The route primarily follows the line of the escarpment, with attendant views in good weather. If you're less lucky, warming up at the Air Balloon pub (see p117) is an appealing prospect, and it's worth lingering at **Crickley Hill** (see p117), both to explore the hill fort and surrounding area and for the excellent visitor centre – when it's open, that is.

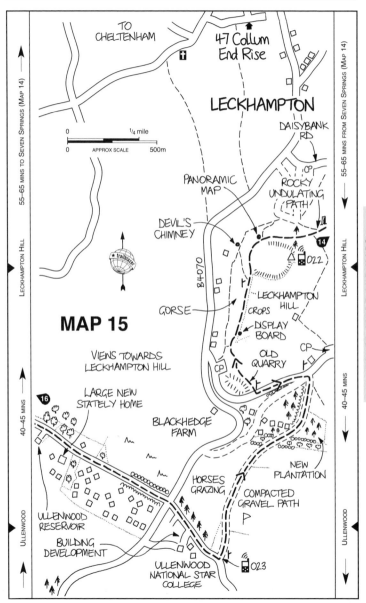

TO CHELTENHAM

47 Collum End Rise

LECKHAMPTON

DAISYBANK RD

CP

ROCKY UNDULATING PATH

PANORAMIC MAP

DEVIL'S CHIMNEY

14

022

LECKHAMPTON HILL

CROPS

GORSE

DISPLAY BOARD

CP

OLD QUARRY

CP

MAP 15

VIEWS TOWARDS LECKHAMPTON HILL

LARGE NEW STATELY HOME

16

BLACKHEDGE FARM

NEW PLANTATION

HORSES GRAZING

COMPACTED GRAVEL PATH

ULLENWOOD RESERVOIR

BUILDING DEVELOPMENT

ULLENWOOD NATIONAL STAR COLLEGE

023

★ trailblazer

0   ¼ mile
0   APPROX SCALE   500m

B4070

55–65 MINS TO SEVEN SPRINGS (MAP 14)

55–65 MINS FROM SEVEN SPRINGS (MAP 14)

LECKHAMPTON HILL

LECKHAMPTON HILL

40–45 MINS

40–45 MINS

ULLENWOOD

ULLENWOOD

ROUTE GUIDE AND MAPS

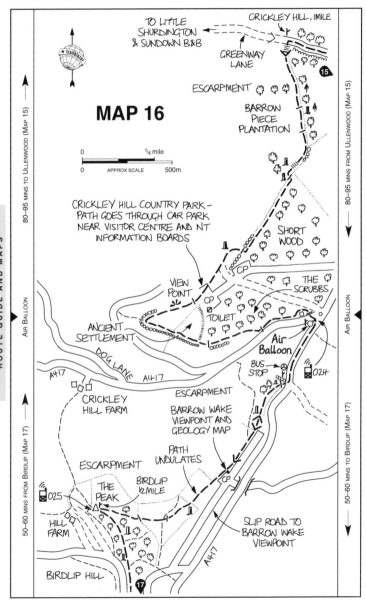

MAP 16

trailblazer

0   ¼ mile
0   APPROX SCALE   500m

80–95 MINS TO ULLENWOOD (MAP 15)

AIR BALLOON

50–60 MINS FROM BIRDLIP (MAP 17)

CRICKLEY HILL, 1MILE

TO LITTLE
SHURDINGTON
& SUNDOWN B&B

GREENWAY
LANE

ESCARPMENT

BARROW
PIECE
PLANTATION

15

SHORT
WOOD

80–95 MINS FROM ULLENWOOD (MAP 15)

CRICKLEY HILL COUNTRY PARK-
PATH GOES THROUGH CAR PARK
NEAR VISITOR CENTRE AND NT
INFORMATION BOARDS

CP

THE
SCRUBBS

VIEW
POINT

CP

TOILET

AIR BALLOON

ANCIENT
SETTLEMENT

Air
Balloon

DOG LANE

A417

A417

BUS
STOP

024

CRICKLEY
HILL FARM

ESCARPMENT

BARROW WAKE
VIEWPOINT AND
GEOLOGY MAP

PATH
UNDULATES

50–60 MINS TO BIRDLIP (MAP 17)

ESCARPMENT

025

THE
PEAK

BIRDLIP
½MILE

CP

HILL
FARM

BIRDLIP HILL

SLIP ROAD TO
BARROW WAKE
VIEWPOINT

A417

17

LITTLE SHURDINGTON   off MAP 16

One of a small group of houses clustered at the end of a quiet lane, *Sundown* (☎ 01242-863353, Whitelands Lane; anna242@btin ternet.com 1S/1T/1D) is a chalet bungalow where B&B costs £40 in a single room sharing a bathroom, or £60 for two sharing, en suite. About a mile (1.6km) west of the trail, it is best accessed down Greenway

Lane. Follow this downhill for at least half a mile (1km), then take the footpath to the left just behind Greenway Hotel. At Whitelands Lane, turn left and you'll find Sundown on the left, near Yew Tree Farm. A couple of pubs around half a mile away on the main A46 serve evening meals.

AROUND CRICKLEY HILL   MAP 16

Popular locally with families and dog walkers, **Crickley Hill Country Park** covers 143 acres (58 ha) protecting both the site of an ancient hill fort (see box p121) and a natural environment which attracts a broad diversity of birds, butterflies and wild flowers, including the rare bee orchid. The introduction of scooter hire for those with limited mobility is an added bonus. There are picnic facilities here, but no café, and the toilets are open only when the visitor centre is manned – which does not always include weekends.

For somewhere to eat, head for the *Air Balloon* (☎ 01452-862541, www.airball oon-pub-gloucestershire.co.uk; daily noon-

9.45pm), a big, friendly pub with a garden that is especially popular on Sundays. The menu covers the full works, from soup (£3.49) to steaks (£12.39-16.99), not to mention pies, pasta and plenty of vegetarian choices. There are sandwiches, wraps and jackets until 5pm, too, plus coffee, tea and pastries.

Several **buses** stop near the pub, including Pulhams' 852 between Gloucester and Cirencester via Birdlip. See public transport table and map, p46.

If you're planning to stop in this area, note that Little Witcombe (see p119) is almost as close to Birdlip Hill as it is to Cooper's Hill.

BIRDLIP   MAP 17, p118

Although the Cotswold Way passes within 200m of Birdlip, it is easy to miss the tiny village entirely. But negotiate the steep and busy road and you'll come to the stone-built *Royal George Hotel* (☎ 01452-862506, 💻 www.theroyalgeorge-hotel .com; 7T/23D/2F, all en suite 🛏; WI-FI; 🐕 by arrangement). B&B in large rooms is around £94 per room, or £115 for a family

room, though rates vary and special deals are regularly available. **Meals** (daily noon-10.00pm) can be taken in the restaurant, or more informally in the bar or garden, or on the terrace.

Pulhams' 852 **bus** operates between Cirencester and Gloucester, stopping here about 100m up the road from the hotel; see public transport table and map, p46.

BIRDLIP TO PAINSWICK   MAPS 17-20

For much of the next 6³/₄ **miles (10.9km, 3¹/₂-4hrs)** you'll continue along the Cotswold escarpment through a woodland fringe, which opens out occasionally to reveal hillside areas such as **Cooper's Hill** (where the annual cheese-rolling competition has long been held, see box p119), and tantalising glimpses north-west to the Malvern Hills. Be particularly careful to follow the way-marked path up here, and not to wander off the edge of the escarpment in misty weather; the rough picket fence would do little to break a fall.

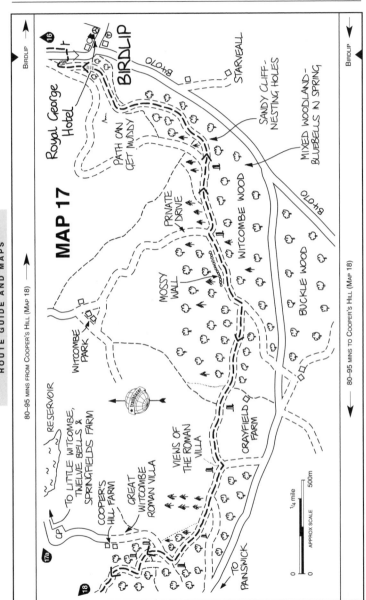

BIRDLIP →

80–95 MINS FROM COOPER'S HILL (MAP 18) →

MAP 17

Royal George Hotel

BIRDLIP

B4070

STARVEALL

PATH CAN GET MUDDY

SANDY CLIFF – NESTING HOLES

MIXED WOODLAND – BLUEBELLS IN SPRING

PRIVATE DRIVE

WITCOMBE WOOD

B4070

MOSSY WALL

BUCKLE WOOD

WITCOMBE PARK

RESERVOIR

TO LITTLE WITCOMBE, TWELVE BELLS & SPRINGFIELDS FARM

COOPER'S HILL FARM

GREAT WITCOMBE ROMAN VILLA

VIEWS OF THE ROMAN VILLA

CRAYFIELD FARM

TO PAINSWICK

17a

18

16

¼ mile

APPROX SCALE

500m

0

0

← BIRDLIP

← 80–95 MINS TO COOPER'S HILL (MAP 18)

Painswick Beacon, site of an Iron-Age hill fort (see box p121) follows, before you reach one of the trail's architectural highlights: **Painswick**. It was east of the town, in the Slad Valley, that the three-year-old Laurie Lee was famously 'set down from the carrier's cart', thus beginning his evocative autobiographical work, *Cider with Rosie*. While the world has moved on, many of the views along this part of the route are probably little changed – at least superficially – since Lee's childhood.

❑ **Cheese rolling**

Picture the scene at Cooper's Hill near Brockworth on the Whitsun Bank Holiday Monday at the end of May. At the top, a group of contestants is set on chasing a giant Double Gloucester cheese down the almost sheer hillface for no other reason than to win the cheese – and the glory. Add in the unpredictable English weather and it's a spectacle that will gladden the heart of anyone who thought British eccentricity was dying out. It's a risky affair, with paramedics kept busy throughout the five races, but that's never stopped the proceedings – until now.

Sadly, this once strictly village event has become a victim of its own success. As numbers increased, so did the pressure on marshals, police and paramedics, such that in 2010 the authorities decided not to stage the event. All the same, cheese rolling has a long history in this neck of the woods, and local rivalries are not that easily put down. So while there is no longer an official event, keep well clear of any large cheese headed your way if you're timing your walk at the end of May.

LITTLE WITCOMBE   MAP 17a

A steep walk down from the trail brings you to **Great Witcombe Villa**, which was constructed during Roman times, but abandoned around the 5th century AD. The foundations are still clearly visible, but almost as interesting is an unmown section of grass which in summer yields numerous wild flowers, including the pyramidal orchid.

About 1¼ miles (2km) from the trail – or the villa – the Bickell sisters have been welcoming **B&B** guests to *Springfields Farm* (☎ 01452-863532; 2S/1D; shared bathroom ✎) since the war. It's a traditional place, warm and welcoming, with a cosy guest lounge and an excellent breakfast. B&B costs £25 per person and a packed lunch is available on request. You can sometimes arrange to be collected from close to the trail, and returned in the morning.

Just a short walk across the main road is the *Twelve Bells* (☎ 01452-862521; Sun-Thu noon-10pm, Fri-Sat noon-11pm), part of the Beefeater chain, with both food and service of a higher-than-average standard.

The accommodation here is a ***Premier Inn*** (🖥 www.premierinn.com; 19D/28F all en suite ✎; WI-FI). Pricing is 'dynamic', with huge variations both up and down, especially online, but £50-70 for a double room is a rough guide. Breakfast – taken at the pub – is £5.25 for a continental breakfast, or £7.99 for a buffet-style English breakfast.

Little Witcombe

MAP 17a

CRANHAM CORNER/CRANHAM

MAP 18

Not so much a village as a point on the map where the road to Cranham (and the Cotswold Way) meets the A46, Cranham Corner is nevertheless served by a **bus**, Stagecoach's No 46 between Cheltenham and Forest Green via Painswick. On Wednesday's Cotswold Green's No 256

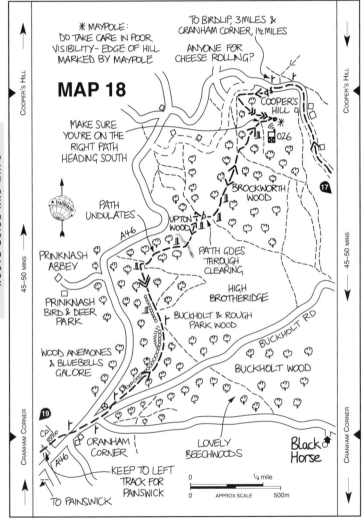

*MAYPOLE: DO TAKE CARE IN POOR VISIBILITY– EDGE OF HILL MARKED BY MAYPOLE

TO BIRDLIP, 3 MILES & CRANHAM CORNER, 1½ MILES

ANYONE FOR CHEESE ROLLING?

MAP 18

COOPER'S HILL

MAKE SURE YOU'RE ON THE RIGHT PATH HEADING SOUTH

□ 026

★ trailblazer

PATH UNDULATES

BROCKWORTH WOOD

17

A46

UPTON WOOD

PATH GOES THROUGH CLEARING

PRINKNASH ABBEY

HIGH BROTHERIDGE

PRINKNASH BIRD & DEER PARK

BUCKHOLT & ROUGH PARK WOOD

BUCKHOLT RD

WOOD ANEMONES & BLUEBELLS GALORE

BUCKHOLT WOOD

19

CP

CRANHAM CORNER

LOVELY BEECHWOODS

Black Horse

KEEP TO LEFT TRACK FOR PAINSWICK

A46

TO PAINSWICK

0   ¼ mile
0   APPROX SCALE   500m

COOPER'S HILL

COOPER'S HILL

45–50 MINS

CRANHAM CORNER

CRANHAM CORNER

ROUTE GUIDE AND MAPS

45–50 MINS

service also calls here. See public transport table and map, p46.

Just quarter of a mile (0.4km) from the junction on the A46 is a **pub**, the *Royal William* (Map 19; ☎ 01452-813650, 🖥 www.royalwilliam.co.uk), where a wide-ranging menu is served daily noon-9pm. Take your pick from burgers to baguettes, salads to steaks, and more, washed down with real ale.

In Cranham itself, almost a mile (1.3km) east of the trail along the road (or slightly shorter through Buckholt Wood), there's B&B for £55 in a small, no frills room at **The Black Horse Inn** (Map 18; ☎ 01452-812217, 1D en suite; 🐕). An open fire welcomes walkers into the bar (Tue-Sun noon-2pm, Tue-Sat 6.30-9.30pm), where the ploughman's (£5.75) and faggots (£9) are great value. The village was a favourite with Gustav Holst (see p109), who composed the music here for *In the Bleak Midwinter*.

If a spot of exotic wildlife appeals, **Prinknash Bird and Deer Park** (☎ 01452-812727, 🖥 www.thebirdpark.com; daily summer 10am-5pm, winter 10am-4pm; £6.80) might appeal. It's located west of the trail, off the A46, and is home to both deer and an array of exotic birds.

❏ **Hill forts**

Painswick Beacon (see Map 19, p122), also known as Kimsbury Camp, is just one of 35 Iron-Age hill forts that have been identified in Gloucestershire, this one dating back to around 400BC. From the layman's perspective, it is arguably the fort that gives greatest vent to the imagination along the Cotswold Way, with steep sides leading up to the fort area from where there are extensive views. Although golf has been played here since 1891, and quarrying has left its mark, the outline of the fort on the ground can still clearly be seen. Today, steps have been cut into the hill to prevent further damage to the ramparts.

Other notable hill forts along the Cotswold Way include those at **Leckhampton Hill** (see Map 15, p115), **Crickley Hill** (see Map 16, p116), **Haresfield Beacon** (see Map 21, p128) and – just off the trail – **Uley Bury** (see Map 26, p137). Some of the earlier settlements, including the one at Crickley Hill, are at least 5000 years old, although the hill fort there is far more modern, occupied around 500BC. Although little of these sites is visible on the ground today, there are some excellent interpretive panels along the trail, including an artist's impression at Crickley Hill of how a hill fort might have looked.

The thin soil on these sites, and the fact that they have never been ploughed, means not only that it is relatively easy to make out the lines of the forts on the ground, but also that they are particularly rich environmentally, and several – including Painswick Beacon – have been designated as SSSIs (see p59).

PAINSWICK — MAP 20a, p125

The small town of Painswick, which harks back to the Domesday Book, may come as something of a surprise for those more familiar with the Cotswold villages further north. The off-white stone of the buildings, many built by wool merchants during the 18th century, comes without the golden hue found further north, and the whole style is more elegant. If you've the energy, count the 99 yew trees in the grounds of **St Mary's Church** (legend has it that the Devil won't let the 100th one grow) or seek out the spectacle stocks by the churchyard wall. And while you're there, note the clock on the tower, erected to celebrate the millennium.

The Arts & Crafts movement (see box p75) was influential here in the early 20th century and the tradition continues. Today's

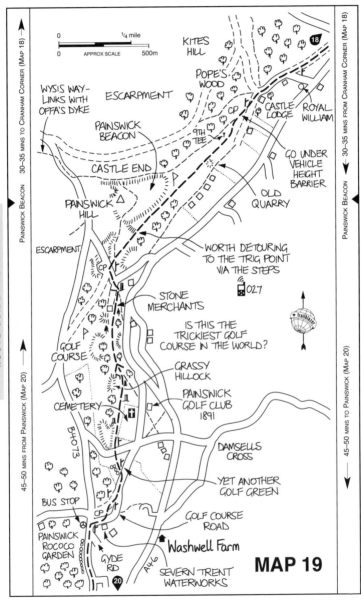

0 — 1/4 mile
0 — 500m
APPROX SCALE

KITES HILL

POPE'S WOOD

18

WYSIS WAY -
LINKS WITH
OFFA'S DYKE

ESCARPMENT

CASTLE LODGE

ROYAL WILLIAM

PAINSWICK
BEACON

9TH TEE

CP

CASTLE END

GO UNDER
VEHICLE
HEIGHT
BARRIER

PAINSWICK
HILL

OLD
QUARRY

ESCARPMENT

CP

WORTH DETOURING
TO THE TRIG POINT
VIA THE STEPS

027

STONE
MERCHANTS

IS THIS THE
TRICKIEST GOLF
COURSE IN THE WORLD?

GOLF
COURSE

GRASSY
HILLOCK

PAINSWICK
GOLF CLUB
1891

CEMETERY

B4073

DAMSELLS
CROSS

YET ANOTHER
GOLF GREEN

BUS STOP

CP

GOLF COURSE
ROAD

PAINSWICK
ROCOCO
GARDEN

GYDE
RD

A46

Washwell Farm

20

SEVERN TRENT
WATERWORKS

MAP 19

★ trailblazer

artists exhibit at the **Painswick Centre** on Bisley St, which showcases the work of the Gloucestershire Guild of Craftsmen (☎ 01452-814745, 🖳 www.guildcrafts.org.uk; Tue-Sat 10am-5pm; admission free).

Transport

The No 46 **bus** between Cheltenham and Stroud, operated by Stagecoach, stops outside the church every day. Cotswold Green's 256 calls here en route between Stroud and Gloucester. For details, see the public transport map and table, p46.

For a **taxi**, try Ted's Cabs (☎ 01452-813599) or JW Goddard (☎ 01452-812240).

Services

Painswick's **tourist information centre** (mob ☎ 07503-516924; Mon-Fri 10am-1pm, 2-4pm, Sat 10am-1pm) is in the Town Hall on Victoria St and is run by volunteers.

There is no bank in the town, but cash can be obtained and foreign currency exchanged at the half-timbered **post office** building on New St. An attraction in its own right, it is claimed to be the oldest working post office in the country, dating back to the 15th century. There's an ATM at the small best-one **supermarket** (Mon-Sat 7am-8pm, Sun 8am-5pm) on St Mary's St. More upmarket foodwise is Oliva's **deli** (see p126). Those in search of **books** will be saddened to learn that the Little Fleece Bookshop has closed, abandoning its 17th-century home on Bisley St that was restored in Arts & Crafts style in 1935.

There's a doctor's **surgery** (☎ 01452-812545) to the north of the town at Hoyland House on Gyde Rd, off Gloucester St, and the handy **Painswick Pharmacy** on New St. Public **toilets** are located by the church and in the car park on the A46 south of town.

Where to stay

Most of Painswick's places to stay are near the town centre. Three **B&Bs** are close to each other on Gloucester St, along the trail. At ***Troy House*** (☎ 01452-812339, 🖳 www.troy-house.co.uk; 1T/1D, both en suite; ☛ in T; WI-FI; 🐕), where the rooms are in a separate cottage, you'll pay £70 a night, or £50 for single occupancy. ***St Anne's*** (☎ 01452-812879, 🖳 www.st-annes-painswick.co.uk; 1T/2D en suite; WI-FI; 🐕 £5 by arrangement), where the rates are £70 or £45 for single occupancy. The neighbouring ***Ashton House*** (☎ 01452-812738, 🖳 www.ashtonhousebedandbreakfast.co.uk; 1S/1T/2D 1☛ in D; WI-FI; 🐕), charges £70 for a room with en suite or private bathroom (single occupancy £60), and £45 for the single room.

Both central and on the trail is the ***Falcon Inn*** (☎ 01452-814222, 🖳 www.falconpainswick.co.uk, New St; 3T/ 5D/3F en suite; ☛; WI-FI; 🐕), a 16th-century coaching inn. Broadly, £59-95 will secure a twin or double room (less £5 for single occupancy), rising to £115 for three or four people in a family room. That said, rooms can be booked online and prices fluctuate considerably, with the highest at weekends.

❑ Painswick Rococo Garden — Map 19

Just half a mile (0.8km) north of Painswick on the B4073, this garden (☎ 01452-813204, 🖳 www.rococogarden.org.uk; mid Jan to end Oct daily 11am-5pm; £6) is claimed to be the only complete English Rococo garden still in existence. It was planted in the 1740s, but so quickly did the fashion change that the original was soon replanted, and the garden was later abandoned. Over 240 years later, in 1984, restoration was put in hand thanks to a painting made in 1748 showing the original design. Flights of fancy characterise a fairly structured and geometric layout, with fruit and vegetables forming a part of the whole rather than hidden away. A maze created to commemorate the garden's 250th anniversary is an added attraction, and the gardens are renowned for their display of snowdrops in early spring. Coffee, tea, cakes and light lunches are served in the old coach house.

ROUTE GUIDE AND MAPS

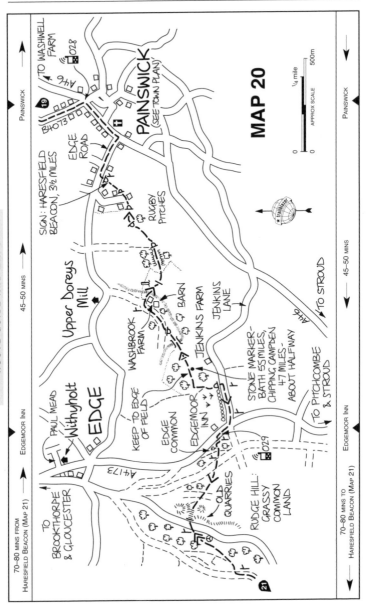

MAP 20

PAINSWICK (SEE TOWN PLAN)

TO WASHWELL FARM

☐28

A46

B4073

19

PAINSWICK

EDGE ROAD

SIGN: HARESFIELD BEACON, 3½ MILES

RUGBY PITCHES

Upper Doreys Mill

Withyholt EDGE

PAUL MEAD

KEEP TO EDGE OF FIELD

WASHBROOK FARM

BARN

JENKINS FARM

JENKINS LANE

EDGE COMMON

EDGEMOOR INN

STONE MARKER—BATH 55 MILES, CHIPPING CAMPDEN 47 MILES—ABOUT HALFWAY

TO PITCHCOMBE & STROUD

A4173

TO BROOKTHORPE & GLOUCESTER

☐29

OLD QUARRIES

RIDGE HILL: GRASSY COMMON LAND

21

TO STROUD

A46

½ mile

APPROX SCALE   500m

PAINSWICK ►

◄ 45-50 MINS →

PAINSWICK ►

EDGEMOOR INN

EDGEMOOR INN

◄ 45-50 MINS →

70-80 MINS FROM HARESFIELD BEACON (MAP 21) →

← 70-80 MINS TO HARESFIELD BEACON (MAP 21)

TO BROOKTHORPE & GLOUCESTER

Opposite the churchyard, *St Michael's Restaurant* (☎ 01452-814555, 💻 www.st michaelsrestaurant.co.uk; 3D en suite, Indian 🍽; WI-FI; 🐾 £10) on Victoria St is a self-styled 'restaurant with rooms'. No ordinary rooms, though: the names Art Deco, Rococo and Indian room hint at the style that would be yours for £85-110 a night (single occupancy from £65). Although they accept dogs, they ask that they are not left unattended in the rooms.

Around the corner at The Cross, there's an air of grandeur about *Cardynham House* (☎ 01452-814006, 💻 www.cardynham.co.uk; 6D/3F en suite, 🍽, WI-FI), too. Here there are four grades of room, costing £87-110 (single occupancy £65-95), depending on the day and time of year; for true indulgence, how about the pool room at £200?

At *Tibbiwell Lodge* (☎ 01452-812748, 💻 www.tibbiwelllodgepainswick.webs.com; 1T private facilities/1D/1D or F, both en suite; 🍽; WI-FI; 🐾), a short way down Tibbiwell Lane, there's an interesting choice of rooms, with higher prices charged at weekends. One double, with an extra single bed, has a balcony overlooking the valley,

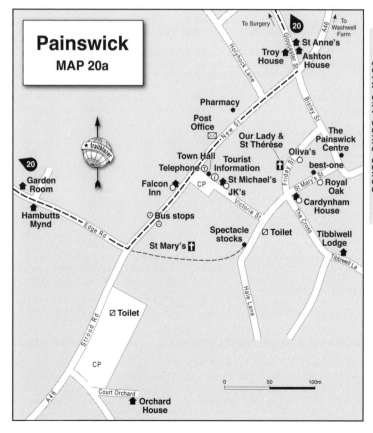

Painswick
MAP 20a

To Surgery
20
St Anne's
Troy House
Ashton House
To Washwell Farm

Holyhock Lane
Gloucester St
A46
Bisley St

Pharmacy
Post Office
Our Lady & St Thérèse
Oliva's
The Painswick Centre
best-one

★ trailblazer
20

Town Hall
Tourist Information
St Michael's
JK's
Friday St
St Mary's St
Royal Oak
Cardynham House

Telephone
New St
CP

Garden Room
Falcon Inn

Hambutts Mynd
Edge Rd

Bus stops
Victoria St
The Cross

Spectacle stocks
Toilet
Tibbiwell Lodge
Tibbiwell La

St Mary's

Stroud Rd
Hale Lane

Toilet

CP
A46

0   50   100m

Court Orchard
Orchard House

and costs £75-85, plus £15 for a third person, or £45-80 for single occupancy. The other, with a terrace, is £85-95, (single £55-90), and the twin costs £65-75 (single £39-70).

At the western edge of the town, right on the trail overlooking fields, *Hambutts Mynd* (☎ 01452-812352, 🖳 ewarland@ supanet.com; 1S/1T/1D en suite; ☞) lies rather appropriately on Edge Rd. B&B in en suite rooms with a bath costs £66 for two people, or £36 for the single with a shower.

Also on Edge Rd is the *Garden Room* (☎ 01452-810879, 🖳 www.thegarden room.biz; 1T or D en suite; WI-FI; 🐾), set on its own in a beautiful garden right on the trail, and costing £85-90 for B&B.

Just off the Stroud Rd is *Orchard House* (☎ 01452-813150, 🖳 www.orchard housepainswick.co.uk, 4 Court Orchard; 1T/1D, ☞; WI-FI) in a small cul-de-sac near the car park, but surrounded by mature gardens and overlooking the valley. The en suite twin room with its own lounge costs £70 a night, while the double with private bathroom is £60 – or £45 for single occupancy.

North of Painswick, about half a mile (0.8km) from the Cotswold Way along the main A46, Richard Hinds has **self-catering** rooms available on a one-night basis at *Washwell Farm* (map 19, mob ☎ 07836-788666, 🖳 rhindsandsons@yahoo.co.uk; 2D/1F all en suite; WI-FI), a working farm that's signposted simply 'Farmhouse B&B'. For £60 a night, you get a double room, or a family with three single beds, plus use of a kitchen, lounge and laundry facilities. There's tea and coffee available, but for most other provisions you'll need to bring your own – or pop into the village for a meal.

Where to eat and drink

Painswick is something of a mecca for foodies, so it could be worth timing your

walk for a stop here at some stage of the day. At *The Royal Oak* (☎ 01452-813129, 🖳 www.theroyaloakpainswick.co.uk; daily 11.30am-3pm) on St Mary's St, they serve Stroud Brewery ales to accompany lunchtime sandwiches or British dishes such as casseroles, steaks, venison and the traditional Painswick puppy-dog pie (£8.50 – and don't panic; this is 'dog' in name only). More prominent is the *Falcon Inn* (see opposite; daily 11.30am-2.30pm, Mon-Sat 6.30-9.30pm, Sun to 8.30pm), with plenty of lunchtime goodies and a seasonal dinner menu that might include the likes of duck breast in a port and redcurrant sauce with new potatoes & vegetables (£12.75).

The **bistro** at *Cardynham House* (see p125; Tue-Sun noon-3pm & Tue-Sat 6.30-9.30pm) serves everything from baguettes and jacket potatoes at lunchtime, to a regularly changing menu in the evening that will set you back around £25 for two courses with wine. Opened at the end of 2011, *JK's at St Michael's* (☎ 01452-813832; Tue-Sat noon-11pm, Sun noon-3pm) aims for a more relaxed atmosphere than its predecessor. At lunchtime, they expect home-cooked ham and pies to feature as well as sandwiches, and weekend menus are à la carte, but during the week themed evenings at £17.50 feature an all-you-can-eat oriental menu on Wednesday, and – on Tuesday and Thursday – 'rustic dining': a hearty three-course Mediterranean meal.

If you fancy something lighter, search out *Oliva's* (☎ 01452-814774; daily 10.30am-5pm) on Friday St, which operates both as a deli and a licensed coffee shop serving soups, salads, sandwiches and tapas; note that they may close earlier on Sunday.

For a more rural repast, consider the Rococo Gardens (see box p123).

PAINSWICK TO STONEHOUSE/EBLEY   MAPS 20-23

This **8¹/₂-mile (13.4km, 4¹/₄-4³/₄hr)** section marks the halfway point along the Cotswold Way; indeed, you'll pass a milestone stating 'Bath 55' on one side – and 'Chipping Campden 47' on the other. After the open countryside of the first few miles the trail enters a narrow strip of woodland, following the edge of the escarpment as it twists and turns around **Haresfield Beacon**. With unimpeded (not to mention spectacular) views in almost every direction, and sheer slopes on two sides, it's no surprise that it was chosen as the site of an Iron-Age hill fort (see box p121).

The descent through woods and fields to the **Stroudwater Canal (Ebley Canal)**, gives little indication of the urban sprawl to the east that is the town of Stroud. No wonder, then, that the appearance of first the railway, then two busy parallel roads, jars the senses. Yet the canal between these, just a few metres above sea level and the lowest point along the route, is one of the few areas of water along the Cotswold Way (or will be, once restoration is complete!), and introduces a very different environment.

EDGE MAP 20, p124

Right on the Cotswold Way on the busy A4173 opposite the entrance to Edge Common (now part of Rudge Hill National Nature Reserve), ***The Edgemoor Inn*** (☎ 01452-813576, 💻 www.edgemoorinn.com; daily noon-2pm, Mon-Sat 6.30-9pm) could be a good staging post. Expect daily specials on the menu, and a range of real ales such as Wickwar's BOB.

The hamlet of Edge itself has a couple of **B&Bs**, both north of the trail. Closest is ***Upper Doreys Mill*** (☎ 01452-812459, 💻 www.doreys.co.uk; 1D/1T or F both en suite; twin with ☕; WI-FI) lying in rural isolation near the bottom of a steep lane, just a short walk from the trail at Washbrook Farm. B&B here is £35 per person (£45 single occupancy), with a minimum two-night stay; note that they accept credit and debit cards, but not cheques. For an evening meal, there's plenty of choice within half a mile or so.

Just off the A4173, on Paul Mead, the modern ***Withyholt Guest House*** (☎ 01452-813618, 💻 www.thewithyholtbedandbreakfast.com; 1T/1D en suite; ☕; WI-FI; 🐕) is particularly walker (and dog) friendly. Set among trees in a big garden, it offers B&B at £65 (single £35). Guests may use the drying room and washing machine; a packed lunch (£6-7) is available with advance notice; and there's even a full-size billiard table.

ROUTE GUIDE AND MAPS

RANDWICK/WESTRIP MAP 22, p129

On the western outskirts of Stroud are the villages of Randwick and Westrip, a short but steep walk down from the trail.

In **Randwick**, the 17th-century ***Court Farm*** (☎ 01453-764210, 💻 dwt6@talktalk.net; 1T/1D/1D or F, all en suite or with private bathroom; 🐕) offers B&B in a rambling farmhouse building that has long been the family home of the Taylors. B&B costs £30 per person. You can get there via a steep ¼-mile (0.4km) footpath off the Cotswold Way, or there's a longer but easier route along the road. If neither of the pubs within walking distance is open, the Taylors will usually run guests without transport to the pub in Cashes Green (see p130), charging a nominal £2 to cover fuel.

With advance booking, **campers** are in luck at **Westrip**, where ***Croft Farm*** (☎ 01453-764376; 💻 croftfarmcampsite@juliacurrie.co.uk; May-Oct) charges £7 per person per night. It's a small, simple, level site, with just cold water and a toilet, though you can use the shower in the house for an additional £1.50. As well as the local pubs, there is a small supermarket a ten-minute walk away, plus a couple of takeaways.

Local **pubs** do a good job of satisfying walkers' hunger pangs – except on Sunday and Monday evenings. Up the hill from Court Farm is ***Vine Tree Inn*** (☎ 01453-763748, 💻 www.thevinetreerandwick.co.uk; Wed-Fri noon-2pm, Tue-Sat 7-9pm, Sun noon-2.30pm). *(cont'd on p130)*

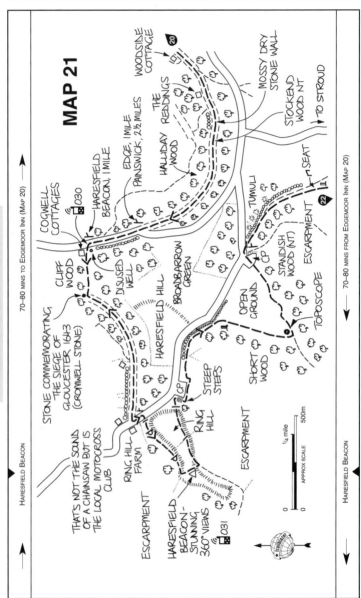

MAP 21

70–80 MINS TO EDGEMOOR INN (MAP 20)

70–80 MINS FROM EDGEMOOR INN (MAP 20)

HARESFIELD BEACON

HARESFIELD BEACON

WOODSIDE COTTAGE

MOSSY DRY STONE WALL

STOCKEND WOOD NT

TO STROUD

THE REDDINGS

HALLIDAY WOOD

EDGE, 1 MILE
PAINSWICK, 2½ MILES

SEAT

COGWELL COTTAGES
030

HARESFIELD BEACON, 1 MILE

TUMULI

CLIFF WOOD

DISUSED WELL

BROADBARROW GREEN

STANDISH WOOD (NT)

ESCARPMENT

CP

OPEN GROUNDS

TOPOSCOPE

STONE COMMEMORATING THE SIEGE OF GLOUCESTER 1643 (CROMWELL STONE)

HARESFIELD HILL

SHORT WOOD

THAT'S NOT THE SOUND OF A CHAINSAW BUT IS THE LOCAL MOTOCROSS CLUB

RING HILL FARM

CP

STEEP STEPS

RING HILL

ESCARPMENT

ESCARPMENT

HARESFIELD BEACON – STUNNING 360° VIEWS
031

¼ mile

500m

APPROX SCALE

0

0

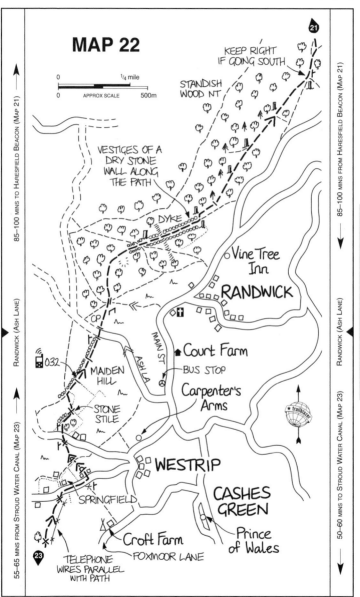

MAP 22

0   ¼ mile
0   APPROX SCALE   500m

KEEP RIGHT
IF GOING SOUTH

STANDISH
WOOD NT

VESTIGES OF A
DRY STONE
WALL ALONG
THE PATH

DYKE

Vine Tree
Inn

RANDWICK

CP

□32

MAIDEN
HILL

STONE
STILE

MAIN ST

ASH LA

Court Farm

BUS STOP

Carpenter's
Arms

WESTRIP

SPRINGFIELD

CASHES
GREEN

Croft Farm

FOXMOOR LANE

Prince
of Wales

TELEPHONE
WIRES PARALLEL
WITH PATH

★ trailblazer

85–100 MINS TO HARESFIELD BEACON (MAP 21)

RANDWICK (ASH LANE)

55–65 MINS FROM STROUD WATER CANAL (MAP 23)

85–100 MINS FROM HARESFIELD BEACON (MAP 21)

RANDWICK (ASH LANE)

50–60 MINS TO STROUD WATER CANAL (MAP 23)

ROUTE GUIDE AND MAPS

(cont'd from p127) In the other direction, at **Westrip**, is the ***Carpenter's Arms*** (☎ 01453-762693; Sat noon-2pm, Sun noon-2.30pm, Tue-Sat 6-9pm). A reliable third option is down the road in **Cashes Green**, where the ***Prince of Wales*** (☎ 01453-763175, 💻 www.princeofwalesstroud.co

.uk; daily noon-2pm, Mon-Sat 6-9pm, Sun 6-8pm) serves real ale alongside specials; chicken and mushroom pasta bake is £8.95.

Cotswold Green's 230 **bus** (Mon-Sat, 3-4/day) from Ebley stops in Cashes Green and Randwick. See public transport map and table, p46.

STONEHOUSE/EBLEY MAP 23

The Cotswold Way follows a line between Stonehouse to the west and Ebley to the east, running for a short while along Ryeford Rd. With two busy roads and a fair amount of urban degradation it's not the most picturesque of spots, and there's little to delay the walker. There is, though, a **B&B**, ***Merton Lodge*** (☎ 01453-822018; 3D; 🛏), 250m east of the trail on the B4008, screened by trees and set well back from the road. One of the rooms here is en suite and the other two share a bathroom; you'll pay £28-30 per person for B&B.

A few steps east along the road, the Murco garage (daily 7am-9pm) sells

drinks and snacks, but the nearest pub for an evening meal is about a mile (1.6km) away in Stonehouse.

The **railway** station at Stonehouse is a stop on the service between London Paddington and Cheltenham operated by First Great Western, offering straightforward access to the Cotswold Way at this point. Stagecoach's **bus** No 20 between Uley and Stroud via Dursley and Lower Cam stops on the B4008. There's also the No 230, operated by Cotswold Green, to Cashes Green and Randwick. See public transport map and table, p46.

STONEHOUSE/EBLEY TO PEN WOOD MAPS 23-24

At this point, the Cotswold Way offers two alternatives. The **shorter route** of the two, which runs close to King's Stanley, is only **1¹/₂ miles (2.4km)** long, taking about **45-50 minutes** to walk. Predominantly urban with an agricultural fringe, its attractions are of a practical nature, with several B&Bs, plus a pub and a useful shop in King's Stanley.

The more **scenic route**, which crosses Selsley Common, is just over **3 miles (4.6km, 1¹/₂-1³/₄hrs)**, so about twice the distance, but there is a pub within half a mile (0.8km) of the trail. Following restoration of the canal, it is planned to reroute the Cotswold Way along the towpath to Ebley Mill. At present, however, this section has been diverted along the parallel road and cycle path. Even so, unless time is of the essence, or you need to pick up supplies, opt for the longer walk; the rewards are infinitely greater, with the common itself one of the trail's highlights. Open and windswept, it offers glorious walking at any time of year, but is at its best in summer when the grass is thick with orchids and other wild flowers. Both routes converge in Pen Wood, above (almost literally) Middleyard.

ROUTE GUIDE AND MAPS

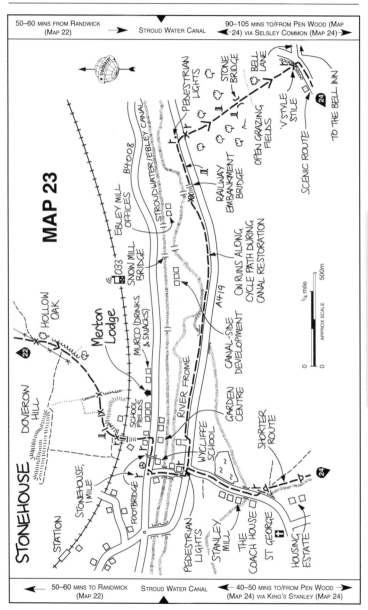

MAP 23

STONEHOUSE

STATION

STONEHOUSE, 1 MILE

HOLLOW OAK

DONERON HILL

Merton Lodge

EBLEY MILL OFFICES

B4008

0033

SNOW MILL BRIDGE

MURCO (DRINKS & SNACKS)

STROUDWATER/EBLEY CANAL

PEDESTRIAN LIGHTS

STONE BRIDGE

BELL LANE

V-STILE

TO THE BELL INN

OPEN GRAZING FIELDS

SCENIC ROUTE

RAILWAY EMBANKMENT BRIDGE

CW RUNS ALONG CYCLE PATH DURING CANAL RESTORATION

A419

CANAL-SIDE DEVELOPMENT

RIVER FROME

GARDEN CENTRE

SCHOOL FIELDS

FOOTBRIDGE

WYCLIFFE SCHOOL

SHORTER ROUTE

STANLEY MILL

THE COACH HOUSE

ST GEORGE

HOUSING ESTATE

PEDESTRIAN LIGHTS

¼ mile

500m

APPROX SCALE

0

0

ROUTE GUIDE AND MAPS

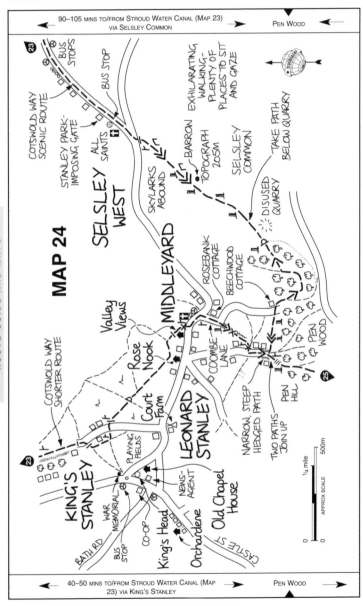

PEN WOOD

23

BUS STOPS

BUS STOP

COTSWOLD WAY SCENIC ROUTE

STANLEY PARK-IMPOSING GATE

ALL SAINTS

EXHILARATING WALKING-PLENTY OF PLACES TO SIT AND GAZE

BARROW

TOPOGRAPH 205M

SELSLEY COMMON

TAKE PATH BELOW QUARRY

SKYLARKS ABOUND

SELSLEY WEST

MAP 24

DISUSED QUARRY

ROSEBANK COTTAGE

BEECHWOOD COTTAGE

MIDDLEYARD

Valley Views

Rose Nook

PEN WOOD

COTSWOLD WAY SHORTER ROUTE

Court Farm

COOMBE LANE

PEN HILL

25

LEONARD STANLEY

NARROW, STEEP HEDGED PATH

TWO PATHS JOIN UP

KING'S STANLEY

PLAYING FIELDS

NEWS-AGENT

Old Chapel House

23

WAR MEMORIAL

BUS STOP

CO-OP

King's Head

Orchardene

CASTLE ST

BATH RD

¼ mile

APPROX SCALE

500m

0

0

PEN WOOD

KING'S STANLEY
(SHORTER ROUTE)   MAP 24

Only a short walk east of the trail across playing fields, King's Stanley offers most of the services essential to walkers.

The **Co-op** (Mon-Fri 9am-5.30pm, Sat 9am-12.30pm) has all the necessities, including a **post office** counter and a useful **ATM**. Opposite is a small newsagent, Yew Tree Stores.

Stagecoach **buses** Nos 14/14B between Stroud and Gloucester, via Selsley and Stonehouse, stop here daily. For details, see the public transport map and table, p46.

Campers can pitch a tent for £3.50 per person at *Court Farm* (☎ 01453-823127), up the hill towards Middleyard, where there's space for around five tents. There are outside toilets and hot and cold water, but no showers.

For **B&B** accommodation, try *Old Chapel House* (☎ 01453-826289, ☐ jean hannaoldchapelhouse@hotmail.com, Broad St; 2S/1T/1D/1F; ☛; WI-FI) which, as the name suggests, is in a converted (red-brick) chapel. In the singles and twin,

which share a bathroom with bath, you'll pay £30 per person, rising to £32 in the en suite double or family rooms.

Heading away from the shops along Castle St, down a narrow drive, you'll come to the 19th-century stone *Orchardene* (☎ 01453-822684, ☐ www.orchardene.co .uk; 1T en suite/1D with private ☛; WI-FI; 🐾), where B&B costs £60 per room, or £40 single. It's a friendly place, offering local organic food, including homemade bread and – if booked in advance – an evening meal at around £15.

A range of **food** options is available at the newly renovated *King's Head* (☎ 01453-828293, ☐ www.thekingsheadinn .co.uk; Mon-Sat noon-9pm, Sun noon-3pm), by the **war memorial**. From light bites to traditional pub favourites, it's all here, with a couple of special nights at £5 a head to add to the mix: Monday night is fish and chips night; on Wednesday it's a curry. Their **coffee shop** (Mon-Sat 8.30am-3.30pm, Sun 10am-2pm) serves all-day breakfasts, including bacon baps.

MIDDLEYARD
(SHORTER ROUTE)   MAP 24

The Cotswold Way runs through Middleyard, a small ribbon of old and new stone houses up the hill from King's Stanley, yet within easy walking distance of the larger village's facilities. Backing on to farmland and away from the road, the aptly named *Valley Views* (☎ 01453-827458, ☐ www .valley-views.com, 12 Orchard Cl; 1T/ 2D; ☛; WI-FI) is a modern house, clearly signposted right on the trail. B&B here comes in at £65-70, the higher rate for a large double with its own balcony; single occupancy is £50. A two-course evening meal

can be organised for walkers at £14 a head.

On the main road through the village, *Rose Nook* (☎ 01453-791697, ☐ www .rosenook.co.uk; 1T/1D private facilities; ☛; WI-FI) charges £65 for two sharing, or £45 for single occupancy (when there's a minimum two-night stay). In the evening, they'll drive walkers to the Bell at Selsley for a meal, to return by taxi.

Stagecoach **buses** Nos 14/14B run daily between Stroud and Gloucester, via Selsley, King's Stanley and Stonehouse. See the public transport map and table, p46.

SELSLEY
(SCENIC ROUTE)   MAP 24

Divided by the common that bears its name, the village of Selsley is notable for the Victorian **All Saints' Church**, clearly visible on the hill from the canal. The

church was influential in the development of the Arts and Crafts movement (see box p75), its stained-glass windows being one of the first commissions for William Morris's design company. Work was contributed by

Dante Gabriel Rossetti and Edward Burne-Jones, as well as by Morris himself. The common itself is a haven for any number of wild flowers, including the pyramidal orchid (see photo opposite p64).

The No 14 or 14B Stagecoach **bus** between Stroud and Gloucester stops daily, travelling via King's Stanley and Stonehouse. See public transport map and table, p46.

Sustenance is on hand at the nearby *Bell Inn* (off map 23; ☎ 01453-764910; daily noon-9pm) in the form of sandwiches and pub grub, including a pie of the day, and a roast on Sunday.

PEN WOOD TO DURSLEY   MAPS 24-27

Further ribbons of beech woods characterise this **8-mile (12.9km, 4-4³/₄hrs)** stretch, broken up by two significant highlights as well as a couple of interesting long barrows.

The views from **Coaley Peak** look not just west to the Severn, but onward to Cam Long Down and the Tyndale Monument – a taste of things to come. **Cam Long Down** itself is all too short, the steep climb up being richly rewarded with 360° views: a place to be savoured before the descent into Dursley. Be careful up here if the weather is poor; there are some sheer drops.

The area is also home to two of the trail's most interesting long barrows, at **Nympsfield** and **Uley** (see box below), and to two very different mansions: **Woodchester Mansion** and **Owlpen Manor** (see boxes on p136), although this last is no longer open to the public.

❑ **What is a long barrow?**
Essentially another name for a communal burial ground, the long barrow is known locally as a tump. These were the graveyards of the Neolithic people, early settlers who were the first to farm the land over 5000 years ago. In addition to human remains, archaeologists have identified the remains of fires that indicate some form of ritual or religious activity.

Of almost 100 long barrows in the Cotswolds, several are along the Cotswold Way, including the **Nympsfield Long Barrow** near Coaley Peak, dating from 2500BC, and others at Leckhampton Hill and in Standish Wood. Notable among them are **Belas Knap** (see box p101) and – just off this stretch of the route – **Uley Long Barrow**, more evocatively known as Hetty Pegler's Tump. Best approached along the road rather than by scrambling up the steep hill through the woods, Hetty Pegler is worth the detour, since here you can crawl inside the chamber itself. You'll need a torch (if not, a camera flash will do) – but don't spend too long, for folklore has it that, if you do, the fairies will start to work their magic on the passing of time.

NYMPSFIELD   **off MAP 25**
About half a mile (0.8km) off the trail from Coaley Peak, in the heart of the village of Nympsfield, the *Rose and Crown Inn* (☎ 01453-860240, 🖳 www.theroseandcrowninn.com; 2D/1D or F, all en suite, ♥; WI-FI) offers an appealing mix of **B&B**, an interesting menu and real ale. They charge £80 for two sharing, £90 for three, and £60 for single occupancy. In the **restaurant** (Mon-Sat noon-2.30pm & 6-9pm, Sun 12-5pm), old favourites rub shoulders with seasonal specials that might include faggots, and there's a bar menu too.

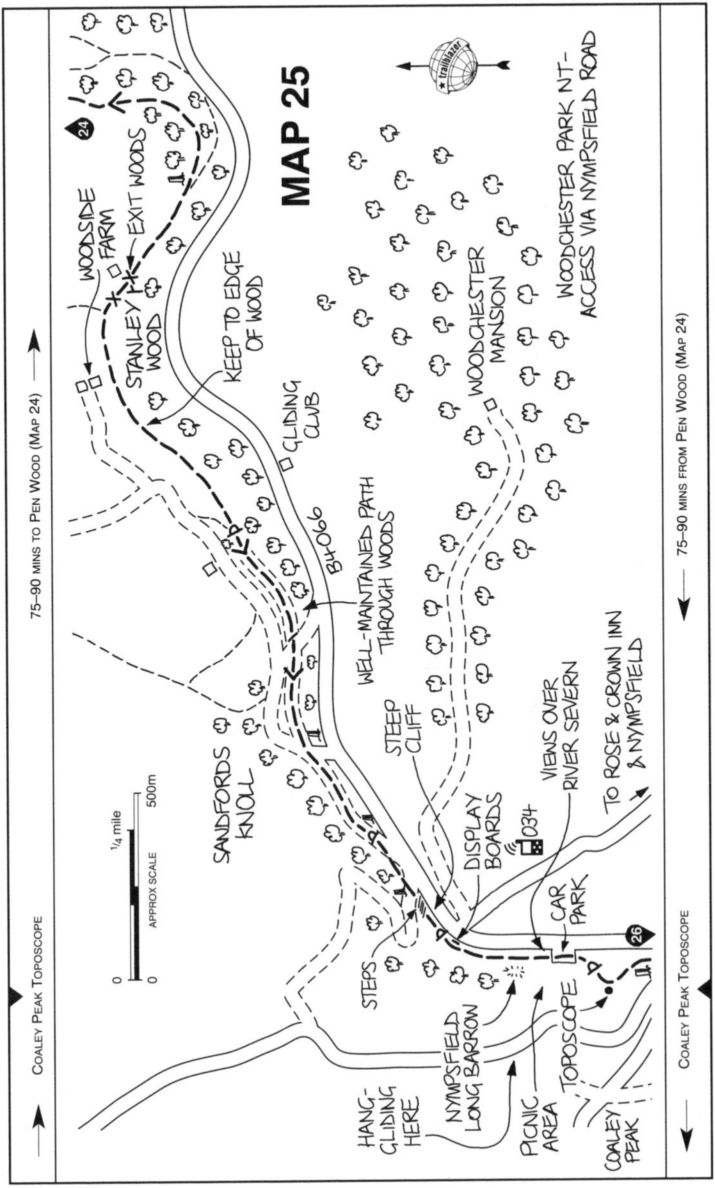

MAP 25

75–90 MINS TO PEN WOOD (MAP 24)

COALEY PEAK TOPOSCOPE

¼ mile
500m
APPROX SCALE

SANDFORDS KNOLL

STEPS

HANG-GLIDING HERE

NYMPSFIELD LONG BARROW

PICNIC AREA

TOPOSCOPE

COALEY PEAK

COALEY PEAK TOPOSCOPE

STEEP CLIFF

WELL-MAINTAINED PATH THROUGH WOODS

DISPLAY BOARDS

VIEWS OVER RIVER SEVERN

TO ROSE & CROWN INN & NYMPSFIELD

CAR PARK

B4066

GLIDING CLUB

KEEP TO EDGE OF WOOD

STANLEY WOOD

WOODSIDE FARM

EXIT WOODS

WOODCHESTER MANSION

WOODCHESTER PARK NT-ACCESS VIA NYMPSFIELD ROAD

75–90 MINS FROM PEN WOOD (MAP 24)

ROUTE GUIDE AND MAPS

24

26

□ **Woodchester Mansion and Park**   **Map 25, p135**

Despite its imposing architecture, the Victorian **Woodchester Mansion** (☎ 01453-861541, 🖳 www.woodchestermansion.org.uk; £6.50, or £5.50 to NT and English Heritage members) near Nympsfield was never finished, its rooms being inhabited by five species of bat, but never by humans. It is usually open to the public from Easter to October on Wednesdays, Thursdays, Saturdays, Sundays and bank holidays, between 11am and 5pm, but do check their website first. The mansion is set in the grounds of **Woodchester Park**, a peaceful wooded valley with a chain of lakes that is owned by the National Trust (☎ 01452-814213, 🖳 www.nationaltrust.org.uk; daily dawn-dusk, parking £2, NT members free). Designated as an SSSI (see p59), the estate is notable not just for the bats, but for a broad diversity of birds and wild flowers. Waymarked trails through the grounds are accessible to the public all year.

ULEY   MAP 26

Although it's over half a mile (1km) from the Cotswold Way, Uley does at least justify the diversion. Probably many people's idea of a proper village, it boasts a pub, a decidedly imposing church, St Giles, and a **post office cum shop** (Mon-Fri 8am-1pm & 2-5.30pm, Sat 8am-4pm, Sun 9am-noon); it even has its own brewery, and a posh manor house a short distance away. Stagecoach's No 20 **bus** service runs from Dursley; see public transport map and table, p46.

The whitewashed *Old Crown Inn* (☎ 01453-860502, 🖳 www.theoldcrownuley .co.uk; 2T/2D, all en suite; WI-FI; 🐾 1 room only), with a terrace garden at the rear, does **B&B** at £45 single, £75 double, or £85 for a twin. A standard **pub menu** is served daily noon-2pm & 6-9pm, with plenty of real-ale choices to accompany it.

□ **Owlpen Manor**   **off Map 26**

Almost hidden from view in a valley along a short avenue of trees, Owlpen Manor (☎ 01453-860261, 🖳 www.owlpen.com) is an enchanting Tudor manor house, complete with great hall, dating in part back to 1450. It was abandoned early in the 19th century, but was rescued in 1926 in line with the principles of the Society for the Protection of Ancient Buildings (🖳 www.spab.org.uk), a body formed by William Morris, founder of the Arts and Crafts movement. While most of the furniture and decoration date to an earlier era, the Arts and Crafts movement is also represented. Outside, the formal gardens with their neatly clipped yews lead to beech woods with a series of walks, while above looms an elaborate Victorian church.

Sadly, the estate, which remains in private hands, is no longer open to the public except for private functions, though if you'd like to explore you could always spend a few days in one of the cottages on the estate.

DURSLEY   MAP 27a, p139

In the words of one local resident, Dursley has been 'very successfully ruined' by the planning authorities – and it's hard not to echo those sentiments. While a hint of longevity remains in the form of the pillared **Georgian Market House**, and **St James** the Great Church, gone are many of the natural stone buildings in favour of practical but characterless replacements and – the *pièce de résistance* – a modern, tinted-glass library which, although it is exceptionally efficient, stands out like a sore thumb.

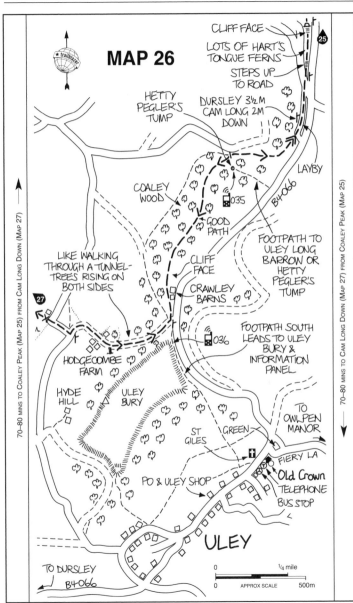

MAP 26

★ trailblazer

25

CLIFF FACE

LOTS OF HART'S TONGUE FERNS

STEPS UP TO ROAD

HETTY PEGLER'S TUMP

DURSLEY 3½ M CAM LONG 2 M DOWN

LAYBY

COALEY WOOD

B4066

035

GOOD PATH

FOOTPATH TO ULEY LONG BARROW OR HETTY PEGLER'S TUMP

LIKE WALKING THROUGH A TUNNEL- TREES RISING ON BOTH SIDES

27

CLIFF FACE

CRAWLEY BARNS

036

FOOTPATH SOUTH LEADS TO ULEY BURY & INFORMATION PANEL

HODGECOMBE FARM

HYDE HILL

ULEY BURY

TO OWLPEN MANOR

ST GILES

GREEN

FIERY LA

PO & ULEY SHOP

Old Crown TELEPHONE BUS STOP

ULEY

TO DURSLEY B4066

0   ¼ mile

0   APPROX SCALE   500m

70–80 MINS TO COALEY PEAK (MAP 25) FROM CAM LONG DOWN (MAP 27)

70–80 MINS TO CAM LONG DOWN (MAP 27) FROM COALEY PEAK (MAP 25)

ROUTE GUIDE AND MAPS

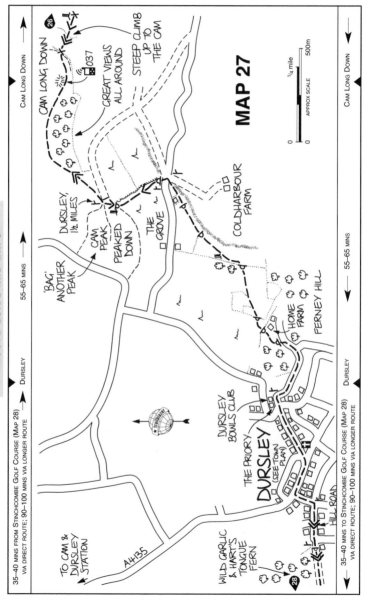

35–40 MINS FROM STINCHCOMBE GOLF COURSE (MAP 28) ← 55–65 MINS → DURSLEY ← CAM LONG DOWN →
VIA DIRECT ROUTE; 90–100 MINS VIA LONGER ROUTE

MAP 27

¼ mile
0
0   500m
APPROX SCALE

CAM LONG DOWN

STEEP CLIMB
UP TO
THE CAM

GREAT VIEWS
ALL AROUND

☐037

26

DURSLEY, 1½ MILES

CAM
PEAK

PEAKED
DOWN

THE GROVE

COLDHARBOUR
FARM

'BAC'
ANOTHER
PEAK

trailblazer

FERNEY HILL

HOME
FARM

DURSLEY
BOWLS CLUB

THE PRIORY

DURSLEY
(SEE TOWN
PLAN)

HILL ROAD

TO CAM &
DURSLEY
STATION

A4135

WILD GARLIC
& HART'S
TONGUE
FERN

28

35–40 MINS TO STINCHCOMBE GOLF COURSE (MAP 28) ← 55–65 MINS → DURSLEY ← CAM LONG DOWN →
VIA DIRECT ROUTE; 90–100 MINS VIA LONGER ROUTE

Despite this, Dursley retains a strong sense of community and, with a decent range of traditional shops and facilities, it is a good place to sort out practical issues. Then there's the advent of a new supermarket which, far from blighting the town, seems to have given it a lift. For the walker, Dursley also has one significant card up its sleeve: the CAMRA award-winning Old Spot pub (see p141), which is one of the best along the trail.

Like many other Cotswold towns, Dursley was founded on the wool trade; later it was home to the Lister family, of engineering fame. To get an idea of the town's history, including its industrial past, take a look at the **Heritage Centre** (☎ 01453-542953; Tue, Thu, Fri, Sat 10.30am-12.30pm).

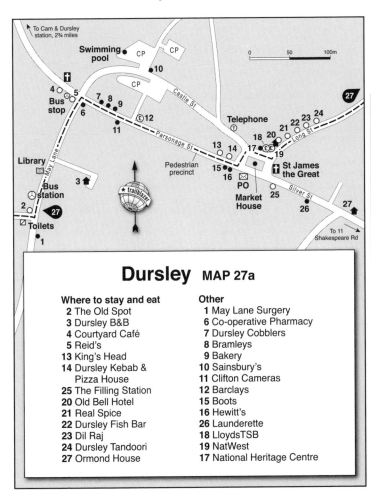

Dursley MAP 27a

Where to stay and eat
2 The Old Spot
3 Dursley B&B
4 Courtyard Café
5 Reid's
13 King's Head
14 Dursley Kebab & Pizza House
25 The Filling Station
20 Old Bell Hotel
21 Real Spice
22 Dursley Fish Bar
23 Dil Raj
24 Dursley Tandoori
27 Ormond House

Other
1 May Lane Surgery
6 Co-operative Pharmacy
7 Dursley Cobblers
8 Bramleys
9 Bakery
10 Sainsbury's
11 Clifton Cameras
12 Barclays
15 Boots
16 Hewitt's
26 Launderette
18 LloydsTSB
19 NatWest
17 National Heritage Centre

ROUTE GUIDE AND MAPS

Transport

Trains run to Cam and Dursley station, a good 2¹/₂ miles (4km) north of the town, from where Swansbrook run the 210 rail-link service into Dursley more or less hourly Monday to Saturday, with additional services during the morning rush hour. Buses coincide with train departures.

The town's **bus station** is on May Lane, squeezed between the library and the Old Spot – the old and the new – with regular services except on Sunday. Probably the most useful bus for those on the Cotswold Way is First's 311 from Thornbury, stopping at North Nibley and Wotton-under-Edge. Also helpful is Stagecoach No 20 between Stroud and Uley via Ebley and Dursley. See the public transport map and table, p46.

For **taxi** services, try Al's Taxis (☎ 01453-519354), CLS Taxis (mob ☎ 07717-750452), or Martins (☎ 01453-511115).

Services

Although there are signs up indicating a **tourist information** centre, these are misleading; there are leaflets available at the swimming pool and the **library** (☎ 01453-543059; Mon & Thu 9am-5.30pm, Tue & Fri 9am-7pm, Sat 9am-4pm), where the staff are extremely helpful, but no dedicated centre. Three of the main high street **banks** have branches in the town, two with ATMs. The **post office**, with a bureau de change and ATM, is by the Market House, at the end of Parsonage St.

The arrival of Sainsbury's **supermarket** (Mon-Sat 8am-10pm, Sun 10am-4pm) has brought a new dimension to Dursley, but its traditional shops along the pedestrianised Parsonage St are hanging on. This is where you'll find an independent **bakery**, and an excellent **greengrocer**, Bramleys. Crisps, sandwiches and drinks can also be bought at Hewitt's the **newsagent**. A **farmers' market** is held on the second Saturday of each month at the Market Hall, from 9am to 1pm.

If you've any problems with your **boots**, The Dursley Cobbler (☎ 01453-542918; Mon, Tue, Thu & Fri 9am-5pm, Wed & Sat 9am-4pm), on Parsonage St, may be able to repair them, while for **cam-**era issues try Clifton Cameras (☎ 01453-548128; Mon-Sat 9am-5.30pm) opposite. And while you're at it, you could get to grips with muddy clothes at The Washtub **launderette** on Silver St.

Although there's a branch of Lloyds **pharmacy** attached to the May Lane surgery almost right on the trail about two minutes' walk from the library, more central are two other chemists – Boots and the Co-op – along Parsonage St.

If you've any energy left after a day's walking, you could always try Dursley's **swimming pool** (☎ 01453-546441). Call ahead for times of public sessions, which vary according to the time of year.

Where to stay

Those planning to stay in Dursley will find that options are limited. Most central is the 18th-century **Dursley Bed & Breakfast** at 7 Prospect Place (☎ 01453-543445, 🖳 www.dursleybedandbreakfast.co.uk; 1S/1T/1D; 🛥; WI-FI; 🐾), set back from May Lane. It may be in need of a facelift, but the welcome is warm, the décor eclectic, and it's close to the trail. B&B comes in at £34 per person in rooms sharing a bathroom and shower room, or £37 for single occupancy.

Well recommended is *The Garden Flat* (☎ 01453-545312; 1T, 🛥; WI-FI), a self-contained annexe of **Ormond House** at 13 Silver St. Large, light and airy, with its own kitchen and bathroom, it looks over a pretty garden and costs £32 per person B&B; the fridge is well stocked so that guests can cook their own substantial breakfast.

Further out in this direction, at *11 Shakespeare Road* (☎ 01453-547080, 🖳 ronnieh@talktalk.net; 1S/1D; 🛥), walkers are welcomed with tea and cake and the potential of a hot bath. Rooms, with sole use of a bathroom, are £25 per person, and for £4 the owner will prepare a packed lunch. To get there, you can either turn right at the end of Bull Pitch, then left on to Byron Rd, left again on to Tennyson Rd and first right on to Shakespeare Rd (passing the New Inn on the way), or phone for directions from the Priory on Long St.

The *Old Bell Hotel* (☎ 01453-542821; 2S/5T/1F, 🛥; small 🐾 no charge), on Long

St, also does B&B in recently refurbished rooms at £48-60 for two sharing, the latter en suite, or £24-30 single. The downside is that rooms are above a busy bar, with a nightclub operating in the latter half of the week.

Where to eat and drink

Arguably the best reason for stopping in Dursley is to pay a visit to *The Old Spot* (☎ 01453-542870, 🖳 www.oldspotinn.co.uk; daily 11-3pm, Mon 6.30-9.30pm). Regularly featured among the top CAMRA awards, it is so popular among ale drinkers (see box p22) that food is served only at lunchtime and on Monday evenings (though do phone ahead to check). That's a shame, because they've an excellent chef, and the prices – £7.25 for soup and a salad at lunch, or £14.95 for a two-course 'supper' that would do a posher place proud – very reasonable.

Late 2011 saw the arrival of *Reid's Cucina Italiana* (☎ 01453-549459; daily 11am-11pm) on Parsonage St. With an upstairs restaurant focusing on Italian dishes alongside steaks and fresh fish, and a wine bar below, it could be just what is needed.

More established options are largely on Long St. Choose from a standard menu of steaks and grills at the *Old Bell Hotel* (see above; Mon-Sat 10am-9pm, Sun 11am-9pm), or a trio of Indians: *Real Spice* (☎ 01453-519711/2; daily 5-11pm), *Dursley Tandoori* (☎ 01453-548833; Sat-Thu noon-2pm, daily 5.30-11.30pm), and *Dil Raj* (☎ 01453-543472; Sun-Thu 5.45-11.30pm, Fri-Sat 5.30pm-midnight). Otherwise you'll be looking at a takeaway. Among these are the good *Dursley Fish Bar* (☎ 01453-547865; Mon-Sat 11.30am-2pm, Mon-Thu & Sun 5-10pm, Fri-Sat 4.45-10pm), and *Dursley Kebab and Pizza House* (☎ 01453-544188; daily 3pm to the small hours.

For lighter meals during the day, try the *Courtyard Café* (☎ 01453-544246; Mon-Fri 9am-4pm, Sat 9am-2pm), on Parsonage St, for breakfast, coffee, lunchtime snacks or afternoon tea, or the aptly named *Filling Station* (☎ 01453-542609; Mon-Fri 8am-3pm, Sat 9am-2pm), on Silver St, which serves the likes of sandwiches and jacket potatoes. The *King's Head* (☎ 01453-543205; Mon-Sat 11am-3pm) also serves affordable pub grub – think sandwiches, ploughman's or pasta – or an all-day breakfast, all for under £5.

DURSLEY TO WOTTON-UNDER-EDGE　　　　　MAPS 27-30

The Cotswold Way offers another choice at this stage. The **longer route**, a **6³/₄-mile (11km, 3¹/₂-4¹/₄hrs)** stretch, climbs steeply from Dursley and circumnavigates Stinchcombe Hill – and the golf course – before coming almost full circle. (As an aside, this section has been designated the Korean Friendship Trail, effectively a twinning link with South Korea's Jeju Olle trail.) The **more direct route** (just **4¹/₂ miles/7.2km, 2¹/₄-2¹/₂hrs**) cuts straight across what looks on the map like the stem of a leaf. Unless the weather is great and you've all the time in the world to follow the wood around a golf course, albeit with some fine views from Drakestone Point, going straight across is the better option. Either way, you'll have the opportunity to climb the **Tyndale Monument** to see those views from on high.

NORTH NIBLEY　　　　MAP 29, p143

This thriving village boasts all the essentials – a church, a school, a **post office** and **shop** with **ATM** (Mon-Fri 9am-1pm & 3-6pm, Sat 9am-1pm, Sun 9.30am-12.30pm), and a decent pub – not to mention a range of accommodation.

A regular **bus** service, the 311 operated by First, connects Thornbury and Dursley, via Wotton-under-Edge and North Nibley. The 201, run by Mike's Travel between Gloucester and Thornbury, includes the same stops. *(cont'd on p144)*

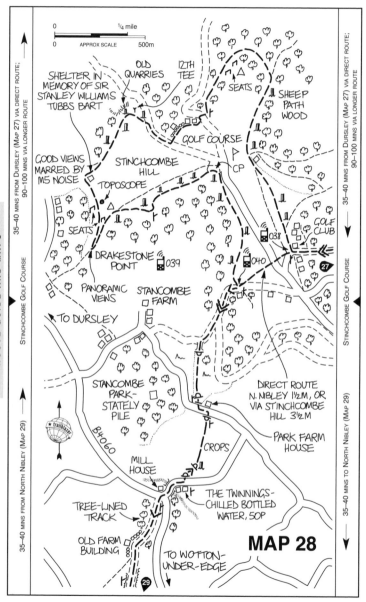

0   ¼ mile
0   APPROX SCALE   500m

SHELTER IN MEMORY OF SIR STANLEY WILLIAMS TUBBS BART

OLD QUARRIES

12TH TEE

SEATS

SHEEP PATH WOOD

GOLF COURSE

CP

GOOD VIEWS MARRED BY M5 NOISE

STINCHCOMBE HILL

TOPOSCOPE

GOLF CLUB

SEATS

☐038

27

DRAKESTONE POINT

☐039

☐040

PANORAMIC VIEWS

STANCOMBE FARM

TO DURSLEY

STANCOMBE PARK- STATELY PILE

B4060

DIRECT ROUTE N. NIBLEY 1½M, OR VIA STINCHCOMBE HILL 3½M

PARK FARM HOUSE

CROPS

MILL HOUSE

TREE-LINED TRACK

THE TWINNINGS- CHILLED BOTTLED WATER, 50P

OLD FARM BUILDING

TO WOTTON-UNDER-EDGE

MAP 28

29

★ trailblazer

35-40 MINS FROM DURSLEY (MAP 27) VIA DIRECT ROUTE; 90-100 MINS VIA LONGER ROUTE

STINCHCOMBE GOLF COURSE

35-40 MINS FROM NORTH NIBLEY (MAP 29)

35-40 MINS FROM DURSLEY (MAP 27) VIA DIRECT ROUTE; 90-100 MINS VIA LONGER ROUTE

STINCHCOMBE GOLF COURSE

35-40 MINS TO NORTH NIBLEY (MAP 29)

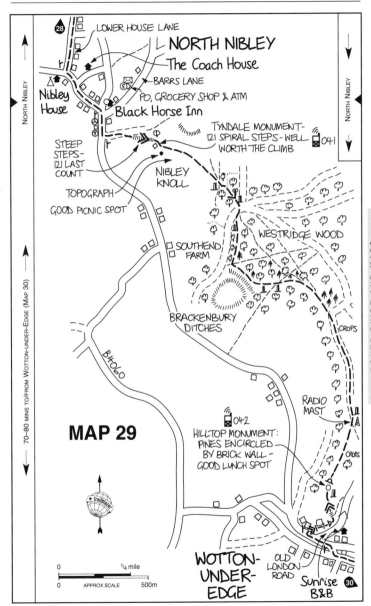

MAP 29

LOWER HOUSE LANE

NORTH NIBLEY

The Coach House

BARRS LANE

PO, GROCERY SHOP & ATM

Black Horse Inn

Nibley House

TYNDALE MONUMENT-
121 SPIRAL STEPS - WELL
WORTH THE CLIMB

041

STEEP
STEPS -
121 LAST
COUNT

NIBLEY
KNOLL

TOPOGRAPH

GOOD PICNIC SPOT

SOUTHEND
FARM

WESTRIDGE WOOD

BRACKENBURY
DITCHES

CROPS

B4060

RADIO
MAST

042

HILLTOP MONUMENT:
PINES ENCIRCLED
BY BRICK WALL -
GOOD LUNCH SPOT

CROPS

trailblazer

0   1/4 mile

0   APPROX SCALE   500m

**WOTTON-
UNDER-
EDGE**

OLD
LONDON
ROAD

Sunrise
B&B

NORTH NIBLEY

70–80 MINS TO/FROM WOTTON-UNDER-EDGE (MAP 30)

NORTH NIBLEY

ROUTE GUIDE AND MAPS

(cont'd from p141) For details, see the public transport map and table, p46.

This is one place where **campers** don't have to trudge far for the night, as there's a campsite at *Nibley House* (☎ 01453-543108, 🖳 johneeley@btconnect.com, 🖳 www.nibleyhouse.co.uk; 2T or F, both en suite; 🐾 £5), just a few yards off the trail towards St Martin's Church. It's a working farm, where campers pay £5 a head, with an outside toilet and shower, and plenty of space to explore. Those with delusions of grandeur might prefer to lord it over the campers in the Georgian manor house itself, a family home set in extensive flower gardens: the rooms are large (one room can sleep up to four people and the other three) and cost £40 per person sharing for **B&B**, or £45 for single occupancy. For £7 a head, they'll even do breakfast for campers who'd like a taste of the good life for themselves.

In the other direction, right on the route, *The Coach House* (☎ 01453-456754, 🖳 kirsten_marlow@hotmail.co .uk; 2D en suite; 🛒; 🐾) is a self-contained house with kitchen, lounge and dining room, which is available for walkers at £80 for a double room. A substantial continental breakfast can be organised for £7.50 a head.

The village pub, the *Black Horse Inn* (☎ 01453-543777, 🖳 www.blackhorse northnibley.co.uk, Barrs Lane; 3D/1F; WI-FI; 🐾 £10), is on the trail too, and offers en suite B&B accommodation for £70 a night double (£50 single occupancy), as well as a restaurant and bar. The pub is open for **food**, too (Tue-Fri noon-2pm & 6-9pm, Sat noon-3pm, Sun noon-4.45pm).

After the steep climb through the woods from North Nibley, the additional ascent of the stone **Tyndale Monument** (entry 50p) on Nibley Knoll may seem 121 steps too far. It's worth it, though, for some splendid views in every direction. The monument was erected in 1866 to the memory of Sir William Tyndale, who in defiance of the authorities translated the New Testament into English. He was burnt at the stake for heresy in 1536.

WOTTON-UNDER-EDGE
MAP 30a, p147

It's a friendly place, Wotton-under-Edge, and very community spirited. Almost everything happens on the appropriately named Long St, which morphs from High St, extending downhill the length of the town. The Cotswold Way runs along this street, passing most of the shops and many pubs and cafés, as well as two of three sets of **almshouses**. One of these, on Church St, incorporates a small chapel where visitors are welcome.

The trail continues past the 13th-century parish church of **St Mary the Virgin** before rejoining open countryside. More visible than any of these from above the town is the old **Tabernacle Church**, now an auction room.

East of the town, the Cotswold Way passes through the grounds of **Newark Park** (see Map 30; ☎ 01453-842644, 🖳 www.national trust.org; Mar-Oct, Wed, Thu, Sat, Sun & bank holidays, 11am-5pm, last entry 4.30pm; £6.80), with almost direct footpath access from the Cotswold Way. Built as a Tudor hunting lodge, it has commanding views to the south-west from its ridge-top location. Following a chequered history, during which it was converted to a fashionable house, it was finally abandoned during the war years, and was given to the National Trust in 1949. Since then, both house and garden have been restored and the place is once again inhabited, with an eclectic collection of art on view to the public.

Transport

The 86 **bus**, operated by Wessex Connect, connects Wotton-under-Edge with Kingswood via Alderley, Hillesley and Hawkesbury Upton. There is also First's 311 service to Thornbury, and Stagecoach's 40 service to Stroud. For details, see the public transport map and table, p46.

For **taxis**, try A1's Taxis (☎ 01453-519354) or Coombe Valley Taxis (☎ 01453-845071).

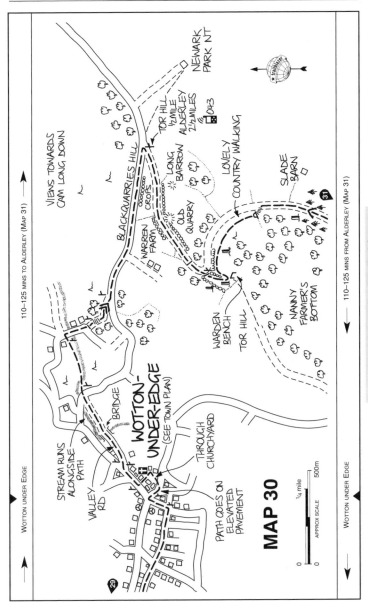

MAP 30

VIEWS TOWARDS CAM LONG DOWN

BLACKQUARRIES HILL

NEWARK PARK NT

TOR HILL ½ MILE
ALDERLEY 2½ MILES

LONG BARROW

WARREN FARM CROPS

OLD QUARRY

LOVELY COUNTRY WALKING

SLADE BARN

31

WARDEN BENCH

TOR HILL

NANNY FARMER'S BOTTOM

STREAM RUNS ALONGSIDE PATH

BRIDGE

VALLEY RD

WOTTON-UNDER-EDGE
(SEE TOWN PLAN)

THROUGH CHURCHYARD

PATH GOES ON ELEVATED PAVEMENT

29

¼ mile
APPROX SCALE
500m

110–125 MINS TO ALDERLEY (MAP 31)

110–125 MINS FROM ALDERLEY (MAP 31)

WOTTON UNDER EDGE

WOTTON UNDER EDGE

ROUTE GUIDE AND MAPS

Services

For **tourist information** find your way to the purpose-built Heritage Centre (☎ 01453-521541, 🖳 www.wottonheritage .com; all year Tue-Fri 10am-1pm, summer 2-5pm, winter 2-4pm, Sat 10am-1pm), tucked away behind Long St on The Chipping. It's privately run, and has good displays relating to the town's history.

Of the **banks**, NatWest has a branch on the High St, while Barclays and Lloyds TSB (both with ATMs) are close together on Long St. The **post office** is almost opposite, as is a **bookshop**, the Cotswold Book Room. If your **camera** is in need of repair, Don Clark Camera Repairs (☎ 01453-842102), also on Long St, may be able to help.

The town's main **supermarket**, the Co-op (Mon-Sat 7am-10pm, Sun 10am-4pm), is some way down Long St, with Tesco Express (daily 7am-10pm) just a few yards further on. More personal are the Relish Deli (with soup, pasties, pizza and home-made cakes – and space to eat in) and Parson's **bakery**, with another bakery further down

the road, and a second deli in the offing. A **farmers' market** is held at 9am-1pm on the first Saturday of each month, except January, in the Town Hall on Market St.

The **pharmacy**, a branch of Lloyds, is here, too, with two **medical surgeries** relatively close by: Chipping Surgery (☎ 01453-842214) on Symn Lane, and Culverhay (☎ 01453-843252) on Culverhay. There are public **toilets** south of Long St on Rope Walk, and on Old Town.

The town scores on the entertainment stakes, all run by volunteers. The Electric Picture House **cinema** (☎ 01453-844401, 🖳 www.wottoneph.co.uk) on Market St has 11 screenings a week. Close to the car park, **Under the Edge Arts** (🖳 www.utea .org.uk), a community venture in Chipping Hall hosts regular displays and a programme of events throughout the year. There's even a week-long Arts Festival (see p15) every year at the end of April/early May.

If you still have energy at the end of a day's walking, you could always check out the open-air **swimming pool** on Symn Lane

WOTTON-UNDER-EDGE

Where to stay
3 Elmside House
9 Orchard House
16 Swan Hotel
33 Carlton House
38 Old Town Mill

Where to eat and drink
5 Bunter's Café
6 Wotton British Takeaway
7 Royal Oak
16 The Swan Hotel
17 The Star
18 Pizza Planet
19 Reg's Kebab, Chicken & Pizza
20 McQuigg's
21 Singing Teapot
35 Hong Kong Kitchen
36 India Palace

Other
1 Auction Rooms (formerly Tabernacle Church)
2 Almshouses
4 Fuel station
8 NatWest Bank
10 Chipping Surgery
11 Swimming pool

Other (cont'd)
12 Under the Edge Arts
13 Heritage Centre & Tourist Information
14 Cinema
15 Town Hall
22 Lloyds Pharmacy
23 Parson's Bakery
24 Co-op
25 Relish Deli
26 Tesco Express
27 Cotswold Book Room
28 Lloyds TSB & ATM
29 Barclays & ATM
30 Proposed new deli
31 Don Clark Camera Repairs
32 Post Office
34 Almshouses & chapel
37 War memorial
39 Culverhay Surgery
40 Almshouses

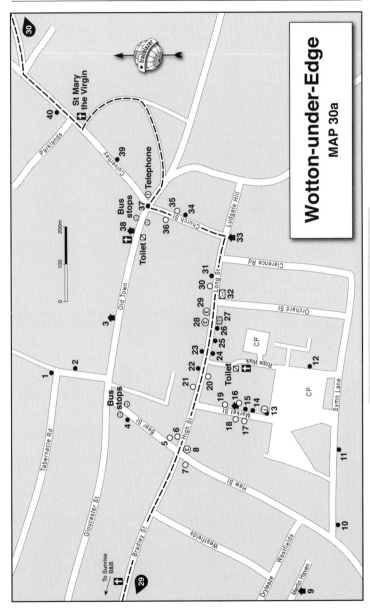

Wotton-under-Edge
MAP 30a

(🖥 www.wottonpool.co.uk; May-mid Sep, Mon-Fri 3-4.30pm & 6.30-8pm, Sat/Sun 2-4pm) – with slightly different hours in school holidays).

Where to stay

B&B in Wotton comes in several guises. That rarity along the Cotswold Way, **budget** accommodation, appears at *Old Town Mill* (☎ 01453-842208, 🖥 www.oldtownmill.co.uk; 1D/1F sharing bathroom; WI-FI), on Old Town. Here, £25 per person will secure **B&B**, to include a continental breakfast. If you're travelling in a group, and have your own bedding and towels, they'll put extra beds in the larger room for £15 per person, or £19 to include breakfast.

Also on Old Town, but further up the hill, is *Elmside House* (☎ 01453-843446, mob ☎ 07748 682934; 1S/1T/1D; 🐾) at 41 Old Town, where B&B is £70 for the twin room with private facilities or the en suite double, and £40 for the single en suite.

At the other end of the spectrum, how about staying in Jacobean splendour? At the bottom of Long St, right next to the Cotswold Way signpost, *Carlton House* (☎ 01453-844183, 🖥 www.carltonhouse-bedandbreakfast.co.uk; 1S/2D/1F all en suite; 📶; WI-FI) offers just that. A fully restored 17th-century home, it does B&B at £70-80, or £65-75 for single occupancy. At breakfast, focusing on local produce, you might even be served smoked salmon with scrambled egg.

To the west, set back off the Old London Rd, *Sunrise House* (Map 29; ☎ 01453-842322; 1T/1D/1T or F; 📶; 🐾 £4) has an en suite family room costing £38 per person for two people, £29 for three, or £45 single occupancy. Their double and twin rooms share a bathroom, with rates at £31 per person, or £34-35 if only one of the rooms is booked.

Also in this direction is *Orchard House* (☎ 01453-842613, 🖥 jchaines@tiscali.co.uk; 1T/1D; 📶; WI-FI), on Merlin Haven, whose rooms share a bathroom and cost £53 for B&B in the double, or £33 per person in the twin. It can be reached by following Westfields into Dryleaze, then turning left and left again into Merlin Haven.

Back in town, the helpful and welcoming *Swan Hotel* (☎ 01453-843004, 🖥 www.swanhotelwotton.co.uk; 2S/2T/4D; WI-FI; 🐾) on Market St has attractive rooms, many with wooden beams, and all en suite except the singles, which share a bathroom; two of the rooms can be linked for a family or group. B&B rates are £75-85 for two sharing, £50-55 single, £75-85 for two, £100 for three, and £120 for four.

Where to eat and drink

Cafés and takeaways dominate the foody outlets in Wotton-under-Edge, but there are **pubs** too. Of these, *The Star* (☎ 01453-844651; Mon-Fri noon-2pm) offers a daily homemade special such as curry, chilli or pasta for £3.95, alongside the normal pub basics. There's bar food and pastries at the *Swan Hotel* (see above; Mon-Fri noon-3pm, Mon-Thu 5.30-9pm, Fri 5.30-9.30pm, Sat noon-9.30pm, Sun noon-8pm), but for a more formal affair, try their à la carte restaurant, where duck breast with fondant potato cherry and Cointreau sauce (£13.95) is a popular choice. At the time of writing, the *Royal Oak* on Haw St was not serving food, but with the possibility of new management, this could change.

Away from the pubs, Long St will serve you well. Among its offerings, *McQuigg's* (☎ 01453-844108; Mon-Fri 9am-5pm term time, or from 10am in holidays, Sat 10am-4pm) is clearly a local social hub, serving salads, pasta and specials until 2pm every day, after which there's tea, coffee and cakes. On the other side of the road, the *Singing Teapot* (mob ☎ 07769-267455; Mon-Sat 9.30am-4pm) offers tea, cakes and light lunches in a genuinely welcoming environment. If you're tempted by a cooked breakfast, try *Bunter's Café* (☎ 01453-845557; Mon-Wed 7.30-2.30pm, Thu-Fri 7.30-3.30, Sat 8.30-3.30pm), just off Long St, where the full English will set you back just £4.95. And if you're passing through on a Sunday between April and October, it's worth checking at the **Town Hall** on Market St where afternoon tea is usually served 2.30-5pm by one of the local organisations.

Ethnic cuisine comes from the *India*

Palace (☎ 01453-521171; Sun-Thu 5.30-11.30pm, Fri & Sat 5.30pm-midnight), Church St, which has a restaurant as well as a takeaway service, and the nearby *Hong Kong Kitchen* (☎ 01453-843840; Tue-Thu 5.30-10.15pm, Fri & Sat 5-10.15pm, Sun 6-9.45pm), which is takeaway only. Closer to home, foodwise, is *Wotton British Take-away* (☎ 01453-845521; Mon-Sat 11.30am-2pm & 5-10pm) on High St for fish, chicken and pies, or perhaps *Pizza Planet* (☎ 01453-843377; Mon-Sat 4.30-11pm, Sun 4.30-10.30pm) on Market St. *Reg's Kebab, Chicken & Pizza* (☎ 01453-521353; Mon-Thu noon-11pm, Fri-Sat noon-midnight, Sun 3pm-midnight) is also here.

WOTTON-UNDER-EDGE TO OLD SODBURY   MAPS 30-35

This **12¼-mile (19.6km)** section will take about **6-7 hours**, passing through open, rolling fields interspersed with the occasional tract of woodland, and a number of small villages with attractive stone churches. Of these, one of the most intriguing, primarily for its cubed yews, is **St Mary the Virgin** at Hawkesbury, but it's a long downhill detour off the Cotswold Way. Similarly, tantalising glimpses of **Horton Court** (see p152) among the trees might tempt the walker to tackle the very steep path for closer inspection, but most will be happy to stick to the trail and the lovely drovers' road south of Hawkesbury. If the walk lacks drama, it certainly makes up for it in nomenclature: who could resist the appeal of a dip that glories in the name of Nanny Farmer's Bottom? And if you find yourself tiring, there's always the prospect of a sandwich or dinner at the Dog Inn in Old Sodbury to act as a spur.

ALDERLEY   MAP 31, p150
There's an air of exclusivity about Alderley, from the timeless solidity of **St Kenelm's Church** to the old stone houses surrounded by well-maintained gardens.

Wessex Connect's 86 **bus** stops in the village; for details, see the public transport map and table, p46.

HILLESLEY   MAP 31, p150
Little more than a cluster of individual stone cottages with a church and a refurbished gastropub, Hillesley is another attractive village around half a mile (1km) from the trail. There's B&B at *Half Acre Cottage* (☎ 01453-844619, 🖳 jane.kendall @hotmail.co.uk; 1S/1D) along the Kingswood Rd, with the double room from £55-60, or a single from £35 to £40.

The local pub, *The Fleece Inn*, had just closed at the time of writing, and a there's now a campaign in motion (🖳 www.thefleeceinnhillesley.com) to buy it for the local community.

LOWER KILCOTT   MAP 32, p151
To most people there's no compelling reason to stop in Lower Kilcott, but a super **B&B** at *Bridge Farm* (☎ 01454-238254, 🖳 bridgefarm@tiscali.co.uk; 1T/2D, shared bathroom, 🖂; WI-FI) is reason enough for walkers. The mixture of Victorian and Thai artefacts reflects the diverse interests of owners Malcolm and Wendy Watchman. It's a friendly, family place, with B&B from £70 for two sharing (£40 for single occupancy). A very good dinner (including the option of a traditional Thai meal cooked by their Thai daughter-in-law) is available from £16, if booked in advance.

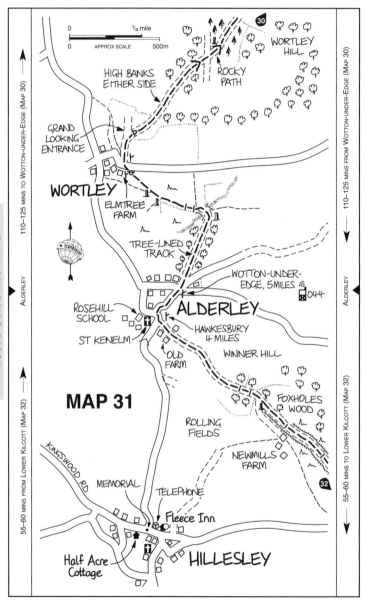

110–125 MINS TO WOTTON-UNDER-EDGE (MAP 30)

110–125 MINS FROM WOTTON-UNDER-EDGE (MAP 30)

ROUTE GUIDE AND MAPS

ALDERLEY

ALDERLEY

55–60 MINS FROM LOWER KILCOTT (MAP 32)

55–60 MINS TO LOWER KILCOTT (MAP 32)

0   ¼ mile

APPROX SCALE   500m

30

WORTLEY HILL

ROCKY PATH

HIGH BANKS
EITHER SIDE

GRAND
LOOKING
ENTRANCE

WORTLEY

ELMTREE
FARM

★ trailblazer

TREE-LINED
TRACK

WOTTON-UNDER-
EDGE, 5MILES   044

ROSEHILL
SCHOOL

ALDERLEY

HAWKESBURY
4 MILES

ST KENELM

OLD
FARM

WINNER HILL

MAP 31

FOXHOLES
WOOD

ROLLING
FIELDS

NEWMILLS
FARM

32

KINGSWOOD RD

MEMORIAL

TELEPHONE

Fleece Inn

Half Acre
Cottage

HILLESLEY

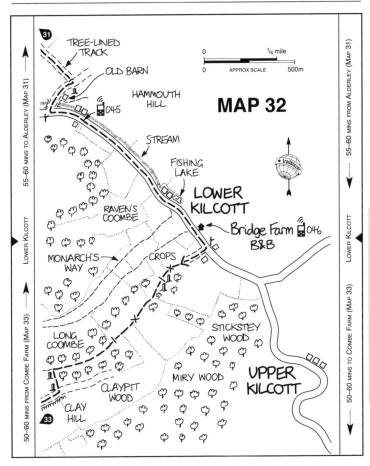

MAP 32

HAWKESBURY UPTON
MAP 33, p153

Is there no end to the attractive villages in this area? This one lies about quarter of a mile (0.4km) off the Cotswold Way, but with a pleasant B&B pretty close and a range of other facilities, it has plenty to offer the walker.

Down a quiet lane just east of the trail, *Coombe Farm* (Map 33; ☎ 01454-238202, 🖳 karen.hasted@lineone.net; 3T en suite;

☛) has compact rooms in a modern annexe at £32 per person B&B (single occupancy £42). One of the rooms has a bath and its own kitchen.

Within half a mile (0.8km) of the farm, the *Beaufort Arms* (Map 33; ☎ 01454-238217, 🖳 www.beaufortarms.com; daily noon-2.30pm & 6.30-9.30pm) is one of two real ale pubs in the village, both listed in the *Good Beer Guide*. It's a friendly place, with scarcely a nod to the 21st century. Standard pub meals are served in portions designed for different appetites; the 'old codger's' cod and chips at £7.50 is enough for all but the most ravenous of walkers. On Sundays, there's a regular roast.

At the far end of the village, about half a mile (0.8km) from the trail, *The Fox Inn* (☎ 01454-238219, 1T/2D/1F, all en suite; ✖; 🐾), has accommodation at £46 for single occupancy, £72 for two people and £78 for three in a family room, including breakfast. The pub, with a garden at the back, serves

food Tue-Fri 4-9pm, and Sat-Sun noon-9pm.

Also up this way is the village **shop** (Mon-Sat 8am-6pm, Sun 8am-12.30pm), with all the basics and a good range of filling pastries. The **post office** is located a short way beyond the pub.

Bus No 86 between Wotton-under-Edge and Kingswood stops here, operated by Wessex Connect. They also run a direct service from Bath to Old Sodbury, the 620, stopping at the Cross Hands on the A46. See the public transport map and table, p46, for details.

HORTON   MAP 34, p154

While the village of Horton is on the Cotswold Way, most walkers will bypass its main attraction, the National Trust property of **Horton Court** (☎ 01225-833977, 🖳 www.nationaltrust.org.uk), which lies at the bottom of a steep footpath off the Cotswold Way (or you could walk back along the road from the village school). For details of limited opening times, you'll need to contact them directly.

It's a rather grand name for the seemingly modest but picturesque property that

sits in a cottage-style garden close to the church of **St James the Elder**. At its heart is a 12th-century Norman hall, all that remains of what may be the oldest rectory in England. Other parts of the building date to Tudor times, with significant expansion and the addition of an Italianate loggia during the 16th century, and further changes in the 1920s.

Wessex Connect's 86 **bus** stops in the village *en route* to Wotton-under-Edge; see public transport table and map, p46.

LITTLE SODBURY   MAP 34, p154

This pretty village is set apart by the hilltop church of St Adeline, offering a perfect vantage point from which to survey the landscape unrolling ahead.

Walkers on the Cotswold Way are welcome to **camp** at *Willowfield* (mob ☎ 07958 620283), the first house on the left along Portway Lane, and about half a mile (0.8km) west of the trail. Facilities are limited to cold water and a long-drop toilet, but the cost, £7.50 per person, includes firewood, and for an extra £5 they'll lend you a two-man tent with roll mats and basic cooking equipment. This, and their offer (with advance notice) to buy in the basics for an evening meal or breakfast, means that all

you need to carry is a sleeping bag. Those who don't want to cook can borrow bikes to cycle to the nearest pub for a meal.

For **B&B**, try *New Crosshands Farm* (☎ 01454-316366, www.newcrosshands farm.co.uk; 1T/ private shower/2D en suite ✖), whose versatile accommodation also includes a self-contained apartment, with a double and a twin room sharing a bathroom and kitchen, that can be booked on a B&B basis during the summer months. You'll pay £35 per person per night; a packed lunch (£3.50-5) is available with advance notice; and in the evening they'll drive walkers to the Cross Hands (see p156) for dinner; they can then walk back or get a taxi.

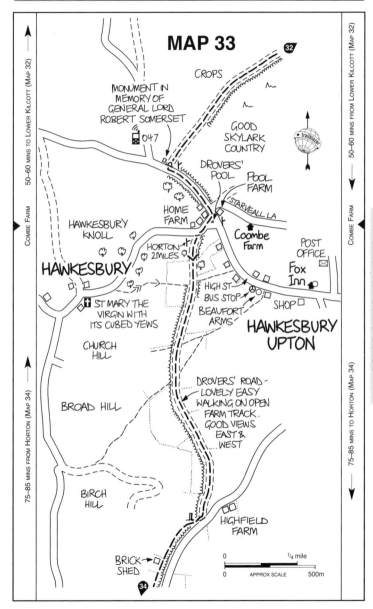

MAP 33

32

CROPS

MONUMENT IN
MEMORY OF
GENERAL LORD
ROBERT SOMERSET

☎ 047

GOOD
SKYLARK
COUNTRY

trailblazer

DROVERS'
POOL

POOL
FARM

STARVEALL LA

HOME
FARM

Coombe
Farm

POST
OFFICE ✉

HAWKESBURY
KNOLL

HORTON
2 MILES

Fox
Inn

HAWKESBURY

HIGH ST
BUS STOP

SHOP

BEAUFORT
ARMS

HAWKESBURY
UPTON

✝ ST MARY THE
VIRGIN WITH
ITS CUBED YEWS

CHURCH
HILL

DROVERS' ROAD -
LOVELY EASY
WALKING ON OPEN
FARM TRACK.
GOOD VIEWS
EAST &
WEST

BROAD HILL

BIRCH
HILL

HIGHFIELD
FARM

BRICK
SHED

0   ¹/₄ mile

0   500m
APPROX SCALE

34

◄ COMBE FARM

50-60 MINS TO LOWER KILCOTT (MAP 32)

75-85 MINS FROM HORTON (MAP 34)

50-60 MINS FROM LOWER KILCOTT (MAP 32)

COMBE FARM ►

75-85 MINS TO HORTON (MAP 34)

ROUTE GUIDE AND MAPS

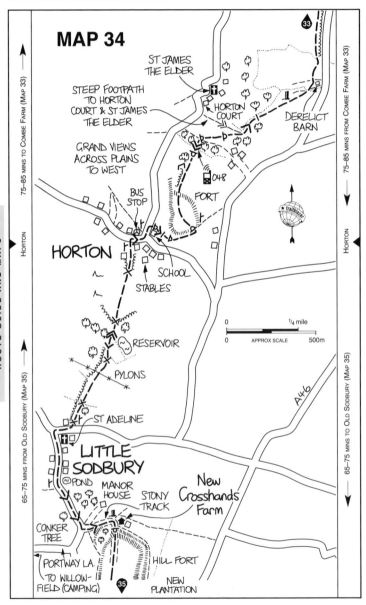

MAP 34

75-85 MINS TO COMBE FARM (MAP 33) ──➤

HORTON ──➤

65-75 MINS FROM OLD SODBURY (MAP 35) ──➤

75-85 MINS FROM COMBE FARM (MAP 33) ──➤

HORTON

65-75 MINS TO OLD SODBURY (MAP 35) ──➤

33

ST JAMES
THE ELDER

STEEP FOOTPATH
TO HORTON
COURT & ST JAMES
THE ELDER

HORTON
COURT

DERELICT
BARN

GRAND VIEWS
ACROSS PLAINS
TO WEST

☐ 048

FORT

BUS
STOP

★ trailblazer

HORTON

SCHOOL

STABLES

RESERVOIR

PYLONS

0   ¼ mile
0   APPROX SCALE   500m

A46

ST ADELINE

LITTLE
SODBURY

POND

MANOR
HOUSE

STONY
TRACK

New
Crosshands
Farm

CONKER
TREE

PORTWAY LA.
TO WILLOW-
FIELD (CAMPING)

35

HILL FORT

NEW
PLANTATION

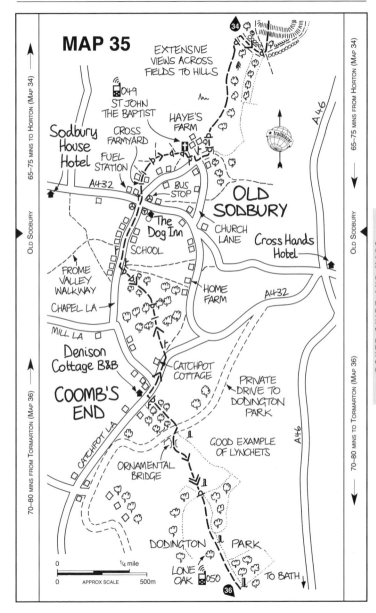

OLD SODBURY   MAP 35, p155

The trail passes through the grounds of the beautiful **St John the Baptist Church**, up on the hill, before dropping down to the village itself. In the shadow of its larger neighbour to the west, Chipping Sodbury, the village nevertheless has a lot to recommend it to the walker.

Wessex Connect's No 620 **bus** connects Bath with Old Sodbury, stopping at the Cross Hands on the A46. Andybus's No 41 also stops there between Malmesbury, Tormarton and Yate. See the public transport map and table, p46, for details.

For **taxis**, try Grab-a-Cab (☎ 01454-313883, 🖳 www.grab-a-cab-online.co.uk) in Chipping Sodbury.

In the centre of the village, and right on the trail, the popular *Dog Inn* (☎ 01454-312006, 🖳 www.the-dog-inn.co.uk; 1S/ 4T/ 4D/2F; ✒; 🐾) offers a welcome respite. **B&B** in a twin or double room (three with bath) costs £80 en suite or £60 sharing a bathroom, and the family room is £90 for three adults. Single walkers pay £25 sharing a bathroom, or £57.50 for single occupancy of a larger room. In the bar, real ales and a broad menu (daily noon-2.30pm & 6-9pm) are the order of the day. Vegetarians won't go hungry – and with a good choice of curries as well as steaks, plenty of fresh fish, pasta and jacket potatoes, nor will anyone else. For £30, a hungry twosome could even tuck into a paella.

Some 300 yards (270m) from the trail is the more upmarket *Sodbury House Hotel* (☎ 01454-312847, 🖳 www.sodbury house.co.uk; 9D/6S, all en suite; ✒ in 4D; WI-FI), which offers B&B in a double for £88 and £60 for a single. In the evening, most guests gravitate towards The Dog Inn for dinner or – in the other direction – The Bell.

Rather over half a mile (1km) in the other direction, on the main A46, the *Cross Hands Hotel* (☎ 01454-313000, www.old-englishinns.co.uk/old-sodbury; 4S/2T/14D/ 1F rooms, all en suite; ✒; WI-FI; 🐾) is just by the bus stop. Prices are variable, but average £59 single, and £79-89 for a twin or double – some of which have baths. They also have a restaurant (daily noon-10pm).

The **fuel station** (closed Sun) near the pub sells drinks and snacks, a boon now that the shop/post office up the road has closed.

OLD SODBURY TO COLD ASHTON   MAPS 35-39

Despite being split in half by the M4, this **8¹/₂-mile (13.7km, 4¹/₄-4³/₄hrs)** part of the walk has much to recommend it. In place of many (but not all!) of the ups and downs further north are broad expanses of farmland, an unexpectedly rewarding walk across **Dodington Park**, and the glimpsed glory of **Dyrham Park** (see p158), which most certainly merits a visit.

COOMB'S END   MAP 35, p155

B&Bs don't come much more conveniently located than the white-washed *Denison Cottage* (☎ 01454-311510; 1T; 🐾), which is right on the path. Formerly home to the butler at Dodington Park, it's an attractive place with a two-acre walled garden. A Scandinavian cabin in the garden provides accommodation for guests, who have access to a private bathroom in the house. B&B costs £65 (£40 for single occupancy).

TORMARTON   MAP 36

In spite of its proximity to the busy M4, the village of Tormarton remains relatively unscathed by noise or even by the 21st century, so it's an unexpectedly good place to stop for the night. There's no longer a shop in the village, but there's a welcoming hotel, a pub with rooms, a choice of B&Bs, and even a place to camp.

The village is served by the 41 **bus**, run by Andybus between Malmesbury and Yate, which also stops at Old Sodbury; see the public transport map and table, p46.

Rather unexpectedly, **campers** can pitch a tent free of charge at *The Compass Inn* (☎ 01454-218242, 🖳 www.compass inn.co.uk; 7T/13D/6F; ☕; WI-FI; 🐕 £4.50) – though donations to their charity box are welcome. There are no outdoor facilities,

but when the inn is open you can use the hotel's toilets, for which you'll be given a key. The hotel itself is something of a rabbit warren, independently owned but marketed under the Best Western umbrella, and with extensive gardens. It's about a quarter of a mile (0.4km) from the village, quite close to the motorway and within sight of the A46, so noise is a factor, but it's not too bad. Indoors you'll find en suite **rooms**

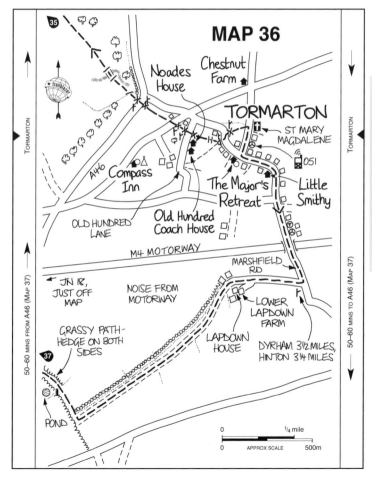

MAP 36

Noades House

Chestnut Farm

TORMARTON

ST MARY MAGDALENE

Compass Inn

The Major's Retreat

Little Smithy

OLD HUNDRED LANE

Old Hundred Coach House

M4 MOTORWAY

MARSHFIELD RD

JN 18, JUST OFF MAP

NOISE FROM MOTORWAY

LOWER LAPDOWN FARM

GRASSY PATH – HEDGE ON BOTH SIDES

LAPDOWN HOUSE

DYRHAM 3½ MILES, HINTON 3¼ MILES

POND

0   ¼ mile

0   500m

APPROX SCALE

TORMARTON

TORMARTON

50-60 MINS FROM A46 (MAP 37)

50-60 MINS TO A46 (MAP 37)

ROUTE GUIDE AND MAPS

with all the accoutrements of a business hotel, costing £77.50-87.50 plus breakfast at £3.95-9.95. Service is formal but friendly and the **food** (daily 7am-9.30pm in the bar, restaurant or garden) is a pleasant surprise; good sandwiches at lunchtime, from £4.95, come up with a proper salad.

With the Cotswold Way at the bottom of the garden, *Noades House* (☎ 01454-218278, ☐ www.noadesstudio.co.uk; 1T/1D; ☛; WI-FI). on the quiet Old Hundred Lane is exceptionally well placed. Rates for both the en suite twin and the double with a private bathroom are £70, or £40-45 for single occupancy. Right next door, *Old Hundred Coach House* (☎ 01454-218420, ☐ deedaveb@yahoo.co.uk; 1T, D or F, shared bathroom; ☛; WI-FI; ☙) charges £25 for B&B. A relative newcomer, *Little Smithy* (☎ 01454-218412, ☐ www.little smithy.com; 1T/1D en suite; ☛) is a stone's throw from the pub, and charges £75 for two sharing, or £60 single. Added perks are a guest lounge, drying facilities and the possibility of a packed lunch (£5).

In the village centre, the *Major's Retreat* (☎ 01454-218263; 3T/1F sleeps up to 4; ☙) offers basic but functional B&B rooms at £45 for a twin, £60 for the family room, and £35 for single occupancy; all the rooms have shower facilities. No-nonsense **pub grub** (daily noon-2pm & 7-9pm), is excellent value, from £2.95 for a doorstep sandwich. Real ales may include Pig's Ear from Uley (see p22) and Mole Catch from Mole's Brewery.

Up the road and over the crossroads, the rooms at *Chestnut Farm* (☎ 01454-218563, ☐ www.chestnut-farm.co.uk; 1T/4D/cottage sleeping 4; all en suite; WI-FI; ☙) are grouped together in a converted barn, or in a separate cottage. You'll pay £55 per room here (£40 single occupancy), with breakfast taken in the main house.

SOUTH OF THE M4　　　MAP 37

South of Tormarton, on the main A46 about 500m from the trail, *The Crown* (☎ 01225-891166, ☐ www.ohhcompany.co.uk/the_crown; daily noon-9.30pm) offers bar meals and sandwiches until 6pm, and an à la carte menu in the evening. On the opposite corner, at Marshfield **Bakery** (Mon-Fri 8am-5pm, Sat 10am-4pm), biscuits and cakes are sold alongside sandwiches and pasties to present the perfect packed lunch.

❑ **Dyrham Park**　　　　　　　　　　　　　　**Map 37 & Map 38 p160**
As the Cotswold Way wends through the tiny village of Dyrham, it passes the ornamental gates of Dyrham Park (☎ 0117-937 2501, ☐ www.nationaltrust.org.uk; park daily 10am-5pm, garden mid Feb-Jun & Sep-Oct Fri-Tue 10am-5pm, Jul-Aug daily 10am-5pm, Nov-mid Dec Sat-Sun 10am-4pm, house mid Mar-Jun & Sep-Oct Fri-Tue 11am-5pm, Jul-Aug daily 11am-5pm, last entry 1hr before closing; admission house, garden & park £11.90, garden & park only £4.80, park only £3, NT members free), affording a splendid vista up the long drive to the house and church. It's a tantalising view, and if you're not pushed for time it's well worth exploring further.

Familiar to many film buffs as the set location for *Remains of the Day*, the Baroque-style house nestling at the bottom of a steep valley was built at the end of the 17th century. A strong Dutch influence pervades the original décor and furnishings, and the Victorian kitchens give an indication of how life must have been for those below stairs. The church alongside, however, is medieval, and the estate itself dates back to Saxon times. Visitors can explore both the house and the formal gardens, as well as 274 acres (110 hectares) of rolling parkland.

Note that the National Trust bus between Bath and Dyrham Park is no longer operating.

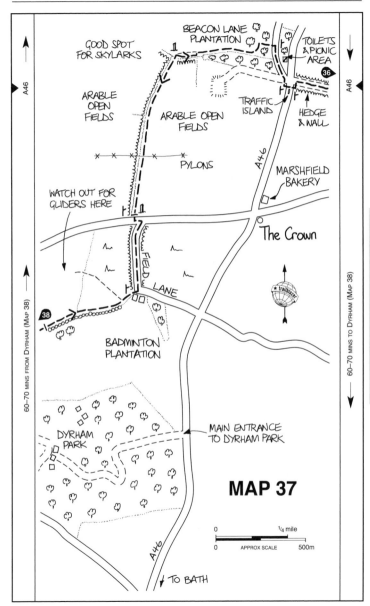

BEACON LANE PLANTATION

GOOD SPOT FOR SKYLARKS

TOILETS & PICNIC AREA

36

ARABLE OPEN FIELDS

ARABLE OPEN FIELDS

TRAFFIC ISLAND

HEDGE & WALL

× × × × ×
PYLONS

A46

MARSHFIELD BAKERY

WATCH OUT FOR GLIDERS HERE

The Crown

FIELD LANE

38

BADMINTON PLANTATION

60–70 MINS FROM DYRHAM (MAP 38)

60–70 MINS TO DYRHAM (MAP 38)

A46

A46

★ trailblazer

DYRHAM PARK

MAIN ENTRANCE TO DYRHAM PARK

MAP 37

0   ¼ mile
0   APPROX SCALE   500m

A46

↙ TO BATH

ROUTE GUIDE AND MAPS

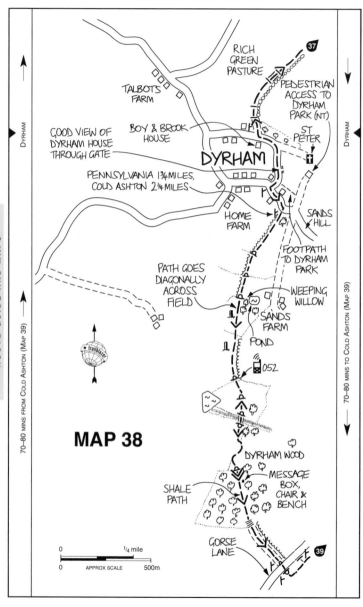

RICH GREEN PASTURE

37

PEDESTRIAN ACCESS TO DYRHAM PARK (NT)

TALBOTS FARM

ST PETER

GOOD VIEW OF DYRHAM HOUSE THROUGH GATE

BOY & BROOK HOUSE

DYRHAM

DYRHAM

DYRHAM

PENNSYLVANIA 1¾ MILES, COLD ASHTON 2¼ MILES

SANDS HILL

HOME FARM

FOOTPATH TO DYRHAM PARK

PATH GOES DIAGONALLY ACROSS FIELD

WEEPING WILLOW

SANDS FARM

POND

052

trailblazer

MAP 38

DYRHAM WOOD

MESSAGE BOX, CHAIR & BENCH

SHALE PATH

GORSE LANE

39

70–80 MINS FROM COLD ASHTON (MAP 39)

70–80 MINS TO COLD ASHTON (MAP 39)

0   ¼ mile

0   APPROX SCALE   500m

PENNSYLVANIA   MAP 39, p162

Right on the A46, this isn't the quietest of locations and the only pub has closed, but there is a good **B&B** on the trail: *Old Swan Cottage* (☎ 01225-891419, 🖥 www.old-swan-cottage.co.uk; 1S or D/1T/1F, all en suite). The welcome is friendly and rooms – at £50 for a small double (£40 single), £65 for a twin or family room (with a double and a single bed), or £75 for three – are modern and well appointed. Ideally walkers should time their arrival for after 3pm,

except by special arrangement. Those in search of an evening meal have a half-mile (0.8km) walk across the fields to Folly End Farm (see Cold Ashton, below); if the weather is inclement or it's dark, the owners may be able to give guests a lift. Alternatively you could buy a snack from the adjacent **fuel station** (daily 6am-10pm) and put your feet up in front of the TV in your room.

COLD ASHTON   MAP 39, p162

With its location between the busy A420 and the even busier A46, Cold Ashton might seem to be blighted, but the reality is entirely different. Most of the village lies along a quiet lane to the south, beyond the church, and its cluster of small stone houses stands peacefully against a backdrop of rolling fields.

With the village pub, the White Hart, closed at the time of writing, the neighbouring *Folly End Farm* (☎ 01225-891849, 🖥 winetoyou@live.co.uk, Mon-Fri 8am-4pm, Sat & Sun 9am-5pm) has come to the rescue. Already open daily for breakfast, lunch, tea and home-made cakes, owner Sarah Parsons now provides homely evening meals by prior arrangement for those staying at local B&Bs. The café is licensed, and as an added bonus, Sarah will drive walkers back to their accommodation after an evening meal. **Campers** don't miss out, either; you can pitch a tent here for £3.50 with access to cold water and an outside toilet.

Without doubt the best-placed **B&B** in the area is the stone-built *Laburnum Cottage* (☎ 01225-891669, 🖥 www.laburnumcottage.info; 1T/1D; 🛏; WI-FI; 🐾), in a peaceful setting opposite the church, yet only a short walk to the main road for an evening meal. Rooms here are £60 for the double with private bathroom (and bath), or

£65 for the en suite twin; for single occupancy, expect to pay £43-45.

Outside the village, two further B&Bs lie about half a mile (1km) from the trail, and both benefit from the evening meal option at Folly End Farm. To the south, right on the busy A46 but surprisingly well insulated from the traffic that thunders past, *Whiteways* (off Map 39; ☎ 01225-891333; 2D/2F all en suite; 🛏; WI-FI; 🐾) has two very big and well-equipped family rooms with baths in a purpose-built annexe and two in the main house. B&B is £70 for two people, £85 for three, and £45 for single occupancy. To the west, close to Freezing Hill on the opposite side of the A46, *Toghill House Farm* (Map 40; ☎ 01225-891261, 🖥 www.toghillhousefarm.co.uk; 3T/6D/3F, all en suite; 🛏; WI-FI; 🐾) is set up for B&B at £88 for a double or twin (2 twins have showers, not baths), and £95 for three in a family room. To get there from the Cotswold Way, take the footpath that leads off Greenway Lane just north of the nursery, and follow this to Toghill Barn Farm; from there, turn left onto the A420 to the junction, then left again; the farm is 100m further on the right.

Faresaver's No 79 **bus** to Bath stops outside the (closed) pub on the A420; for details, see the public transport table and map, p46.

ROUTE GUIDE AND MAPS

Symbols used in text 🐾 Dogs allowed with prior notice   🛏 Bathtub in some rooms

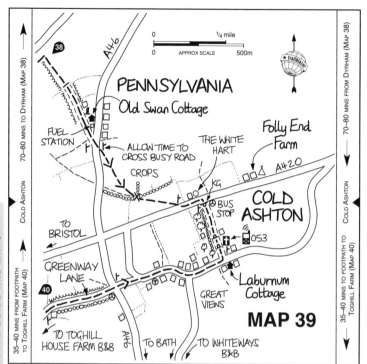

MAP 39

❑ Battle of Lansdown   Map 40 & Map 41, pp164-5

If it were not for the signboards and the monument to Sir Bevil Grenville, the walker on the Cotswold Way might cross the field at the top of Freezing Hill without a second glance. Yet little has changed since the night of 5 July 1643 when the final stages of the Battle of Lansdown were played out between two almost equally matched armies of the Royalists and the Parliamentarians.

    In command of the opposing forces were two friends of long standing: Sir William Waller in charge of the Parliamentarian defence of Bath against a Royalist attack under Sir Ralph Hopton. It was a bloody affair, with 'legs and arms flying all over the place', during which the Royalist Grenville was mortally wounded, having led the Cornish infantry in the charge up Lansdown Hill. While the battle itself was indecisive, casualties were severe. The Parliamentarians withdrew under cover of darkness, and the Royalists were thwarted in their pursuit of capturing Bath and moving on to the richer prize of Bristol.

COLD ASHTON TO BATH   MAPS 39-43

After Cold Ashton comes the final **10-mile (16km, 5-5³/₄hrs)** stretch towards
Bath. Leaving behind the busy A46, the Cotswold Way returns to rolling hills
dotted with cattle and sheep, the noise of traffic replaced with birdsong. It's a
gradual climb to the top of Lansdown Hill, where the trail crosses the very field
where the **Battle of Lansdown** (see box opposite) took place in 1643. The area
is clearly demarcated with orange 'flags' and informative signboards, as well as
a memorial; it doesn't take much to conjure up the chaos that must have ensued
that summer evening. As you pass Bath racecourse, do make time to stop at
Prospect Stile (now a kissing gate!), which at 230m (755ft) affords superb
views across Bath (albeit marred by the gasworks), and over the Severn estuary.
The last couple of miles of the trail beyond **Weston** see some unexpected ups
and downs as the route twists to make the most of open terrain, before the final
descent past Lansdown Crescent to the grandeur of Bath Abbey.

If you'd rather stay on the downward slope, you could cut across the golf
course to Lansdown Road and follow this straight into Bath, taking in
Beckford's Tower as you go (see box below) and ending up with Lansdown
Crescent on your right.

□ **Beckford's Tower**   **off Map 41, p165**
Although the Cotswold Way passes a couple of miles to the west of Beckford's Tower
(☎ 01225-460705, 🖳 www.bath-preservation-trust.org.uk; Easter-Oct, Sat, Sun &
bank hol Mon 10.30am-5pm; £3), you can't miss its distinctive outline, and no trip to
Bath would be complete without a brief nod towards William Beckford (1760-1844).
Beckford's grandfather was a 17th-century plantation owner, and his father three
times Lord Mayor of London; Beckford himself inherited a cool £2 million, no mean
fortune in the 18th century. Having built Fonthill Abbey near Salisbury, he retired to
Lansdown Crescent in Bath, where he set about building the tower as a personal
retreat. The land around it was consecrated as a cemetery in 1848, and is where
Beckford was laid to rest.

The tower today is owned by the Bath Preservation Trust, but part of it is leased
to the Landmark Trust (see p60), so it's possible to stay here for a few days. For walkers it's more important to know that, when it's open, the views from the top are worth
the climb. There's also an interesting museum focusing on Beckford's colourful life.
If you fancy the detour – it's nearly two miles (3km) – you could walk from the golf
course to the main road, then downhill along the pavement to the tower.

□ **Important note – walking times**
Unless otherwise specified, **all times in this book refer only to the time spent walking**. You will need to add 20-30% to allow for rests, photography, checking the map,
drinking water etc. When planning the day's hike count on 5-7 hours' actual walking.

ROUTE GUIDE AND MAPS

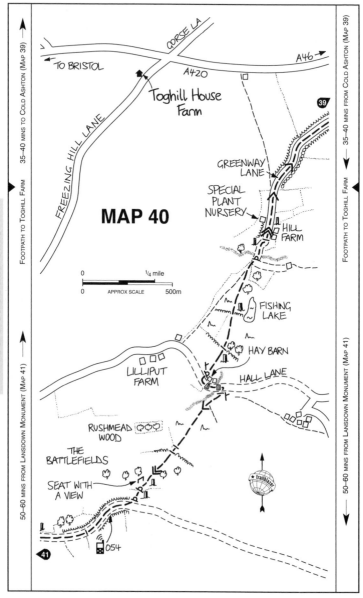

FOOTPATH TO TOGHILL FARM   35-40 MINS TO COLD ASHTON (MAP 39)

50-60 MINS FROM LANSDOWN MONUMENT (MAP 41)

ROUTE GUIDE AND MAPS

35-40 MINS FROM COLD ASHTON (MAP 39)   FOOTPATH TO TOGHILL FARM

50-60 MINS FROM LANSDOWN MONUMENT (MAP 41)

CORSE LA

TO BRISTOL

A420

A46

Toghill House Farm

FREEZING HILL LANE

MAP 40

GREENWAY LANE

SPECIAL PLANT NURSERY

HILL FARM

39

0   1/4 mile
0   500m
APPROX SCALE

FISHING LAKE

HAY BARN

LILLIPUT FARM

HALL LANE

RUSHMEAD WOOD

THE BATTLEFIELDS

SEAT WITH A VIEW

trailblazer

054

41

Map 41 Hanging Hill; Bath city guide 165

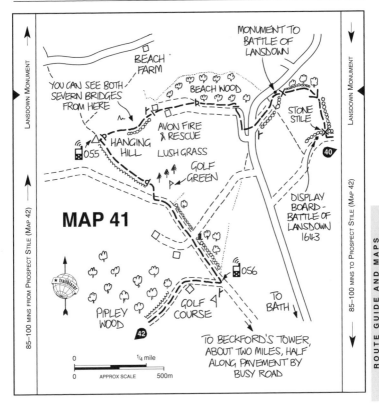

BATH
MAP 43a, p170

'Oh, who can ever be tired of Bath?'
Catherine Morland in **Jane Austen**'s
Northanger Abbey, published in 1817

As the train draws into the station, the announcer used to intone, 'Bath Spa'. It's that word 'spa' that has brought fortune to this western town, attracting 18th-century royalty to take the waters and serving as the catalyst for the construction of what we know today as Georgian Bath.

The city predates Roman times, when it was known as Aquae Sulis, but it is the Georgian buildings that are today revered, and which have been protected as a World Heritage Site since 1987. Although George III (1738-1820) moved his allegiance to Cheltenham, sparking another building frenzy, Bath has never really fallen out of favour.

Today's visitors come not just to bathe in the waters at the smart new Thermae Spa, but to explore the city's history at the Roman Baths, and to marvel at the soaring roof of Bath Abbey. They come, too, to investigate its museums, and – rather more prosaically – to try out any number of restaurants, hotels and bars that are around every corner. All that against a background of architecture that cannot fail to attract even the least-interested observer.

(cont'd on p168)

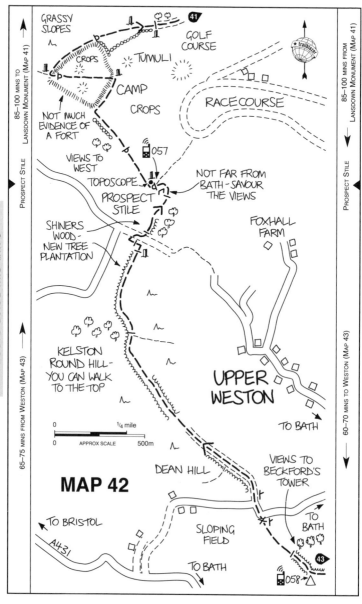

GRASSY SLOPES

41

GOLF COURSE

CROPS

TUMULI

CAMP

CROPS

NOT MUCH EVIDENCE OF A FORT

RACECOURSE

VIEWS TO WEST

057

TOPOSCOPE

NOT FAR FROM BATH - SAVOUR THE VIEWS

PROSPECT STILE

SHINERS WOOD - NEW TREE PLANTATION

FOXHALL FARM

KELSTON ROUND HILL - YOU CAN WALK TO THE TOP

UPPER WESTON

TO BATH

0   1/4 mile

0   500m
APPROX SCALE

DEAN HILL

VIEWS TO BECKFORD'S TOWER

TO BATH

MAP 42

TO BRISTOL

A431

SLOPING FIELD

TO BATH

43

058

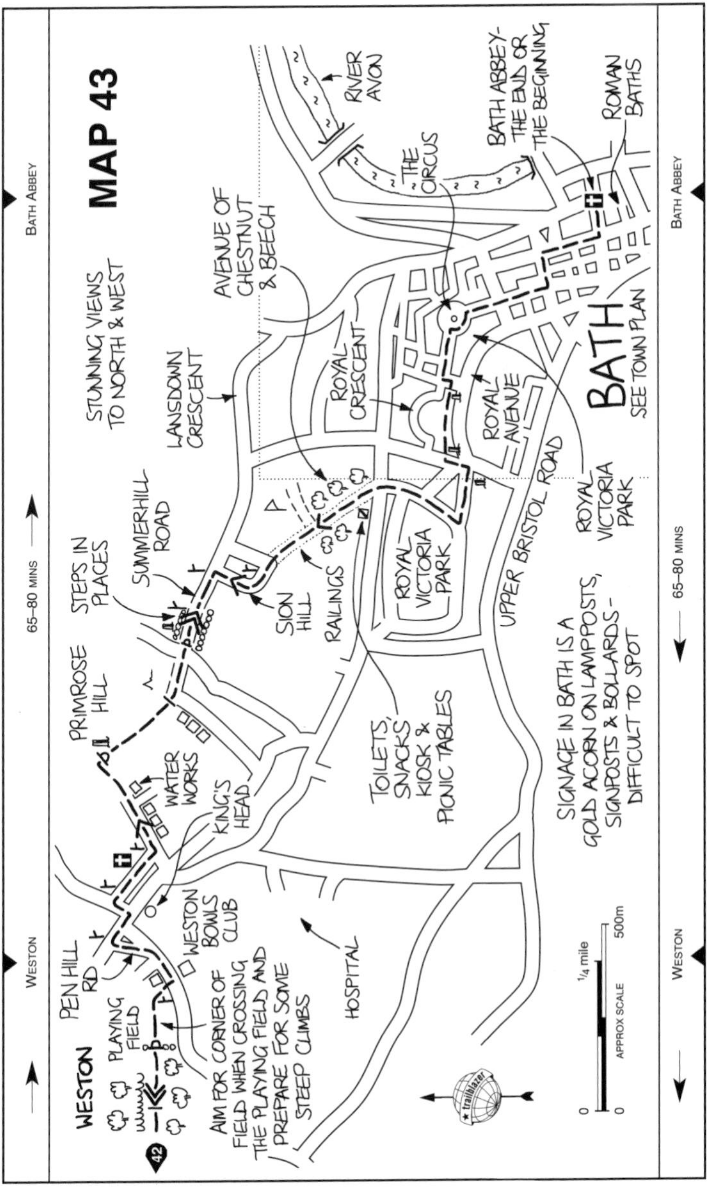

MAP 43

BATH ABBEY

65–80 MINS

BATH ABBEY

STUNNING VIEWS
TO NORTH & WEST

LANSDOWN
CRESCENT

AVENUE OF CHESTNUT & BEECH

RIVER AVON

THE CIRCUS

BATH ABBEY-
THE END OR
THE BEGINNING

ROMAN
BATHS

ROYAL
CRESCENT

ROYAL
AVENUE

BATH
SEE TOWN PLAN

SUMMERHILL
ROAD

STEPS IN
PLACES

PRIMROSE
HILL

SION
HILL

RAILINGS

WATER
WORKS

KING'S
HEAD

PEN HILL
RD

WESTON
BOWLS CLUB

ROYAL
VICTORIA
PARK

ROYAL
VICTORIA PARK

UPPER BRISTOL ROAD

TOILETS,
SNACKS,
KIOSK &
PICNIC TABLES

HOSPITAL

SIGNAGE IN BATH IS A
GOLD ACORN ON LAMPPOSTS,
SIGNPOSTS & BOLLARDS –
DIFFICULT TO SPOT

WESTON

65–80 MINS

WESTON

WESTON

PLAYING
FIELD

AIM FOR CORNER OF
FIELD WHEN CROSSING
THE PLAYING FIELD AND
PREPARE FOR SOME
STEEP CLIMBS

42

¼ mile

500m

APPROX SCALE

0

0

Orientation   (cont'd from p165)

Those unfamiliar with the city will need to keep a sharp eye out for the Cotswold Way signs, which have been reduced to discreet roundels featuring the National Trail acorn in a stylish metallic paint on black. Look out for these on lamp posts and bollards; nothing so rustic as a wooden fingerpost here!

At the heart of the city, and the culmination of the trail, is the abbey. While there's plenty of accommodation close to this focal point, much of it is on the expensive side. The suggestions given on pp169-75 include some more reasonable options, many of them grouped together in one or two areas to the south-east and west of the city, and all within easy reach of the trail.

Arrival and departure

Whether Bath is the grand finale of your walk, or a historic starting point, there is no shortage of ways to get to and from the city.

For more details, see the map and information on public transport, p46.

● **By train** The railway station is at the end of Manvers St, near the river, just a few minutes' walk south of the abbey (and thus the end – or beginning – of the trail). First Great Western trains run up to half-hourly between London Paddington and Bath, or hourly on Sundays.

The station is also on the route between London Waterloo and Bristol, operated by South West Trains; services run up to four times a day.

There's a **taxi rank** at the station.

● **By bus** The bus station is located on Dorchester St, close to both the railway station and the new SouthGate shopping centre which dominates the southern part of the city. National Express runs services to a number of destinations; for details see p45. Journey times between London and Bath average 3hrs 20 minutes during the day, reducing to around 2hrs 40 minutes in the late evening.

● **By road** Bath is about half-an-hour's drive from junction 18 of the M4.

● **By air** The nearest airport to the city is Bristol, a major airport with both domestic and international flights.

Local transport

The centre of Bath is sufficiently compact that most visitors are happy to wander the streets on foot. The introduction of 'Boris **bikes**' in September 2011 means that cyclists can pick up a bike at any one of four docking stations – the railway station [110], Green Park [63], the Holburne Museum [28] and Orange Grove [37] – and drop it back later. You'll need an electronic access card, available from the tourist information centre and 🖥 www.bikeinbath.com. The first half hour is free, regardless of how many times a day it is used. After that, rental is £1 for the next half-hour, then £3 for every subsequent hour, with all-day and weekend cards also available.

At the other end of the energy spectrum, open-top **buses** encircle the tourist areas of the city, anathema to some but a great relief from blistered feet for others. For details of both these and horse-drawn carriages, see p180.

Registered **taxis**, easily spotted by the light on the roof, can be hailed on the streets. Others, such as *Abbey Taxis* [100] (☎ 01225- 444444) and many of those run by *V-Cars* (☎ 01225-464646), must be pre-booked. There's a taxi rank at the station and another behind the abbey.

Services

● **Tourist information** The tourist information centre [82] (☎ 0906-711 2000 – 50p/min, or from overseas ☎ 0844-847 5257, 🖥 www.visitbath.co.uk; Abbey Chambers, Abbey Church Yard; Jun-Sep Mon-Sat 9.30am-6pm, Sun 10am-4pm, Oct-May closes an hour earlier except on Sun) has a prime spot next to the abbey.

It's a large, modern building, with numerous leaflets, a range of maps and guidebooks, as well as an accommodation-booking service. Note, though, that it can get very crowded, so allow plenty of time, particularly at weekends and in the height of the tourist season.

● **Money matters** All the main high street **banks** have branches with **ATMs** across the city. For the visitor, the most central are in Milsom St, where there are branches of Lloyds TSB [48] and HSBC [47], both with ATMs, and on the corner of Henry and Manvers streets, near the railway station, where there's a branch of Barclays [99] with an ATM. **Foreign currency** is handled by these banks, or at the main **post office** [44] on the corner of Broad and Green streets, as well as at Marks & Spencer [85] on Stall St.

● **Shopping** Arguably the most central of the **supermarkets** for those seeking supplies is Waitrose [42] (Mon-Sat 8am-9pm, Sun 11am-5pm), which is in the Podium on Northgate St and scheduled to expand in 2012. There's a large branch of Sainsbury's [62] (Mon-Sat 7am-10pm, Sun 11am-5pm) behind the old Green Park Station, and a smaller Sainsbury's Local (daily 7am-10pm) on Monmouth St. More interesting by far are some of the smaller, **independent shops**, where you can taste the cheese to go in your lunch before buying. Try The Fine Cheese Co [43], on Walcot St opposite the Podium, where you can get coffee and cake at the same time (café ☎ 01225-483407, Mon-Fri 9am-5.30pm, Sat 8.30am-5.30pm), or Chandos Deli [13] (☎ 01225-314418; Mon-Sat 9am-5pm), on George St, which also prepares sandwiches to order and has a café area serving cakes, coffee, soups and sandwiches. There are also several food shops in the **Guildhall Market** [38], and an excellent **farmers' market** in the old Green Park Station in front of Sainsbury's every Saturday 8.30am-1.30pm.

For **outdoor supplies**, such as walking boots, poles and clothing, head for the independent Itchy Feet [11] (☎ 01225-337987, 4 Bartlett St; Mon-Sat 9.30am-5.30pm, Sun 11am-4.30pm), off Alfred St, or BCH Camping & Leisure [98] (☎ 01225-460200; Mon-Sat 9.30am-5.30pm, Sun 11am-5pm) on Southgate St. There are also branches of Blacks [96] (☎ 01225-339678; Mon-Fri 9am-5.30pm, Sat 9am-6pm, Sun 11am-5pm) at Abbey Gate, behind M&S, and Millets [39] (☎ 01225-471500; Mon-Sat 9am-5.30pm, Sun 10.30am-4.30pm) on High St. Mastershoe [23] (☎ 01225-460509; Mon-Sat 9am-6pm, Sun 11am-5pm), on Walcot St, has a good range of

walking boots, but sadly no longer hires them out.

Bath is an easy place to lose a bibliophile, with an excellent independent **bookshop**, Topping & Company [17] (The Paragon, 🖳 www.toppingbooks.co.uk; daily 9am-8pm), at the top of Broad St. Coffee is always on the go, and they have a good range of maps and guides, too, as does the large branch of Waterstone's [49] (Mon-Fri 9am-6pm, Sat 9am-7pm, Sun 11am-5pm) on Milsom St.

● **Health** There's an NHS walk-in centre [60] (☎ 01225-478811; daily 8am-6.30pm) at the Riverside Health Centre west of the main Sainsbury's, The Royal United **Hospital** (☎ 01225-428331) is at Combe Park, about 1½ miles (2.4km) west of the city centre. **Pharmacies** include Boots in the SouthGate centre, and the independent Luther Wilson [2] right on the trail on Brock St near The Circus.

Where to stay

Although seemingly limitless, Bath's accommodation can get booked up very early, especially in the summer, when the tourists descend, and even more so during the Bath Festival (end May-June). Prices almost everywhere vary considerably, taking into account the time of year, the day of the week, the length of stay, and what is going on in the city; those given below are necessarily for guidance, primarily based on a single night midweek during the summer. You can expect to pay at least £5-10 more at weekends, usually defined as Friday and Saturday night, when several places also insist on a minimum two-night stay.

● **Camping** Campers in Bath, as in many places along the Cotswold Way, are in for a hefty hike. The only campsite, *Newton Mill Holiday Park* (☎ 01225-333909, 🖳 www.newtonmillpark.co.uk), is along Newton Rd, some 2½ miles (4km) west of the city, though the good news is that the No 5 bus runs from the bus station to the campsite every ten minutes or so. Camping costs £6.50-7.50 per person, depending on the time of year.

ROUTE GUIDE AND MAPS

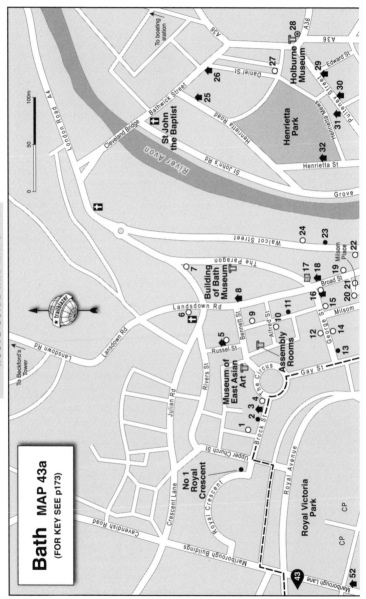

ROUTE GUIDE AND MAPS

Bath MAP 43a
(FOR KEY SEE p173)

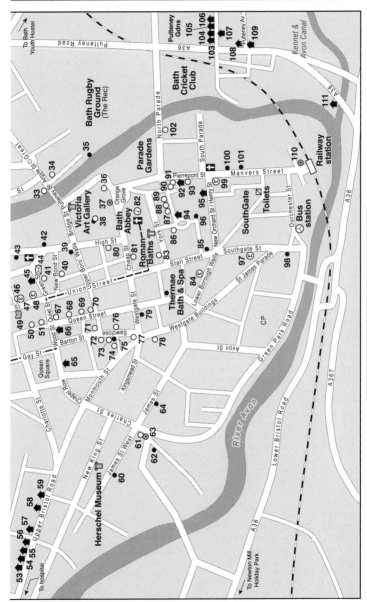

● **Hostels** Basic hostel accommodation that is also central comes in various guises. The largest option, sleeping over 200 people, is the *YMCA* [18] (☎ 01225-325900, ⌨ www.bathymca.co.uk; three 10-bed dorms, one 12-bed, two 14-bed, plus 11S/34T/13F), on Broad Street Place. Some dormitories are single sex and some mixed. Staying here costs £20 per person in a dormitory Monday to Thursday, or £23 at the weekend, with private rooms at £31-35 single, £27-30 per person in a twin, £22-25 triple, and £21-23 quadruple; all rates, include a continental breakfast. There's free WI-FI, a laundry for guests' use, a left-luggage facility, and a gym (at a reduced rate for residents) – though that's unlikely to be of interest at the beginning or end of a 102-mile hike!

For something more personal, head for the privately run *Bath Backpackers* [92] (☎ 01225-446787, ⌨ www.hostels.co.uk; 66 beds; WI-FI), at 13 Pierrepont St, where there's a self-catering kitchen, lounge with satellite TV, and email facilities. Accommodation in 4-, 8- or 10-bed dormitories costs from £12 to £23 per person, depending on various factors including the time of year.

A further option is *St Christopher's Hostel* [45] (☎ 01225-481444, ⌨ www.st-christophers.co.uk/bath-hostels; 54 dorm beds, 1T/2D), at 9 Green St. Beds in 6- to 12-bed dorms (one of them female only) are £15-20 per person, depending on how busy they are, and their twin and doubles (one en suite) are £55 per room. On the down side, it's above the noisy Belushi's pub. The plus? All rates include breakfast.

The city's youth hostel, *YHA Bath* (☎ 01629-592700, ⌨ www.yha.org.uk; 121 beds), is over a mile (1.6km) east of the centre on Bathwick Hill. If you don't mind the walk, and fancy staying in an Italianate mansion, it could be worth considering. A dorm bed costs £14.40-24.90 per person (for members), but expect to pay at least double that in one of the twin-bedded rooms.

● **Guesthouses and B&Bs** Right on the Cotswold Way as you walk into Bath, near The Circus, is *Brocks* [3] (☎ 01225-

338374, ⌨ www.brocksguesthouse.co.uk, 32 Brock St; 1T or D/2D/2D or F/1F, all en suite; ☎; WI-FI; 🐾), where a twin or double room costs £79-89 during the week (the lower price in a standard double without bath), rising to £85-97 at weekends. Not far from here, at 7 Belmont, a pedestrian walkway that runs parallel to but above Lansdown Rd, you'll find *The Belmont* [8] (☎ 01225-423082, ⌨ www.belmontbath.co.uk; 1S/2T /3D; WI-FI), a traditional B&B run by Archie Watson. The single costs £40 with a shared bathroom, or it's £70 for an en suite twin or double room.

At the other end of town, close to the railway station, *The Henry Guest House* [95] (☎ 01225-424052, ⌨ www.thehenry.com; 2S/2T or D/2D/1F sleeping four; ☎; WI-FI) offers contemporary en suite rooms in a Georgian townhouse at £90 for two sharing, rising to £105-115 at weekends, or £65-75 single; one of the singles has private facilities rather than en suite. There is a minimum two-night stay at weekends, as there is at the more central *3 Abbey Green* [94] (☎ 01225-428558, ⌨ www.three abbeygreen.com; 3D/2D or T/2F, all en suite; ☎ in 1F; WI-FI). This family-run guesthouse occupies a listed townhouse just behind the abbey. Charges vary considerably, but expect to pay from £100 a night with a 10% discount for single occupancy. They also have four self-contained apartments (three sleeping four, and the other two people) costing £160-250 per night for a minimum two-night stay.

Across Pulteney Bridge *Ashgrove Guesthouse* [26] (☎ 01225-421911; 3S/1T/5D, all en suite; WI-FI), at 39 Bathwick St, offers rooms at £50-75 for two sharing, or £30-45 for a single, the higher rates in peak season. Round the corner on Henrietta Rd is *Chestnuts House* [25] (☎ 01225-334279, ⌨ www.chestnutshouse.co.uk; 4D/1F, all en suite; ☎; WI-FI; 🐾 1 room) – a stone-built house with rooms from £90-110 for a double, £100-120 for the family room and £80-95 for single occupancy.

Outside the immediate centre, there are two gluts of predominantly terraced B&Bs in residential areas that are within

BATH – MAP KEY (see map pp170-1)

Where to stay

3 Brocks
5 The Queensberry
8 The Belmont
16 Travelodge Bath Central
18 YMCA
25 Chestnuts House
26 Ashgrove Guesthouse
29 Dukes
30 Edgar Townhouse
31 Carfax Hotel
32 Kennard
45 St Christopher's Hostel
52 Marlborough House
53 Bay Tree House
54 Royal Park Guesthouse
55 Waltons
56 Crescent Guesthouse
57 The Albany
58 Dorset Villa
59 The Bath House
65 Francis
66 Harington's Hotel
92 Bath Backpackers
94 3 Abbey Green
95 The Henry Guest House
103 Avon Guesthouse
104 Lynwood
105 Apple Tree Guest House
106 Brindley's
107 White Guest House

Where to stay (cont'd)

108 Membland Guesthouse
109 Radnor Guesthouse
111 Travelodge Bath Waterside

Where to eat and drink

1 Rustico Bistro Italiano
4 The Circus
5 The Olive Tree
6 Grappa Bar
7 Star Inn
9 Casani's
10 Woods
12 The Porter
14 Martini
15 Loch Fyne
16 Wagamama
19 La Tasca
20 Le Parisien
21 Côte Brasserie
22 Sam's Kitchen
24 Schwartz Bros
27 Pulteney Arms
33 Rajpoot
34 River Canteen
36 Browns
38 Market Café
40 Volunteer Rifleman's Arms
41 Old Green Tree
46 Jamie's Italian
50 Salamander

Where to eat and drink (cont'd)

51 Firehouse Rotisserie
61 Green Park Brasserie
67 Eastern Eye
68 The Raven
69 The Canary
70 Butter Pat
71 Gascoyne Place
72 Pizza Express
73 Strada
74 Garrick's Head
76 Schwartz Bros
77 Thai Balcony
78 Mezzaluna
80 Pâtisserie Valerie
81 Roman Baths Café
83 Pump Room
86 Crystal Palace
87 Demuths
88 Tilleys Bistro
89 Sally Lunn's
90 Café du Globe
91 Salathai
93 Yak Yeti Yak
102 OPA

Other

2 Luther Wilson (Chemist)
11 Itchy Feet
13 Chandos Deli
17 Topping & Company

Other (cont'd)

23 Mastershoe
28 Bike in Bath
35 Bath City Boat Trips
37 Bike in Bath
38 Guildhall Market
39 Millets
42 Waitrose (in The Podium)
43 Fine Cheese Co
44 Post Office
47 HSBC Bank & ATM
48 Lloyds TSB Bank & ATM
49 Waterstone's
60 NHS walk-in centre
62 Sainsbury's
63 Bike in Bath
64 Odeon Cinema
75 Theatre Royal
79 Little Theatre Cinema
82 Tourist Information
84 Lloyds TSB Bank & ATM
85 Marks & Spencer
96 Blacks
97 HSBC & ATM
98 BCH Camping
99 Barclays Bank & ATM
100 Abbey Taxis
101 Police Station
110 Bike in Bath

ROUTE GUIDE AND MAPS

easy walking distance of the trail. The first, about ten minutes' walk east of the abbey across the railway, and a short stroll from the Kennet and Avon Canal, runs along Pulteney Rd up Pulteney Gardens. Of these, three are right on the main road, so potentially quite noisy. Colourful flowers enliven **Radnor Guesthouse** [109] (☎ 01225-316159, 🖳 www.radnorguest house.co.uk, 9 Pulteney Terrace; 2D/1T/1F, all en suite; WI-FI), with B&B at around £75-78 for two sharing, £55-60 for single occupancy and £95 for three in the family room. Opposite is **Membland Guesthouse** [108] (mob ☎ 07958-599572, www.memb landguesthouse.co.uk; 3D, all en suite; WI-FI), where rooms come in from £75. Then on the corner of Pulteney Gardens, *Avon Guesthouse* [103] (☎ 01225-313009, 🖳 www.avonguesthousebath.co.uk; 2D/3D or T/1F, all en suite ●) charges £77 per night for two sharing (£50-77 single occupancy), or – in the family room which has a bath – £105-125 for three-four guests.

Pulteney Gardens itself harbours several Victorian homes offering B&B. At No 23, B&B at **White Guest House** [107] (☎ 01225-426075, 🖳 www.whiteguesthouse .co.uk; 1S/1T/3D, all en suite) will set you back from £65 for a double or twin, or £45 for a single. On the opposite side at No 6 is *Lynwood* [104] (☎ 01225-426410, 🖳 www.lynwood-house.com; 1S/1T/3D/1F, all en suite or private bathroom; WI-FI), with rates from £45 for the single, £75 for two sharing and £119 for three in the family room. Right next door, at *Apple Tree Guesthouse* [105] (☎ 01225-337642, 🖳 www.appletreeguesthouse.co.uk, No 7; 2S/3D/1F, all en suite; WI-FI) you'll pay £55 for a single, £85 for a double and £120 for the family room. At the end on the corner, and in another class entirely, is the self-styled 'boutique B&B' *Brindley's* [106] (☎ 01225-310444, 🖳 www.brindleysbath.co .uk; 1T or D/5D; WI-FI). With French-inspired décor, its en suite rooms – four with king-size beds – are priced from £110 during the week to £180 on Friday and Saturday nights, when there's a minimum two-night stay.

To the west of the city, a second clutch

of guesthouses is at Crescent Gardens. This residential road runs above but parallel to the Upper Bristol Rd, and is just a few minutes' walk from the trail – and the centre of Bath. Closest is *The Bath House* [59] (☎ 0117-937 4495, 🖳 www.thebathhouse.org; 1T or D/4D; 3 with ● WI-FI), at No 40, where rooms with en suite king-size or four-poster beds are from £79-119 for B&B – with the higher rate at weekends. They also have two apartments: one twin or double at £99-129; the other at £159-209 for four people, but sleeping up to six. Down the road at No 31, rates at *Dorset Villa* [58] (☎ 01225-425975, 🖳 www.dorsetvilla.co .uk; 1S/2T/2D/1F, all en suite; ●) vary dramatically, from £25-45 for a single, to £59-95 in a twin or double. About half of their rooms have baths; the rest have showers. Rooms at *The Albany* [57] (☎ 01225-313339, 🖳 www.albanybath.co.uk, No 24; 1T/1T or D/2D/1F; ●; WI-FI) are all en suite, except one with a private bathroom, and cost £75-85, or £60 for single occupancy. At *Crescent Guesthouse* [56] (☎ 01225-425945, 🖳 www.crescentbath.co.uk, No 21; 1S/1T/4D all en suite; WI-FI) you can expect to pay £55-75 for the single room, and £75-90 in a double or twin, while rates at *Waltons* [55] (☎ 01225-426528, 🖳 www.waltonsguesthouse.co.uk, No 17; 3S/10D/2F, all en suite; WI-FI) are £50-55 for a single, £80-90 for two sharing and £120-135 for three in a family room. More contemporary is the *Royal Park Guesthouse* [54] (☎ 01225-317651, 🖳 www.royalparkbath.co.uk, No 16; 1S/1T/1D/1F, all en suite or private bathroom; WI-FI), where it's £90 for two sharing, £60 for the single and £110-140 in the family room. Last up is *Bay Tree House* [53] (☎ 01225-483699, 🖳 www.baytreehousebath.co.uk, No 12; 1T/3D/1F, ●; WI-FI), with B&B from £75 for two sharing (en suite except one of the doubles and the twin, which share a bathroom) and £125 for three in the en suite family room.

Further up, a turning to the right leads into Marlborough Lane, where the elegant *Marlborough House* [52] (☎ 01225-318175, 🖳 www.marlborough-house.net; 2D/1T or D/ 3T, D or F; all en suite; ●; WI-

FI; 🐕 £5-10) is in a class of its own. For £95-130 you can have a twin or double room, perhaps with a four-poster or Louis XIV king-size bed (single occupancy £80-95); three sharing a family room will pay £135-145. As at many Bath establishments, there's a two-night minimum stay at weekends.

• **Hotels** With B&Bs climbing steadily up the price ladder, it's not unreasonable to shop around for one of the cheaper hotels, especially if you're happy to find a café for breakfast. The older ***Travelodge Bath Central*** [16] (☎ 0871-984 6219, 🖳 www.travelodge.co.uk; 43D/19F; ☕ in F; WI-FI; 🐕 £20) is indeed central, above a nightclub on George St, whereas the more peaceful ***Travelodge Bath Waterside*** [111] (☎ 0871-984 6407, Rossiter Rd; 19T/97D/4F; ☕ in F; WI-FI; 🐕 £20) is in more tranquil surroundings to the south, on the Kennet and Avon Canal. Prices at both fluctuate significantly, but walk-in rates average around £59.90 for a double room without breakfast. The best rates, however, are found online; with 21 days' notice, rooms can come in as low as £19. Note that there are baths in only the family rooms, and that dogs are charged at £20 per stay, not per night.

To the east of the abbey, over the river, are several small hotels. These include ***Edgar Townhouse*** [30] (☎ 01225-420619, 🖳 www.edgar-townhouse.co.uk; 2S/4T/11D/1F, all en suite; WI-FI) at 64 Great Pulteney St, which offers B&B for £55-69 in a single room, £60-99 in a double or twin, and from £160 for four in the family room; the lower rates being for low season. At other times of the year they have a minimum stay of two nights at weekends. Just along the street at ***Carfax Hotel*** [31] (☎ 01225-462089, 🖳 www.carfaxhotel.co.uk; 6S/20D/1F, all en suite; ☕; WI-FI) there are three types of room. B&B in a double costs £120-180, with a single at £85-105, and £140-170 for the family room. Round the corner at the ***Kennard*** [32] (☎ 01225-310472, 🖳 www.kennard.co.uk; 2S/1T/8D/1F; WI-FI), 11 Henrietta St, the single rooms share a bathroom but the others are all en suite. During the week you'll pay £110-130 for B&B in a double or twin, £65 for a single and £150 for the family room, rising at weekends to £70 single, £130-150 double and £170 family.

Grandly located on the southern side of Queen Square, the ***Francis*** [65] (☎ 01225-424105, 🖳 www.mercure.com; 12S/33T/ 53D all en suite; most with ☕; WI-FI; 🐕 £10) is one of the city's most well-established hotels. Rebuilt in 1953 after being damaged in the Blitz, it is now part of the French Mercure chain, with further refurbishment anticipated in 2012. Prices for B&B start at £133 for an en suite double midweek, topping out at £250, with singles from £123. Equally central but far more personal is ***Harington's Hotel*** [66] (☎ 01225-461728, 🖳 www.haringtonshotel.co.uk, 8-10 Queen St; 1T/9D/3F; ☕; WI-FI), just off the square, where B&B in a twin or double room costs £98-165 (single occupancy £85-165); all rooms are en suite but some have a bath rather than a shower, so do make it clear when booking if you have a preference.

At the top end of the scale, two boutique hotels stand out. Stylish and contemporary, ***The Queensberry*** [5] (☎ 01225-447928, 🖳 www.thequeensberry.co.uk; 29D all en suite; ☕; WI-FI) on Russel St, off The Circus, has double rooms excluding breakfast from £130-255, rising to £195-460 at weekends (continental breakfast £10, English breakfast £15). Then there's the more traditional ***Dukes*** [29] (☎ 01225-787963, 🖳 www.dukesbath.co.uk; 17D, all en suite; 12 with ☕; WI-FI; 🐕), on the corner of Edward St near the end of Great Pulteney St, where a double room with breakfast is £139-199 mid-week, or £159-251 at weekends (single occupancy £99-132).

Where to eat and drink

Eating out in Bath is easy. The problem lies in choosing where to eat and drink from the broad array of pubs, restaurants, cafés and fast-food joints whose menus demand attention at every turn. The following, then, is no more than a selection from the range of options within easy reach of the centre. Others abound, especially around Kingsmead Square, so you'll be spoiled for choice.

• **Traditional and contemporary** As you walk into (or out of) Bath along the Cotswold Way, you'll pass *The Circus* [4] (☎ 01225-466020, 🖳 www.thecircuscafe andrestaurant.co.uk; Mon-Sat 10am-10.30pm), aptly located near the Circus on Brock St. You can have breakfast, elevenses, lunch or tea here, or dine in style. Whatever your choice, the décor is pleasantly informal and the menus seasonal; they even make a 'double dip recession' (smoky aubergine and pomegranate purée, beetroot hummus, with crudités, olives and anchovy toasts at £7.70) sound appealing!

Justifiably popular and very central is *Green Park Brasserie* [61] (☎ 01225-338565, 🖳 www.greenparkbrasserie.com, Charles St; daily noon-2.45pm, Tue-Thu 6-8.45pm, Fri-Sat 6-9.45pm), with the added buzz of live jazz from Wednesday to Saturday. Rather grandly located in the old booking hall of the restored Green Park Station, it spills over on to the old station concourse. During the day choices range from paninis to innovative salads and beefburgers (around £8.95). In the evening eat à la carte or from a set menu (available 6-7pm, £12.95 for two courses) featuring dishes such as salmon and crab fishcakes with chilli crème fraiche and mixed salad.

Just off Queen Square, the *Firehouse Rotisserie* [51] (☎ 01225-482070, 🖳 www.firehouserotisserie.co.uk, John St; Mon-Sat noon-11pm, Sun noon-10pm) is a light and convivial spot that presents a range of innovative 'small plates' along with grills and pizzas from about £12.50.

Close to the Bike in Bath rack on Orange Grove, *Browns* [36] (☎ 01225-461199, 🖳 www.browns-restaurants.co.uk; daily 10am-11pm) could be a good spot to abandon a bike for lunch. The atmosphere is buzzing, the menu broad and the prices affordable (mains £9-15).

Racing paraphernalia adorns the walls of *Woods* [10] (☎ 01225-314812, Alfred St; Mon-Sat noon-2.30pm & 5.30-10pm), David Price's place opposite the Assembly Rooms, setting the scene for one of the best meals in Bath. Come with plenty of time to select from dishes that might include seared Gressingham duck breast marinated with plums, fresh basil and red wine sauce (£17.50), or a starter of chowder with fresh dill, gambas and pancetta (£7.25). A fixed-price menu offers two courses at lunch or an early dinner (5.30-7pm) for £14.95; at other times the menu is à la carte. Enjoy!

If celebration is in order, a classy venue could be appropriate. Round the corner from Woods, on Russel St, *The Olive Tree* [5] (Tue-Sun noon-2pm, daily 7-10pm) is the exclusive and top-quality restaurant at The Queensberry Hotel (see p175), exuding calm and contemporary style. With à la carte mains topping out at £31, this one is strictly for specials.

• **Mediterranean** For classic French cuisine with a contemporary twist, try *Casani's* [9] (☎ 01225-780055, 🖳 www.casanis.co.uk; Tue-Sat noon-2pm & 6-10pm) at 4 Savile Row, near the Assembly Rooms. Think *parfait de crabe* (£8) or *cassolette de poulet provençale* at £14.25. There's more than a passing nod to French café culture at *Côte Brasserie* [21] (☎ 01225-335509, 🖳 www.cote-restaurants.co.uk; Mon-Sat 8am-11pm, Sun 8am-10.30pm) in Milsom Place, where *moules frites* at £10.95 jostle for space on the menu with *poulet breton* (£9.95), and outside seating adds to the ambience. Also with a French bias is *Tilleys Bistro* [88] (☎ 01225-484200, 🖳 www.tilleysbistro.co.uk; Mon-Sat noon-2.15pm & 6-10.30pm, Sun 6-9pm), sandwiched between Sally Lunn's and Demuths on North Parade Passage, where dishes on the dinner menu are conveniently sorted into small, medium or large, offering plenty of flexibility. There are set menus, too, including a two-course lunch or early dinner for £12.50.

Arguably the best Italian in Bath is *Mezzaluna* [78] (☎ 01225-466688, 🖳 www.mezzaluna-bath.co.uk; Mon-Sat noon-2.15pm & 6-10.15pm), on Kingsmead Square, with down-to-earth

---

(Opposite) Top: Bath's magnificent Royal Crescent. **Bottom**: Pulteney Bridge and the River Avon. (Photos © Tricia Hayne).

prices that include a two-course lunch for just £8.95. Altogether more casual is Jamie Oliver's eponymous *Jamie's Italian* [46] (☎ 01225-432340, 🖳 www.jamiesitalian .com, Mon-Sat noon-11pm, Sun noon-10.30pm) in Milsom Place, which links Broad St with Milsom St. Salamis and ham hocks hanging from the ceiling add an authentic touch to a modern building, but you'll often have to wait; only groups of eight or more can pre-book.

Adding a scenic touch to Italian-focused dining is the *River Canteen* [34] (☎ 01225-424800, www.river-canteen.co .uk; Mon-Fri midday-2.30am, 6-10.30pm, Sat midday-11pm, Sun when Bath are playing at home and holiday weekends midday-7pm). Opened in late 2011, it occupies a wood and stainless-steel take on a tradition-al boathouse, in a prime position overlook-ing the weir, next to the Rec. Pizzas from £8.50 and pastas at £10.50 are affordable, but come at lunch during the week and you can indulge in a main course for £6.50, two courses at £9.50, or three for £11.

At the long-standing *Martini* [14] (☎ 01225-460818, 🖳 www.martinirestau-rant.co.uk; Mon-Fri noon-2.30pm, 6-10.30pm, Sat noon-10.30pm, Sun noon-2.30pm, 6-10pm) on George St, the décor may not be up to much, but traditional food and an old-fashioned Italian welcome bring punters back for more. Italian is on the menu at 2 Margaret's Buildings, too, where *Rustico Bistro Italiano* [1] (☎ 01225-310064, 🖳 www.rusticobistroitaliano.co .uk; Tue-Sun noon-2.30pm, 6-10pm) serves hearty helpings of Italian classics, as well as ciabatta sandwiches at lunchtime (£6.95). Then not far away, on Lansdown Rd, pizzas and jazz go together at *Grappa Bar* [6] (☎ 01225-448890, 🖳 www.grap pabar.co.uk; Mon-Sat 5-11pm), where there are cocktails aplenty, too.

The house next to the theatre on Barton St, where Beau Nash lived and died, is today occupied by the Italian restaurant chain *Strada* [73] (☎ 01225-337753; daily 11.30am-11pm). Right next door is *Pizza Express* [72] (☎ 01225-420119; daily 11.30am-11.30pm). The most reliable of the pizza chains, it's one of several Bath restaurants that stay open late.

Sangria rules at the noisy *La Tasca* [19] (☎ 01225-466477, 🖳 www.latasca.co .uk; Mon-Sat 11am-11pm, Sun midday-11pm), on Broad St, with a range of tapas and paellas to mop it up. New on the scene at 1a North Parade is the Moroccan *Café du Globe* [90] (☎ 01225-466437, 🖳 www .cafeduglobe.co.uk; daily 10am-10.30pm). From mezzes to tagines, it's all served in a traditional setting complete with metal fret-work lanterns. And then there's Greek cui-sine, as defined at *OPA* [102] (☎ 01225-317900, 🖳 www.opabath.com; Mon-Sat noon-10.30pm) on North Parade.

● **World cuisines** Even if you're not a huge fan of Indian cuisine (and it's good), the *Eastern Eye* [67] (☎ 01225-422323, 🖳 www.easterneye.com, 8a Quiet St; Mon-Fri noon-2.30pm, Mon-Thu 6-11.30pm, Fri 6pm-midnight, Sat-Sun noon-midnight) is a must for the setting alone. Occupying the first floor of a 19th-century building adorned with sculptures of 'Commerce' and 'Genius', it sits beneath a magnificent three-domed ceiling. For the best Indian food in Bath, however, head below stairs on Argyle St to *Rajpoot* [33] (☎ 01225-466833, 🖳 www.rajpoot.com; daily noon-2.30pm & 6-11pm, weekends to 11.30pm).

Rather less smart is the irresistibly named *Yak Yeti Yak* [93] (☎ 01225-442299, 🖳 www.yakyetiyak.co.uk; daily noon-2pm, Sun-Thu 6-10.30pm, Fri-Sat 5-10.30pm) on Pierrepont St, where Nepalese mains are around £5.50 for vegetarian dish-es, and £8 for others; they also have a three-course menu at lunch and in the early evening for £10.50.

Just a few steps up the road you can head east at *Salathai* [91] (☎ 01225-484663, 🖳 www.salathai-bath.co.uk; daily noon-2.30pm & 6-10.30pm, or 10pm on Sun), where set menus cost from £16.95, or £14.95 for vegetarian. There's also the tran-

---

(Opposite) Bath Abbey (see p181) forms an impressive finish – or start – to the Cotswold Way. (Photo © Tricia Hayne).

❑ **Bath specialities**

● **Bath bun** Created in the 17th century by Sally Lunn, the original Bath bun is a light bread roll, akin to a large French brioche and still served at the eponymous Sally Lunn's (see opposite) in Bath. Later, though, the term 'Bath bun' became associated with a sweetened roll sprinkled with sugar, and this is now the more widely known of the two.

● **Bath Oliver** The plain savoury biscuit served as an accompaniment to cheese was the creation of one Dr Oliver, who practised in Bath during the 18th century. It's widely available in supermarkets and delicatessens.

● **Bath chap** The breadcrumbed boiled cheek of a pig, these normally come in a cone shape. Find them at the Guildhall Market in Bath.

● **Bath soft cheese** An old Bath recipe is said to lie behind the creation of this cheese, which is available at the city's Saturday morning farmers' market.

● **Bath asparagus** Not so much a culinary speciality as a rare summer delicacy, Bath asparagus grows wild in the hills around the city, the locations a closely guarded secret. As you might expect, it is strictly protected.

quil setting of *Thai Balcony* [77] (☎ 01225-444450, 1 Seven Dials; daily noon-2.30pm, Sun-Thu 6-10pm, Fri-Sat 6-10.30pm), above Sainsbury's Local on Sawclose.

For a reliable source of good, inexpensive food with plenty of noodles, you can't beat the relaxed **Wagamama** [16] (☎ 01225-337314, 🖳 www.wagamama.com; Mon-Sat noon-11pm, Sun noon-10pm), next to the Travelodge on the corner of George and Broad streets; it's great for vegetarians, too.

● **Fish** *Loch Fyne* [15] (☎ 01225-750120, 🖳 www.lochfyne.com; daily 7.30-10am, Sun-Thu noon-10pm, Fri-Sat noon-10.30pm) needs little introduction having taken the UK's restaurant scene by storm several years ago. With fresh fish cooked in open kitchens it's a popular concept and the place can get very busy.

● **Vegetarian** Most vegetarians and vegans beat a path to *Demuths* [87] (☎ 01225-446059, 🖳 www.demuths.co.uk, 2 North Parade Passage; Sun-Thu noon-3pm, Sat 11.30am-3.30pm, daily 5-9.30pm), close to the abbey, and go no further. There are alternatives, though, including *The Porter* [12] (☎ 01225-424104, 🖳 www.theporter .co.uk; daily noon-9pm) on George St, where regular live music in the evenings is an added bonus. Check out, too, the places listed under 'world cuisines' above, or try

the veggie options listed by almost all mainstream restaurants.

● **Bars, pubs and pub grub** The opening hours in this section for the most part relate to the hours food is served, but almost all venues serve drinks outside these hours.

The trend towards gastro-pubs has claimed many an erstwhile local, and Bath is no exception, with some excellent results.

Opposite the Theatre Royal on the corner of Sawclose and Barton St, *Gascoyne Place* [71] (☎ 01225-445854, 🖳 www.gas coyneplace.com; Mon-Fri noon-3pm & 6-10pm, Sat noon-3pm & 6-10.30pm, Sun noon-4pm & 6-10pm) is the epitome of contemporary pub chic, with live jazz every Sunday evening.

In a similar location, just behind the theatre, the *Garrick's Head* [74] (☎ 01225-318368, 🖳 www.garricksheadpub.com; Mon-Fri noon-3pm & 5.30-10pm, Sat noon-10pm, Sun noon-9pm) retains the atmosphere of a pub, with a good bar menu and more. Somewhat quirkily it marks the start of the city's ghost walk (see p180) – so presumably Banquo could be among the guests.

Despite the onslaught of modernisation, plenty of pubs remain unscathed. Claiming to be the smallest pub in Bath, *The Volunteer Rifleman's Arms* [40] (☎ 01225-425210; daily noon-4pm) is centrally located on New Bond Street Place. Food here is of the 'any-style-you-like' variety, everything from curry to calamares, washed down with Abbey Ales.

For a quiet drink and well-prepared food, the *Crystal Palace* [86] (☎ 01225-482666, 🖳 www.crystalpalacepub.co.uk; Mon-Fri 11.30-9pm, Sat-Sun 11.30-8pm), on Abbey Green, is absolutely central, and the walled garden behind is an added bonus for lunch in the summer months – that's in a good year, of course. Rather less peaceful is the *Pulteney Arms* [27] (☎ 01225-463923, 🖳 www.thepulteneyarms.co.uk, corner Daniel St and Sutton St; Mon-Fri noon-2.30pm, Mon-Sat 6-9pm; Sat/Sun noon-3pm), behind Great Pulteney St. This is the 'rugby' pub, frequented by players and spectators, and heaving when Bath are playing just across the river at The Rec.

There's simple, no-nonsense fare at *The Raven* [68] (☎ 01225-425045, 🖳 www.theravenofbath.co.uk; Mon-Fri noon-2.30pm & 5-8.30pm, Sat noon-8.30pm, Sun 12.30-8.30pm) on Queen St, which concentrates on pies – lots of them: pork pies, steak pies, vegetarian pies, even Thai pies (about £8.80) – all washed down with real ale.

If you're after nothing more complicated than a good pint, you'd do well to start with the *Old Green Tree* [41] (☎ 01225-448259, Green St; Mon-Sat 11am-11pm; Sun noon-10.30pm), perhaps moving on to the *Salamander* [50] (☎ 01225-428889, 🖳 www.bathales.com/pubs/salamander.html, John St; Sun-Fri 10am-11pm, Sat 10am-midnight) for a more Victorian atmosphere, and ending up at the *Star Inn* [7] (☎ 01225-425072, 🖳 www.star-inn-bath.co.uk; Mon-Fri noon-2.30pm & Mon-Thu 5.30pm-midnight, Fri 5.30pm-1am, Sat noon-1am, Sun noon-midnight), with its four small bars, where real ale is drawn straight from the barrel. Though all of these serve some form of food, in each the beer is a priority, to be drunk in convivial surroundings with little concession to the 21st century. The hours given for these three are pub opening hours.

● **Teahouses and cafés** Walking the Cotswold Way throws up its fair share of trials, from steep hills to unpredictable rain and cold, when a cup of tea is rarely more welcome. Bath doesn't disappoint. Perhaps

this is the time to dress up and treat yourself to afternoon tea at the *Pump Room* [83] (☎ 01225-444477; daily 9.30am-5.30pm), one of the great institutions of Bath. Built between 1795 and 1797, the Pump Room exudes the elegance of the era, with its grand chandeliers and classical music played by the Pump Room Trio. Although you can take morning coffee or lunch here, it's at teatime that it comes into its own. You don't have to have the full works of sandwiches, scones, cakes and pastries (£17.50 per person) – but it's certainly tempting. Tables can be reserved during the week, but not at weekends; at busy periods expect to queue for 20-40 minutes. Note that during festival times or on special occasions, tea may finish an hour or so earlier. If you just want to marvel at the building, you can combine it with a visit to the Roman Baths (see p182).

Old-fashioned tea doesn't have to be quite so posh. The oldest house in Bath, at 4 North Parade Passage, dates back to around 1482 and houses *Sally Lunn's* [89] (☎ 01225-461634, 🖳 www.sallylunns.co.uk; Mon-Thu 10am 9.30pm, Fri-Sat 10am-11pm, Sun 11am-9pm; dinner from 5.30pm). This is the home of the Bath bun (see box opposite), which was created by Ms Lunn when she lived here in the 17th century. Or indulge at *Pâtisserie Valerie* [80] (☎ 01225-444826, 🖳 www.patisserie-valerie.co.uk, 20 High St; Mon-Thu 8am-7.30pm, Fri-Sat 8am-8pm, Sun 8.30am-7pm). Cream cakes, iced cakes, chocolate cakes, sticky gateaux: they serve them all (and light lunches, too).

Another Bath institution, *The Canary* [69] (☎ 01225-462457, 🖳 www.thecanary tearooms.co.uk, daily 9am-9pm), has reopened on Queen St. Long renowned for its Welsh rarebit (£6.95), it now boasts a drinks licence and a more extensive menu, with a roast on Sundays, but the setting remains firmly 'café' in style.

Entirely individual in style is the very chilled *Sam's Kitchen* [22] (☎ 01225-481159, 🖳 www.samskitchendeli.co.uk; Mon-Sat 8am-6pm, Sun 9am-4pm), a licensed café and deli at the southern end of Walcot St offering live music events – and huge meringues!

Should the sun put in an appearance, try a breath of French air at *Le Parisien* [20] (☎ 01225-447147, Milsom Place, 🖳 www.leparisien.co.uk; Mon-Sat 8am-4pm, Sun 9am-4pm). With tables spilling onto an attractive courtyard, it's one of only a handful of places in Bath where you can linger in the sunshine over your coffee or baguette.

And finally, a new one to add to the mix. In spring 2012, the *Roman Baths Café* [81] is scheduled to open opposite the entrance to the baths, and right in front of the abbey. Combining a café and deli with a prime location, this one's sure to attract the crowds.

● **Cheap eats and fast food**   It's not difficult to find some form of fast food among the many outlets around the city, not to mention the occasional 'greasy spoon' joint where you can get a standard fry up, and any number of sandwich bars. First stop should be the indoor Bath Guildhall Market [38] (Mon-Sat 8am-5pm) where – among the pashminas and second-hand books – you'll find the *Market Café*. A full English breakfast here will set you back between £4.35 and £5.20, depending on how hungry you are. Other stalls sell sandwiches and pies – including Bath chaps (see box p178).

For sandwiches and baguettes, try the *Butter Pat* [70] on Upper Borough Walls, off High St, where everything is made to order, and large baguettes are from £3. One of the best proponents of the burger is *Schwartz Bros* (☎ 01225-463613; Mon-Wed 5am-11pm, Thu-Sun around midday-11pm), with a branch on Walcot St [24], and another on Sawclose [76].

What to see and do
For most walkers on the Cotswold Way, the first sense of the city comes from the glimpse of Lansdown Crescent as you descend Lansdown Hill. Royal Crescent follows, leading to the smart new gates of **Royal Victoria Park**, which in themselves represent a symbolic entrance to the city.

Although it is primarily Georgian Bath that draws the crowds, there are hints of medieval times in the ruins of the **city walls** along Barton St, while no trip to Bath

would be complete without visiting the **Roman Baths** (see box p182).

To get a real feel for the city, join one of the 1½- to two-hour **walking tours** that are run by volunteers from outside the Pump Room in front of the abbey. Tours depart at 10.30am and 2pm Sunday to Friday, and just at 10.30am on Saturday; in the summer, between May and September, there's an additional evening walk at 7pm on Tuesday and Friday. There is no charge – and no tips are accepted. Is this one of Bath's best-kept secrets?

A city with this sort of heritage must have the odd ghost hovering in the shadows. If you fancy being scared out of your wits, join a guided **ghost walk** (☎ 01225-350512, 🖳 www.ghostwalksofbath.co.uk; year-round Thu, Fri & Sat 8pm; £7 per person), lasting just short of two hours. To take part, just turn up at the allotted time outside the Garrick's Head pub [71] (see p178), though groups of 10 or more need to pre-book.

For those who prefer to guide themselves, there's a **city trail** (for an upbeat interpretation, see 🖳 www.bath.co.uk) beneath your feet – quite literally: it's marked out with plaques on the pavements. Broadly, the trail starts near the abbey, taking in the Roman Baths and the Pump Room, before moving on to Queen Square and The Circus, Assembly Rooms, then back towards Pulteney Bridge and Parade Gardens, finishing at Abbey Green.

If you've had enough of walking, there are always the double-decker **sightseeing buses** (☎ 01225-330444, 🖳 www.city-sightseeing.com) which operate hop-on, hop-off tours for £12 a head, with a commentary; tickets are valid for 24 hours. Alternatively, you can use the buses as a shuttle service, paying £2 for each leg of the journey. Buses set off from the end of Cheap St, behind Bath Abbey.

Or you could try a **horse-drawn tour** (☎ 01761 471888; 🖳 www.courtyardcarriages.com) which takes in the architectural highlights of Pulteney Bridge, Royal Crescent and The Circus. Trips, at £10 a head, last 25-30 minutes and start opposite Parade Gardens.

When planning your trip, note that several establishments, including the Roman Baths, stop selling tickets up to an hour before closing time, so do be sure to give yourself plenty of time.

● **Assembly Rooms** Built in 1771, the lavishly designed Assembly Rooms (☎ 01225-477789, 🖥 www.nationaltrust.org.uk; Jan-Feb & Nov-Dec daily 10.30am-5pm, Mar-Oct 10.30am-6pm; admission £2, free to National Trust members, except for museum), on Bennett St, were the creation of John Wood the Younger, and *the* place to be seen in fashionable Georgian society. Significant damage was caused by a bomb in 1942, but the Assembly Rooms have since been fully restored. Note that the last admission is an hour before closing, and that the building is sometimes closed for private functions.

On the ground floor is the **Fashion Museum** (☎ 01225-477173, 🖥 www.fashionmuseum.co.uk; £7.50, free to NT members). If you neither know nor care how Georgian formality compares with 20th-century designer chic, perhaps you'd be better off in the chain shops on Stall St. If you do, stay put; you'll even get the chance to try on corsets and crinolines. If you plan to visit the Roman Baths and Pump Room (see p182) as well as it may be worth getting the combined entry ticket (£15.75).

● **Bath Abbey** One of England's most glorious churches, Bath Abbey (☎ 01225-422462, 🖥 www.bathabbey.org; summer Mon 9.30am-6pm, Tue-Sat 9am-6pm, Sun 1-2.30pm & 4.30-5.30pm; winter closes every day at 4.30pm; £2.50 donation requested) is the third church to occupy this site. Visitors are welcome to tour the building, with its magnificent flying buttresses and fan-vaulted rafters, but it is during a service, or a concert, that you can best appreciate the architecture as the sound of choral music soars skywards. Tower tours (£6) are offered hourly Mon-Sat, 10am-4pm, except in bad weather.

Over the years, three separate buildings have occupied the site of the abbey. The first, an Anglo-Saxon church, was replaced by the Normans at the end of the 11th century. When this fell into ruin at the end of the 15th century, the present abbey church was founded, but was abandoned in 1539 at the time of Henry VIII's order for the dissolution of the monasteries. The Gothic church that we see today was rebuilt during the reign of Elizabeth I, and completed in 1616. Today, the Development Project seeks to address the needs of the 21st century – and while this is ongoing, the **Vaults Heritage Museum** is closed.

Take a look at the abbey doors and you'll see the sacred heart and crown of thorns that proclaim its earlier foundation as a Catholic church. To each side of the doors are statues of St Peter and St Paul, to whom the Norman church was dedicated. The statue to the left was decapitated by Roundheads during the reign of Charles I, with the face recarved at a later date to restore the balance – at least in part. The abbey church itself is dedicated to St Peter.

● **Building of Bath Museum** The setting for this fascinating museum (☎ 01225-333895, 🖥 www.bath-preservation-trust.org.uk, The Vineyards, The Paragon; Mar-Oct, Sat, Sun & Mon inc bank holiday Mon 10.30am-5pm; entry £4) is the **Countess of Huntingdon's Chapel**, built in 1765 and in use as a place of worship until 1981. The building is interesting in itself, but the real reason for visiting is to find out why – and how – Georgian Bath was built. Work your way through the grand designs of the architects, including the city's principal visionary John Wood, who designed Queen Square, and his son, also John, who was the inspiration behind both The Circus and Royal Crescent. Discover the challenges faced by the stonemasons, carpenters and roofers, then learn about the interior décor, such as applying gold leaf to the ceiling mouldings. Intricate scale models show how the interiors of the houses were constructed – and depict what went on in each of the rooms. Other museums might shout louder, but this is the one to put at the top of your list.

● **Herschel Museum of Astronomy** Dedicated to five generations of the

Herschel family, this museum (☎ 01225-446865, 🖳 www.bath-preservation-trust .org.uk, 19 New King St; Feb-mid Dec, Mon/Tue & Thu/Fri 1-5pm, Sat/Sun and bank hols 11am-5pm; £5) is as much about the interior of an 18th-century townhouse as about astronomy. Already established as a musician, William Herschel moved here in 1777 with his sister, the astronomer Caroline Herschel. As a form of relaxation, he took up astronomy himself, building his own telescope and going on to discover the planet Uranus from this garden in 1781. Among the exhibits relating to everyday life is a 7ft (210cm) scale model of his 40ft (12m) telescope. Herschel went on to be appointed Astronomer Royal, forcing a move to Datchet in 1782. He died in 1823, and is buried in Berkshire, in the churchyard of St Lawrence, Upton.

● **Holburne Museum of Art** Following substantial restoration and extension, this museum (☎ 01225-388588, 🖳 www.hol burne.org; Mon-Sat 10am-5pm, Sun/bank hol 11am-5pm; admission free except special exhibitions) at the end of Great Pulteney St has emerged with a new sense of light and space. Established in 1893 to showcase the collection of Sir William Holburne, it is a major provincial gallery with a particularly strong emphasis on Georgian portraiture. To miss the rest of the collection would be a shame, however. Do take a look at the smaller exhibits tucked away in drawers – and allow time for a breather in the contemporary café.

● **Museum of East Asian Art** (☎ 01225-464640, 🖳 www.meaa.org.uk, 12 Bennett St; Tue-Sat 10am-5pm, Sun noon-5pm; admission £5) Based on the personal collection of a Hong Kong lawyer, this offers more of an introduction to Asian art than any great insight. Among the exhibits are ceramics, bamboo carvings and an extensive collection of Chinese jade. Find it off The Circus, just a stone's throw from the Cotswold Way as it enters Bath.

● **Parade Gardens** Right in the centre of Bath, the Parade Gardens (Easter-end Sep,

admission £1) is a peaceful place to enjoy the colour of an English formal garden. Bands play here regularly in summer.

● **Roman Baths and Pump Room** Probably the single greatest attraction for visitors to Bath is the **Roman Baths** (☎ 01225-477785, 🖳 www.romanbaths.co.uk, Stall St; daily Nov-Feb 9.30am-5.30pm, Mar-Jun & Sep-Oct 9am-5pm, Jul-Aug 9am-9pm; £12.25, or £12.75 in Jul-Aug; combined ticket with Assembly Rooms and Fashion Museum £15.75). Dating to between the 1st and 5th centuries AD, and constructed of stone, the colonnaded great bath was built to take advantage of a natural spring from which waters rise at a constant temperature of around 46°C. If the changing rooms, saunas and plunge pools are reminiscent of a modern-day spa, the temple dedicated to the goddess Sulis Minerva puts the whole thing firmly back into context. Included in the admission price is entry to the Georgian **Pump Room**, where the spring water may be sampled. For details of afternoon tea at the Pump Room, see p179.

● **Royal Crescent and Lansdown Crescent** At the far right of Royal Crescent, **No 1** was the first house to be constructed, built in the Palladian style by John Wood the Younger. Normally open to the public (☎ 01225-428126, 🖳 www .bath-preservation-trust.org.uk; mid Feb-early Dec, Tue-Sun & bank holiday Mon, 10.30am-5pm, to 4pm in Nov-Feb; admission £6), it will be closed in autumn 2012 while it is being extended to encompass the neighbouring No 1A. The new-look museum will take a more interactive approach while continuing to give visitors a glimpse of life both upstairs and downstairs in fashionable Georgian society.

Royal Crescent may get all the accolades, but it is **Lansdown Crescent** (see Map 43, p167) that is first seen by those heading south on the Cotswold Way. With sheep grazing on the grassy hill in front, and fine views over the city, it arguably runs its more famous neighbour very close.

● **Victoria Art Gallery** Facing Pulteney Bridge (itself designed by Adam, and one of only three river bridges in Europe with shops that are integral to the bridge) is the Victoria Art Gallery (☎ 01225-477233, 🖥 www.victoriagal.org.uk; Tue-Sat 10am-5pm, Sun 1.30-5pm; admission free), built at a time of civic pride to show off the city's attributes. While the name tends to suggest that it focuses on Victorian art, the reality is a far broader mix, from the 17th century to the contemporary, and including a couple of Gainsborough paintings and Rex Whistler's glorious incarnation of British insularity, *The Foreign Bloke*. Some are linked to the city, but most were donated by wealthy Bath residents, or formed part of their collections. Displays also include sculpture, ceramics, glass, porcelain and pottery. The room downstairs plays host to a series of changing exhibitions. On a practical note, there's a self-service machine dispensing hot drinks into china cups (yes, really!) at just £1 a go. And if you're nursing sore feet, note that there is plenty of comfortable seating down the centre of the gallery.

Entertainment

Bath does culture very well, but there's light relief on the agenda too. The place on everybody's lips is the new **Thermae Bath Spa** (☎ 0844-888 0844, 🖥 www.thermae bathspa.com; daily except 25-26 Dec & 1 Jan, 9am-9.30pm; pools closed 9pm) on the gloriously named Hot Bath St. At £26 a head for just a couple of hours, it's expensive – some would say extortionate – but it's a great place to ease all those aches and pains (or to get yourself in a relaxed frame of mind before setting off). If you don't fancy shelling out for the open-air spa at the New Royal Bath (no children under 16), or indeed for one of their 50 treatments and therapies, there's the satellite Cross Bath (daily 10am-8pm, last entry 6.30pm) – open air but without the view – where a 1¹/₂-hour session costs £16. Take your own towel or pay £3 for one of theirs – unless you're on the 3hr twilight package, starting from 4pm (last entry 6.30pm), in which case for £42 a towel, robe and slippers are thrown in, as are a one-course meal at the

Springs Café (Mon-Fri 9.30am-8pm) and a glass of wine or similar. There's something slightly other-worldly about all those cream-robed bodies in the café, though…

Bath's **Theatre Royal** [75] (☎ 01225-448844, 🖥 www.theatreroyal.org.uk) on Sawclose stages a wide range of high-quality productions, and – for theatre buffs – shouldn't be missed. If you've a preference for the silver screen, try the new multi-screen **cinema** [64] (☎ 0871-224 4007, 🖥 www.odeon.co.uk) just below Kingsmead Square, or – for more offbeat offerings – the **Little Theatre Cinema** [79] (☎ 0871-7042061, 🖥 www.picturehouses.co.uk) on St Michael's Place, diagonally opposite Thermae Spa.

River trips can be organised with Bath City Boat Trips [35] (mob ☎ 07974-560197, 🖥 www.bathcityboattrips.com, Apr-Sep daily), with 45-minute trips from 11am to 5pm at £7.95 per adult. On the *Pulteney Princess* (mob ☎ 07791-910650, 🖥 www.pulteneyprincess.co.uk), which plies the Avon between Pulteney Weir and Bathampton Mill up to seven times a day, a round trip of about an hour costs £8; one-way trips are also possible. If you'd rather set off under your own steam, rowing boats, canoes and punts can be hired from Bath Boating Station (☎ 01225-312900, 🖥 www.bathboating.co.uk; Easter-Sep daily 10am-6pm), whose base is at the end of Forester Rd, north-east of Great Pulteney St (off map 43a). Boats cost £7 per person for the first hour, and £3 for every hour after that.

Taking to the skies is a great way to see the city as a whole, though on a **balloon trip** it's pot luck as to which way you will fly – assuming the weather is calm enough to take off. Several companies organise trips: try Bath Balloons (☎ 01225-466888, 🖥 www.bathballoons.co.uk; Mar-Oct), whose balloons take off from Victoria Park and cost £90-155 a head, depending on the day.

Spectators rather than participants can check out what's on at **The Rec** (☎ 01225-325200; 🖥 www.bathrugby.com), home to Bath Rugby Club – though it's a small ground by today's standards, and tickets can be hard to come by. The Rec is also used for concerts.

ROUTE GUIDE AND MAPS

APPENDIX A: GPS WAYPOINTS

MAP	REF	GPS WAYPOINT	DESCRIPTION
Map 1	001	N52° 03.018' W01° 46.913'	Chipping Campden
Map 1	002	N52° 03.525' W01° 47.752'	Kissing gate on Dover's Hill
Map 2	003	N52° 01.862' W01° 49.687'	Fish Hill – toposcope
Map 3	004	N52° 01.458' W01° 50.165'	Broadway Tower
Map 3	005	N52° 02.197' W01° 51.172'	Broadway
Map 3	006	N52° 01.678' W01° 52.427'	Broadway Coppice
Map 4	007	N52° 00.332' W01° 52.842'	Shenberrow – cattle grid
Map 4	008	N52° 00.003' W01° 53.040'	Shenberrow Hill
Map 5	009	N52° 00.403' W01° 54.146'	Stanton
Map 5	010	N51° 59.377' W01° 54.748'	Stanway
Map 6	011	N51° 58.322' W01° 53.473'	Stumps Cross
Map 6	012	N51° 58.070' W01° 54.563'	Beckbury Camp
Map 7	013	N51° 58.157' W01° 55.655'	Hailes Abbey
Map 8	014	N51° 57.218' W01° 57.825'	Winchcombe
Map 9	015	N51° 55.690' W01° 58.255'	Belas Knap
Map 10	016	N51° 56.542' W02° 01.018'	Cleeve Hill car park
Map 10	017	N51° 56.160' W02° 01.328'	Cleeve Hill trig point
Map 11	018	N51° 55.600' W02° 01.325'	Cleeve Hill fort
Map 13	019	N51° 52.606' W02° 01.227'	Dowdeswell Reservoir
Map 14	020	N51° 51.827' W02° 02.207'	Wistley Hill
Map 14	021	N51° 51.193' W02° 02.865'	Seven Springs
Map 15	022	N51° 51.822' W02° 04.550'	Leckhampton trig point
Map 15	023	N51° 50.987' W02° 04.925'	Ullenwood
Map 16	024	N51° 50.598' W02° 05.783'	Air Balloon pub
Map 16	025	N51° 50.073' W02° 06.893'	The Peak
Map 18	026	N51° 49.922' W02° 09.312'	Cooper's Hill
Map 19	027	N51° 48.358' W02° 11.518'	Painswick Hill
Map 20	028	N51° 47.205' W02° 11.592'	Painswick
Map 20	029	N51° 46.808' W02° 13.120'	Edgemoor Inn
Map 21	030	N51° 47.008' W02° 14.685'	Cogwell Cottages (Cliff Wood)
Map 21	031	N51° 46.697' W02° 15.745'	Haresfield Beacon
Map 22	032	N51° 45.325' W02° 15.522'	Maiden Hill
Map 23	033	N51° 44.395' W02° 15.192'	Oil Mills Bridge
Map 25	034	N51° 42.702' W02° 18.037'	Nympsfield display boards
Map 26	035	N51° 41.908' W02° 18.355'	Hetty Pegler's Tump
Map 26	036	N51° 41.527' W02° 18.610'	Uley Bury
Map 27	037	N51° 41.617' W02° 19.482'	Cam Long Down
Map 28	038	N51° 40.818' W02° 22.037'	Stinchcombe Hill Golf Club
Map 28	039	N51° 40.803' W02° 22.938'	Drakestone Point
Map 28	040	N51° 40.725' W02° 22.247'	Stinchcombe Hill Golf Course – South
Map 29	041	N51° 39.528' W02° 22.353'	Tyndale Monument
Map 29	042	N51° 38.492' W02° 21.555'	Monument above Wotton-under-Edge
Map 30	043	N51° 38.347' W02° 19.310'	Blackquerries Hill
Map 31	044	N51° 37.033' W02° 19.995'	Alderley
Map 32	045	N51° 36.318' W02° 19.025'	Lower Kilcott
Map 32	046	N51° 35.972' W02° 18.522'	Bridge Farm

MAP	REF	GPS WAYPOINT		DESCRIPTION
Map 33	047	N51° 35.220'	W02° 19.780'	Somerset Monument
Map 34	048	N51° 33.663'	W02° 20.453'	Wood near Horton Court
Map 35	049	N51° 32.070'	W02° 21.275'	Old Sodbury
Map 35	050	N51° 30.906'	W02° 21.032'	Dodington Park
Map 36	051	N51° 30.427'	W02° 20.087'	Tormarton
Map 38	052	N51° 28.200'	W02° 22.735'	Kissing gate above withy bed
Map 39	053	N51° 27.245'	W02° 21.698'	Cold Ashton
Map 40	054	N51° 25.875'	W02° 23.392'	The Battlefields
Map 41	055	N51° 25.787'	W02° 24.892'	Hanging Hill
Map 41	056	N51° 25.405'	W02° 24.317'	Lansdown Golf Course
Map 42	057	N51° 24.782'	W02° 24.832'	Prospect Stile
Map 42	058	N51° 23.720'	W02° 24.062'	Weston

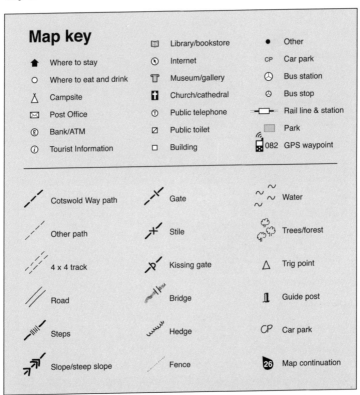

Map key

♠ Where to stay
O Where to eat and drink
⋀ Campsite
⊠ Post Office
£ Bank/ATM
ⓘ Tourist Information

▦ Library/bookstore
◔ Internet
▥ Museum/gallery
✝ Church/cathedral
☏ Public telephone
☑ Public toilet
▢ Building

● Other
CP Car park
Ⓐ Bus station
◔ Bus stop
Rail line & station
Park
082 GPS waypoint

Cotswold Way path
Other path
4 x 4 track
Road
Steps
Slope/steep slope

Gate
Stile
Kissing gate
Bridge
Hedge
Fence

Water
Trees/forest
⋀ Trig point
Guide post
CP Car park
26 Map continuation

Symbols used in text 🐾 Dogs allowed with prior notice ♥ Bathtub in some rooms

	Chipping Campden	Broadway	Stanton	Wood Stanway	Hailes	Winchcombe	Cleeve Hill	Dowdeswell Reservoir	Seven Springs	Crickley Hill	Birdlip
Broadway	6										
	9.5										
Stanton	10.5	4.5									
	17	*7.5*									
Wood Stanway	12.5	6.5	2								
	20	*10.5*	*3*								
Hailes	16	10	5.5	3.5							
	25.5	*16*	*8.5*	*5.5*							
Winchcombe	18	12	7.5	5.5	2						
	29	*19.5*	*12*	*9*	*3.5*						
Cleeve Hill	24	18	13.5	11.5	8	6					
	38.5	*29*	*21.5*	*18.5*	*13*	*9.5*					
Dowdeswell Res'voir	29	23	18.5	16.5	13	11	5				
	46.5	*37*	*29.5*	*26.5*	*21*	*17.5*	*8*				
Seven Springs	32	26	21.5	19.5	16	14	8	3			
	51	*41.5*	*34*	*31*	*25.5*	*22*	*12.5*	*4.5*			
Crickley Hill	37	31	26.5	24.5	21	19	13	8	5		
	59	*49.5*	*42*	*39*	*33.5*	*30*	*20.5*	*12.5*	*8*		
Birdlip	39.5	33.5	29	27	23.5	21.5	15.5	10.5	7.5	2.5	
	63	*53.5*	*46*	*43*	*37.5*	*34*	*24.5*	*16.5*	*12*	*4*	
Cranham Cnr	43.5	37.5	33	31	27.5	25.5	19.5	14.5	11.5	6.5	4
	69.5	*60*	*52.5*	*49.5*	*44*	*40.5*	*31*	*23*	*18.5*	*10.5*	*6.5*
Painswick	46	40	35.5	33.5	30	28	22	17	14	9	6.5
	73.5	*64*	*56.5*	*53.5*	*48*	*44.5*	*35*	*27*	*22.5*	*14.5*	*10.5*
Stonehouse/Ebley	54.5	48.5	44	42	38.5	36.5	30.5	25.5	22.5	17.5	15
	87	*77.5*	*70*	*67*	*61.5*	*58*	*48.5*	*40.5*	*36*	*28*	*24*
Selsley Common	56	50	45.5	43.5	40	38	32	27	24	19	16.5
	89.5	*80*	*72.5*	*69.5*	*64*	*60.5*	*51*	*43*	*38.5*	*30.5*	*26.5*
Dursley	63.5	57.5	53	51	47.5	45.5	39.5	34.5	31.5	26.5	24
	101.5	*92*	*84.5*	*81.5*	*76*	*72.5*	*63*	*55*	*50.5*	*42.5*	*38.5*
North Nibley	68.5	62.5	58	56	52.5	50.5	44.5	39.5	36.5	31.5	29
	109.5	*100*	*92.5*	*89.5*	*84*	*80.5*	*71*	*63*	*58.5*	*50.5*	*46.5*
Wotton-u-Edge	70.5	64.5	60	58	54.5	52.5	46.5	41.5	38.5	33.5	31
	113	*103.5*	*96*	*93*	*87.5*	*84*	*74.5*	*66.5*	*62*	*54*	*50*
Lower Kilcott	76.5	70.5	66	64	60.5	58.5	52.5	47.5	44.5	39.5	37
	122.5	*113*	*105.5*	*102.5*	*97*	*93.5*	*84*	*76*	*71.5*	*63.5*	*59.5*
Little Sodbury	81.5	75.5	71	69	65.5	63.5	57.5	52.5	49.5	44.5	42
	130.5	*121*	*113.5*	*110.5*	*105*	*101.5*	*92*	*84*	*79.5*	*71.5*	*67.5*
Old Sodbury	83.5	77.5	73	71	67.5	65.5	59.5	54.5	51.5	46.5	44
	133.5	*124*	*116.5*	*113.5*	*108*	*104.5*	*95*	*87*	*82.5*	*74.5*	*70.5*
Coomb's End	84	78	73.5	71.5	68	66	60	55	52	47	44.5
	134.5	*125*	*117.5*	*114.5*	*109*	*105.5*	*96*	*88*	*83.5*	*75.5*	*71.5*
Tormarton	85.5	79.5	75	73	69.5	67.5	61.5	56.5	53.5	48.5	46
	137	*127.5*	*120*	*117*	*111.5*	*108*	*98.5*	*90.5*	*86*	*78*	*74*
Pennsylvania	91.5	85.5	81	79	75.5	73.5	67.5	62.5	59.5	54.5	52
	146.5	*137*	*129.5*	*126.5*	*121*	*117.5*	*108*	*100*	*95.5*	*87.5*	*83.5*
Cold Ashton	92	86	81.5	79.5	76	74	68	63	60	55	52.5
	147	*137.5*	*130*	*127*	*121.5*	*118*	*108.5*	*100.5*	*96*	*88*	*84*
Bath	102	96	91.5	89.5	86	84	78	73	70	65	62.5
	163	*153.5*	*146*	*143*	*137.5*	*134*	*124.5*	*116.5*	*112*	*104*	*100*

COTSWOLD WAY
DISTANCE CHART

(route via Selsley Common and Stinchcombe Hill)

miles/*kilometres* (approx)

Cranham Corner	Painswick	Stonehouse/Ebley	Selsley Common	Dursley	North Nibley	Wotton-under-Edge	Lower Kilcott	Little Sodbury	Old Sodbury	Coomb's End	Tormarton	Pennsylvania	Cold Ashton
2.5													
4													
11	8.5												
17.5	*13.5*												
12.5	10	1.5											
20	*16*	*2.5*											
20	17.5	9	7.5										
32	*28*	*14.5*	*12*										
25	22.5	14	12.5	5									
40	*36*	*22.5*	*20*	*8*									
27	24.5	16	14.5	7	2								
43.5	*39.5*	*26*	*23.5*	*11.5*	*3.5*								
33	30.5	22	20.5	13	8	6							
53	*49*	*35.5*	*33*	*21*	*13*	*9.5*							
38	35.5	27	25.5	18	13	11	5						
61	*57*	*43.5*	*41*	*29*	*21*	*17.5*	*8*						
40	37.5	29	27.5	20	15	13	7	2					
64	*60*	*46.5*	*44*	*32*	*24*	*20.5*	*11*	*3*					
40.5	38	29.5	28	20.5	15.5	13.5	7.5	2.5	0.5				
65	*61*	*47.5*	*45*	*33*	*25*	*21.5*	*12*	*4*	*1*				
42	39.5	31	29.5	22	17	15	9	4	2	1.5			
67.5	*63.5*	*50*	*47.5*	*35.5*	*27.5*	*24*	*14.5*	*6.5*	*3.5*	*2.5*			
48	45.5	37	35.5	28	23	21	15	10	8	7.5	6		
77	*73*	*59.5*	*57*	*45*	*37*	*33.5*	*24*	*16*	*13*	*12*	*9.5*		
48.8	46	37.5	36	28.5	23.5	21.5	15.5	10.5	8.5	8	6.5	0.5	
77.5	*73.5*	*60*	*57.5*	*45.5*	*37.5*	*34*	*24.5*	*16.5*	*13.5*	*12.5*	*10*	*0.5*	
58.5	56	47.5	46	38.5	33.5	31.5	25.5	20.5	18.5	18	16.5	10.5	10
93.5	*89.5*	*76*	*73.5*	*61.5*	*53.5*	*50*	*40.5*	*32.5*	*29.5*	*28.5*	*26*	*16.5*	*16*

INDEX

Page references in **bold** type refer to maps

TRAILBLAZER TITLE LIST

Adventure Cycle-Touring Handbook
Adventure Motorcycling Handbook
Australia by Rail
Australia's Great Ocean Road
Azerbaijan
Coast to Coast (British Walking Guide)
Cornwall Coast Path (British Walking Guide)
Corsica Trekking – GR20
Cotswold Way (British Walking Guide)
Dolomites Trekking – AV1 & AV2
Dorset & Sth Devon Coast Path (British Walking Gde)
Exmoor & Nth Devon Coast Path (British Walking Gde)
Hadrian's Wall Path (British Walking Guide)
Himalaya by Bike – a route and planning guide
Inca Trail, Cusco & Machu Picchu
Indian Rail Handbook
Japan by Rail
Kilimanjaro – the trekking guide (includes Mt Meru)
Mediterranean Handbook
Morocco Overland (4WD/motorcycle/mountainbike)
Moroccan Atlas – The Trekking Guide
Nepal Trekking & The Great Himalaya Trail
New Zealand – The Great Walks
North Downs Way (British Walking Guide)
Norway's Arctic Highway
Offa's Dyke Path (British Walking Guide)
Overlanders' Handbook – worldwide driving guide
Peddars Way & Norfolk Coast Path (British Walking Gde)
Pembrokeshire Coast Path (British Walking Guide)
Pennine Way (British Walking Guide)
The Ridgeway (British Walking Guide)
Siberian BAM Guide – rail, rivers & road
The Silk Roads – a route and planning guide
Sahara Overland – a route and planning guide
Scottish Highlands – The Hillwalking Guide
Sinai – the trekking guide
South Downs Way (British Walking Guide)
Tour du Mont Blanc
Trans-Canada Rail Guide
Trans-Siberian Handbook
Trekking in the Annapurna Region
Trekking in the Everest Region
Trekking in Ladakh
Trekking in the Pyrenees
The Walker's Haute Route – Mont Blanc to Matterhorn
West Highland Way (British Walking Guide)

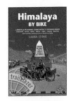

For more information about Trailblazer and our
expanding range of guides, for guidebook updates or
for credit card mail order sales visit our website:

www.trailblazer-guides.com

TRAILBLAZER'S LONG-DISTANCE PATH (LDP) WALKING GUIDES

We've applied to destinations which are closer to home Trailblazer's proven formula for publishing definitive practical route guides for adventurous travellers. Britain's network of long-distance trails enables the walker to explore some of the finest landscapes in the country's best walking areas. These are guides that are user-friendly, practical, informative and environmentally sensitive.

● **Unique mapping features** In many walking guidebooks the reader has to read a route description then try to relate it to the map. Our guides are much easier to use because walking directions, tricky junctions, places to stay and eat, points of interest and walking times are all written onto the maps themselves in the places to which they apply. With their uncluttered clarity, these are not general-purpose maps but fully edited maps drawn by walkers for walkers.

● **Largest-scale walking maps** At a scale of just under 1:20,000 (8cm or 3$\frac{1}{8}$ inches to one mile) the maps in these guides are bigger than even the most detailed British walking maps currently available in the shops.

● **Not just a trail guide – includes where to stay, where to eat and public transport** Our guidebooks cover the complete walking experience, not just the route. Accommodation options for all budgets are provided (pubs, hotels, B&Bs, campsites, bunkhouses, hostels) as well as places to eat. Detailed public transport information for all access points to each trail means that there are itineraries for all walkers, for hiking the entire route as well as for day or weekend walks.

Coast to Coast *Henry Stedman*, 5th edition, £11.99
ISBN 978-1-905864-47-8, 256pp, 110 maps, 40 colour photos

Cornwall Coast Path (SW Coast Path Pt 2) 4th edition, £11.99
ISBN 978-1-905864-44-7, 296pp, 130 maps, 40 colour photos – Due mid 2012

Cotswold Way *Tricia & Bob Hayne* 2nd edition, £11.99
ISBN 978-1-905864-48-5, 192pp, 60 maps, 40 colour photos

Dorset & South Devon (SW Coast Path Pt 3) *Stedman & Newton*, £11.99
ISBN 978-1-905864-45-4, 192pp, 60 maps, 40 colour photos – Due late 2012

Exmoor & North Devon (SW Coast Path Pt I) *Stedman & Newton*, £11.99
ISBN 978-1-905864-43-0, 192pp, 60 maps, 40 colour photos

Hadrian's Wall Path *Henry Stedman*, 3rd edition, £11.99
ISBN 978-1-905864-14-0, 224pp, 60 maps, 40 colour photos

North Downs Way *John Curtin*, 1st edition, £9.99
ISBN 978-1-873756-96-6, 192pp, 80 maps, 40 colour photos

Offa's Dyke Path *Keith Carter*, 3rd edition, £11.99
ISBN 978-1-905864-35-5, 240pp, 98 maps, 40 colour photos

Peddars Way & Norfolk Coast Path *Alexander Stewart*, £11.99
ISBN 978-1-905864-28-7, 192pp, 54 maps, 40 colour photos

Pembrokeshire Coast Path *Jim Manthorpe*, 3rd edition, £9.99
ISBN 978-1-905864-27-0, 224pp, 96 maps, 40 colour photos

Pennine Way *Keith Carter & Chris Scott*, 3rd edition, £11.99
ISBN 978-1-905864-34-8, 272pp, 138 maps, 40 colour photos

The Ridgeway *Nick Hill*, 3rd edition, £11.99
ISBN 978-1-905864-40-9, 192pp, 53 maps, 40 colour photos

South Downs Way *Jim Manthorpe*, 4th edition, £11.99
ISBN 978-1-905864-42-3, 192pp, 60 maps, 40 colour photos – Due mid 2012

West Highland Way *Charlie Loram*, 4th edition, £9.99
ISBN 978-1-905864-29-4, 192pp, 60 maps, 40 colour photos

'The same attention to detail that distinguishes its other guides has been brought to bear here'.
THE SUNDAY TIMES

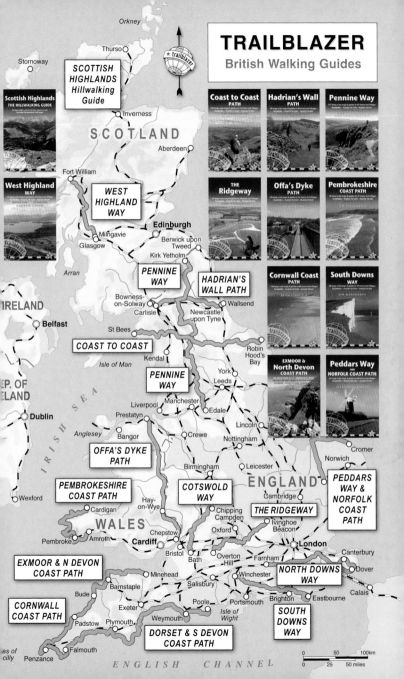

TRAILBLAZER
British Walking Guides

Orkney

Thurso

Stornoway

Scottish Highlands
THE HILLWALKING GUIDE

SCOTTISH
HIGHLANDS
*Hillwalking
Guide*

Inverness

S C O T L A N D

Aberdeen

Fort William

West Highland
WAY

WEST
HIGHLAND
WAY

Edinburgh

Milngavie

Glasgow

Berwick upon
Tweed

Arran

Kirk Yetholm

PENNINE
WAY

HADRIAN'S
WALL PATH

Coast to Coast
PATH

Hadrian's Wall
PATH

Pennine Way

**THE
Ridgeway**

Offa's Dyke
PATH

**Pembrokeshire
COAST PATH**

**Cornwall Coast
PATH**

**South Downs
WAY**

**EXMOOR &
NORTH DEVON
COAST PATH**

Peddars Way
AND
NORFOLK COAST PATH

IRELAND

Belfast

Bowness-
on-Solway

Wallsend

Carlisle

Newcastle
upon Tyne

St Bees

COAST TO COAST

Robin
Hood's
Bay

Kendal

Isle of Man

PENNINE
WAY

York

REP. OF
IRELAND

Leeds

Dublin

Liverpool

Manchester

Prestatyn

Edale

Crewe

Lincoln

Anglesey

Nottingham

Bangor

OFFA'S DYKE
PATH

Birmingham

Leicester

Cromer

Norwich

E N G L A N D

PEMBROKESHIRE
COAST PATH

Wexford

Cardigan

Hay-
on-Wye

W A L E S

Pembroke

Amroth

Chepstow

Cardiff

COTSWOLD
WAY

Chipping
Campden

Oxford

Cambridge

THE RIDGEWAY

Ivinghoe
Beacon

PEDDARS
WAY &
NORFOLK
COAST
PATH

Bristol

Bath

London

Canterbury

EXMOOR & N DEVON
COAST PATH

Minehead

Overton
Hill

Farnham

Winchester

NORTH DOWNS
WAY

Dover

Calais

CORNWALL
COAST PATH

Bude

Barnstaple

Salisbury

Poole

Portsmouth

Brighton

Eastbourne

SOUTH
DOWNS
WAY

Padstow

Exeter

Plymouth

Weymouth

Isle of
Wight

es of
cilly

Penzance

Falmouth

DORSET & S DEVON
COAST PATH

E N G L I S H   C H A N N E L

0   50   100km

0   25   50 miles

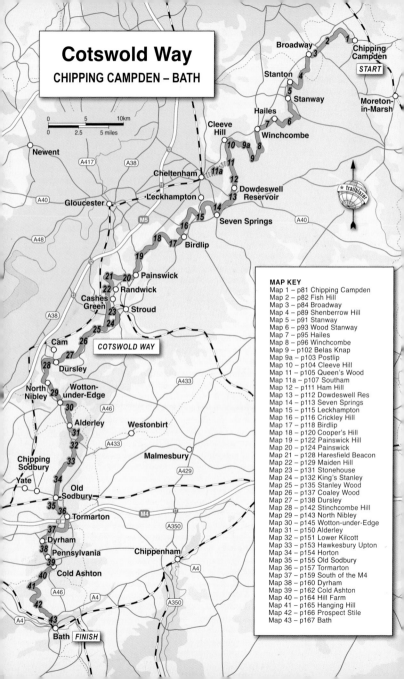

Cotswold Way

CHIPPING CAMPDEN – BATH

Broadway

Chipping
Campden
START

Stanton

Stanway

Moreton-
in-Marsh

Hailes

Winchcombe

Cleeve
Hill

Newent

Cheltenham

Leckhampton

Dowdeswell
Reservoir

Gloucester

Seven Springs

Birdlip

Painswick

Randwick

Cashes
Green

Stroud

Westonbirt

Cam

COTSWOLD WAY

Dursley

Malmesbury

North
Nibley

Wotton-
under-Edge

Alderley

Chipping
Sodbury

Yate

Old
Sodbury

Tormarton

Dyrham

Pennsylvania

Chippenham

Cold Ashton

Bath *FINISH*

trailblazer